T0026589

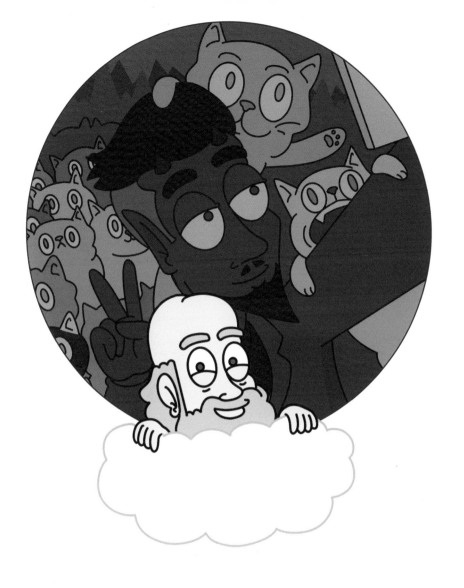

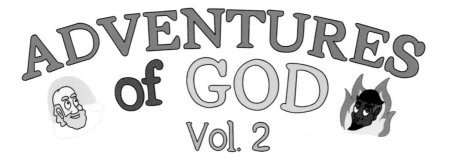

ADVENTURES of GOD

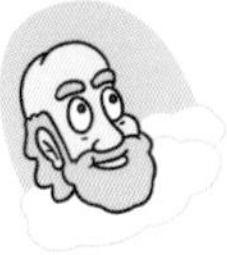

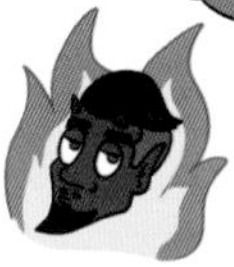

Vol. 2

by Corey & Teo

Layout assists by Nicholas Hogge

Rocketship™

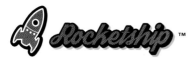

Rocketship Entertainment, LLC

rocketshipent.com

Tom Akel, CEO & Publisher • **Rob Feldman,** CTO • **Jeanmarie McNeely,** CFO
Brandon Freeberg, Dir. of Campaign Mgmt. • **Phil Smith,** Art Director • **Aram Alekyan,** Designer
Jimmy Deoquino, Designer • **Jed Keith,** Social Media • **Jerrod Clark,** Publicity

ADVENTURES OF GOD volume 2 | Softcover Edition ISBN: 978-1-952126-59-8 | Hardcover Edition ISBN: 978-1-952126-94-9
First printing. July 2023.

Tablet of Contents

Page

1 ... Project Adam
4 ... Trolls
7 ... The Way
9 ... Celebration
12 ... All Go to Heaven
15 ... Project Eve
18 ... Greek
20 ... Joke
23 ... Survivor
25 ... Bugs
27 ... Adam & Eve: Trees
30 ... Trick or Treat
34 ... Spam
37 ... VIP
40 ... Escape
43 ... Adam & Eve: The Fall
46 ... The Cloud
50 ... The Cloud 2
53 ... The Box
57 ... Fossil Fuels
60 ... Noah's Ark: 37
62 ... Undercover God
66 ... Undercover God 2
69 ... Up
73 ... Life of Ryan
77 ... Noah's Ark: Snakes on a Boat
80 ... Plan
83 ... Y'all Need Jesus
86 ... Letter to Satan
91 ... Faith Healing
93 ... 2018

Page

95 ... The 9 + 1 Commandments
98 ... Mistake
101 ... Visitors
104... Snow
108 ... Sad Gabe
111 ... Reward
114 ... Lure
116 ... Questions
119 ... Promised
121 ... Cat Duty
124 ... Bad Gabe
128 ... Apocryphal
130 ... Pope?
132 ... Junk
135 ... Belong
139 ... Image
141 ... Fast
143 ... Saint?
145 ... St. Patrick
147 ... Business Trip
150 ... Business Trip 2
152 ... The Whole Truth
155 ... Monk
157 ... Last Words
159 ... Spring Cleaning
162 ... Spring Cleaning 2
166 ... III
168 ... Contract
171 ... Contract 2
174 ... Note
176 ... A Match Made in Heaven

Project Adam

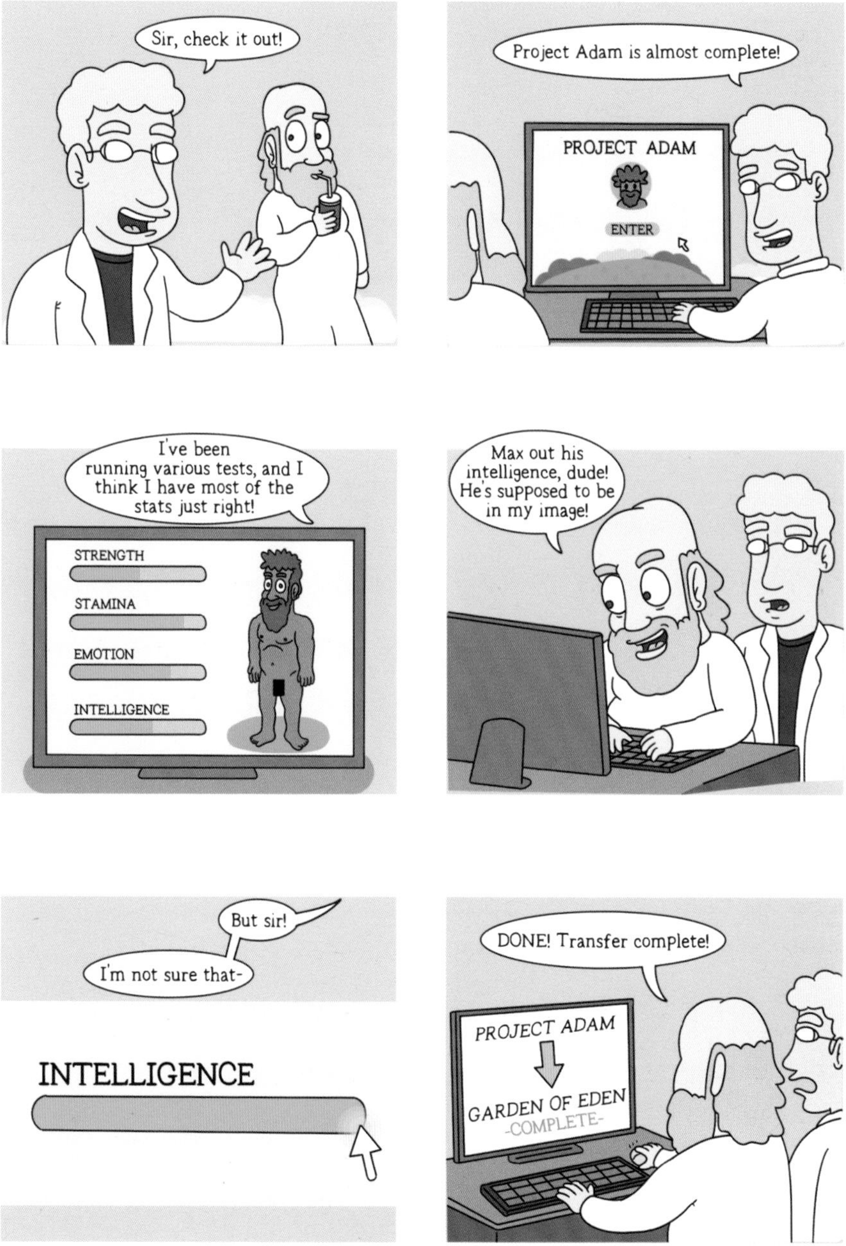

Sir, check it out!
Project Adam is almost complete!
PROJECT ADAM
ENTER
I've been running various tests, and I think I have most of the stats just right!
STRENGTH
STAMINA
EMOTION
INTELLIGENCE
Max out his intelligence, dude! He's supposed to be in my image!
I'm not sure that-
But sir!
INTELLIGENCE
DONE! Transfer complete!
PROJECT ADAM
GARDEN OF EDEN
-COMPLETE-

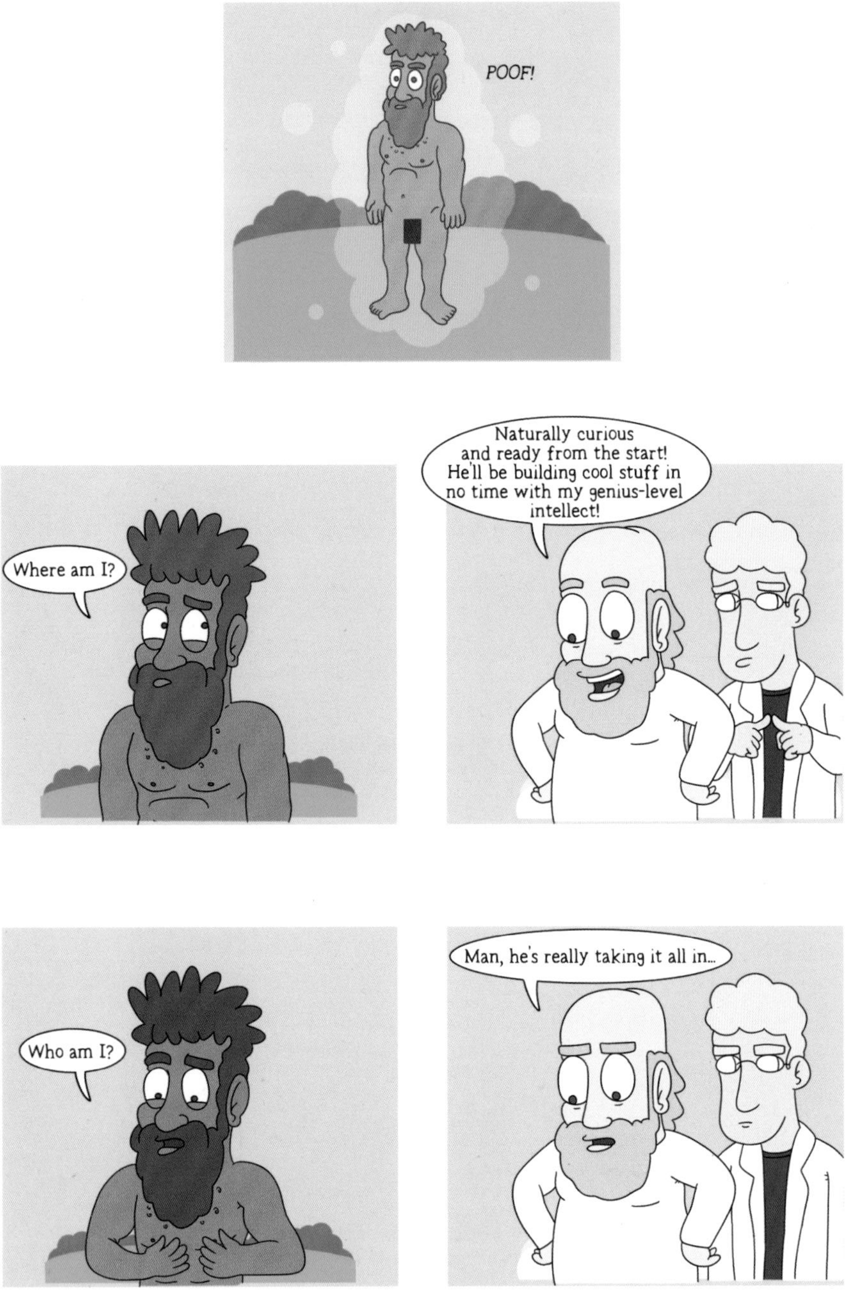
POOF!
Where am I?
Naturally curious and ready from the start! He'll be building cool stuff in no time with my genius-level intellect!
Who am I?
Man, he's really taking it all in...

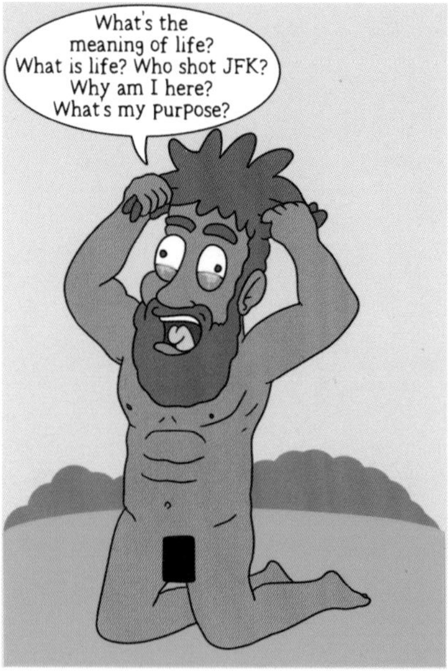
What's the meaning of life? What is life? Who shot JFK? Why am I here? What's my purpose?

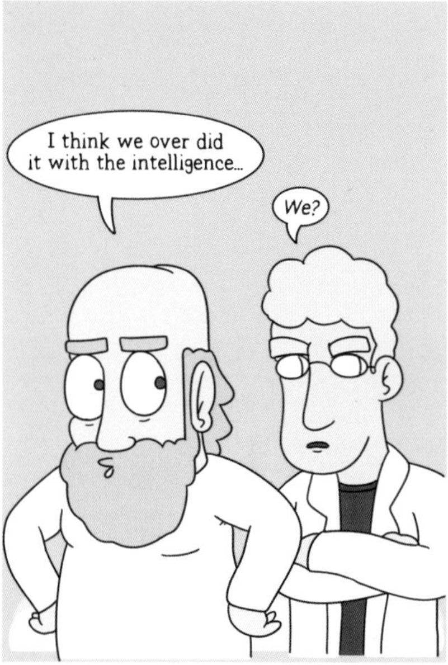
I think we over did it with the intelligence...
We?

BONUS

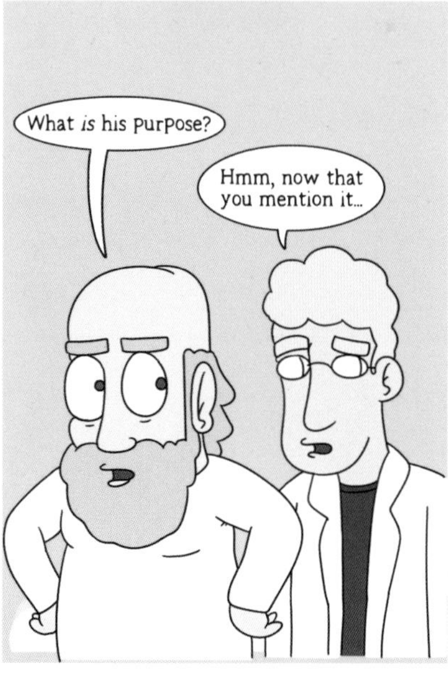
What *is* his purpose?
Hmm, now that you mention it...

Trolls

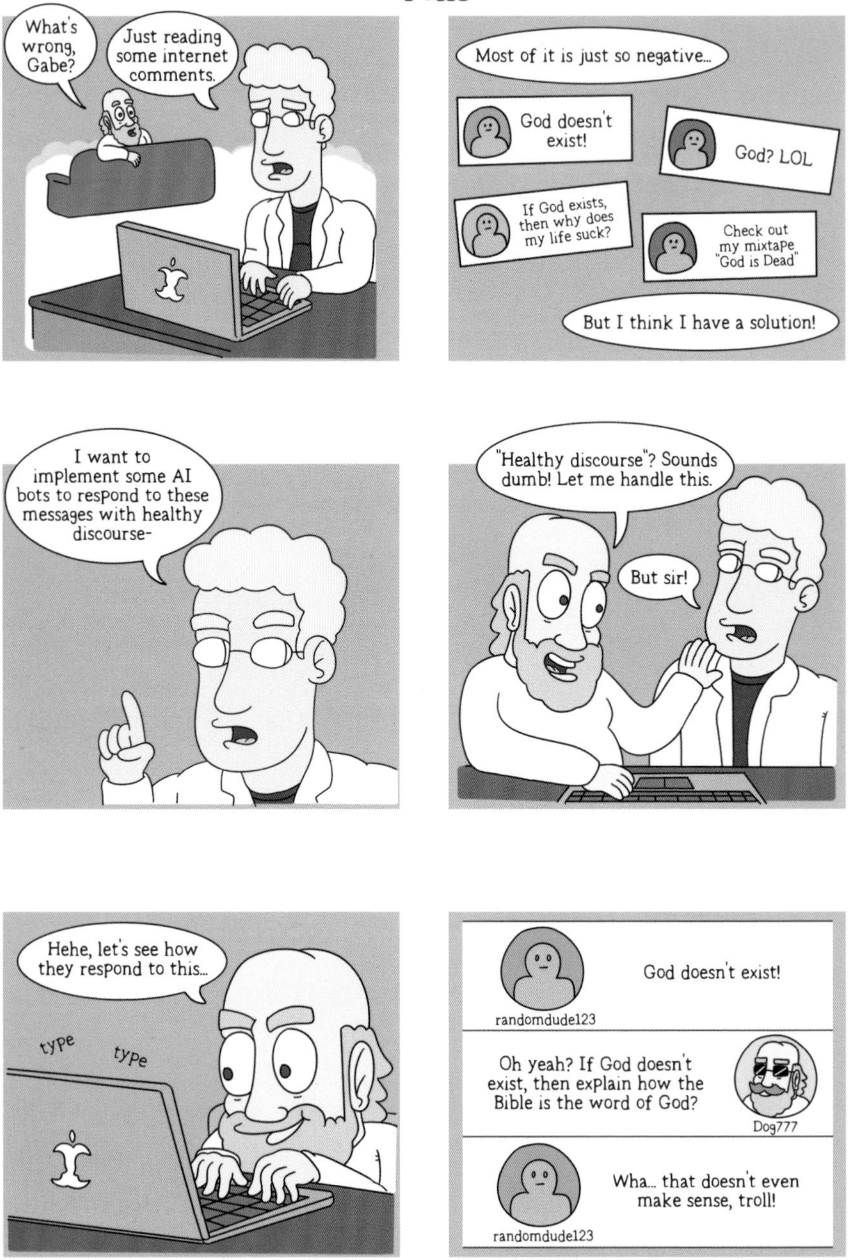

What's wrong, Gabe?
Just reading some internet comments.
Most of it is just so negative...
God doesn't exist!
God? LOL
If God exists, then why does my life suck?
Check out my mixtape "God is Dead"
But I think I have a solution!
I want to implement some AI bots to respond to these messages with healthy discourse-
"Healthy discourse"? Sounds dumb! Let me handle this.
But sir!
Hehe, let's see how they respond to this...
type
type
randomdude123
God doesn't exist!
Oh yeah? If God doesn't exist, then explain how the Bible is the word of God?
Dog777
randomdude123
Wha... that doesn't even make sense, troll!

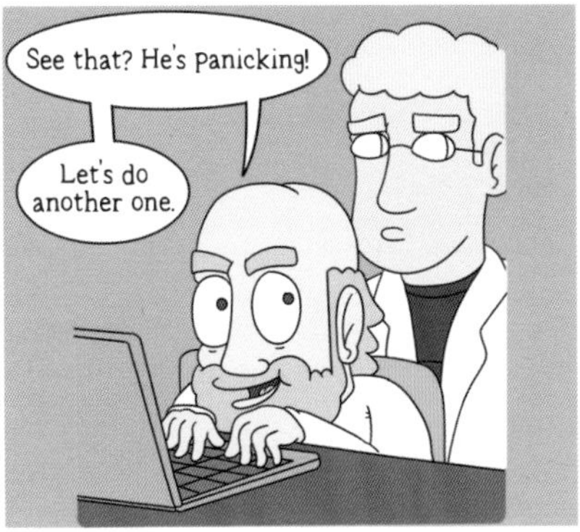
See that? He's panicking!
Let's do another one.

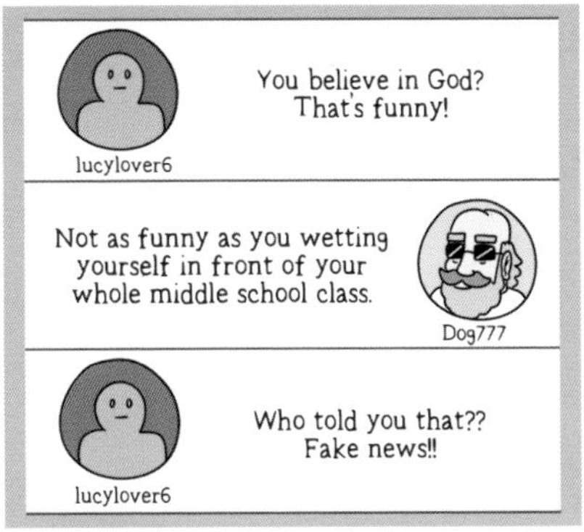
You believe in God? That's funny!
lucylover6
Not as funny as you wetting yourself in front of your whole middle school class.
Dog777
Who told you that?? Fake news!!
lucylover6

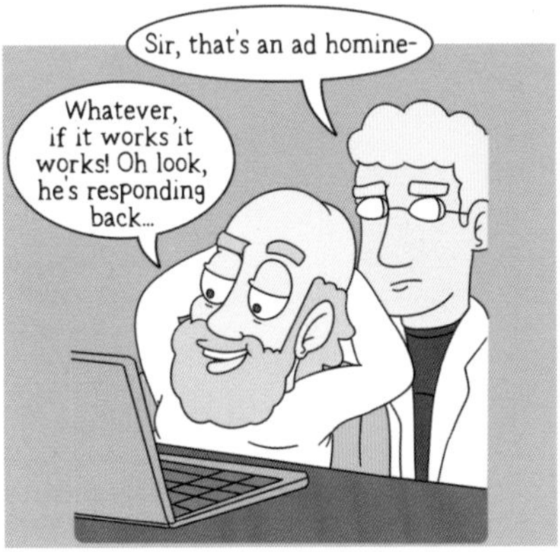
Sir, that's an ad homine-
Whatever, if it works it works! Oh look, he's responding back...

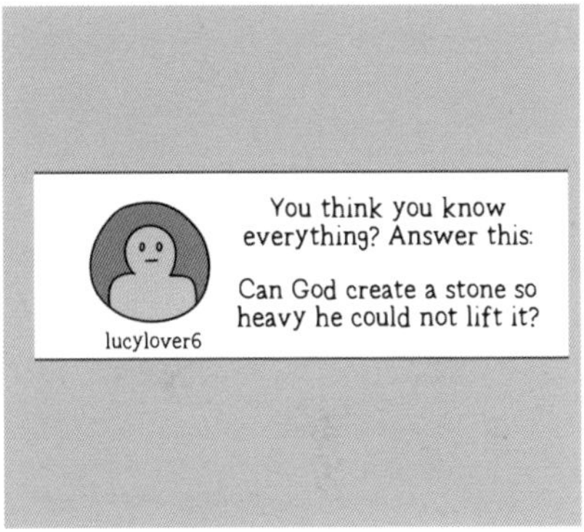
You think you know everything? Answer this:
Can God create a stone so heavy he could not lift it?
lucylover6

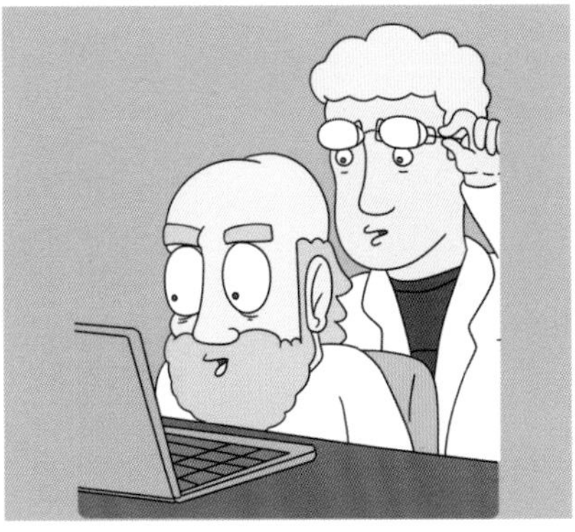

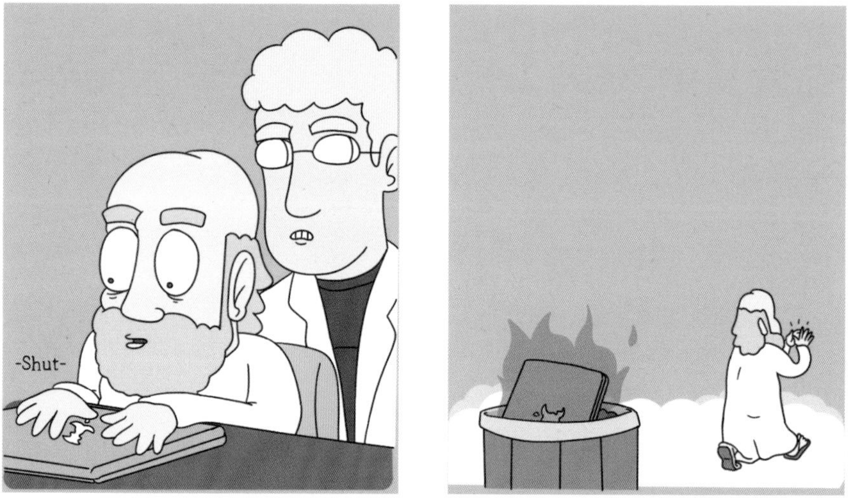
-Shut-

BONUS

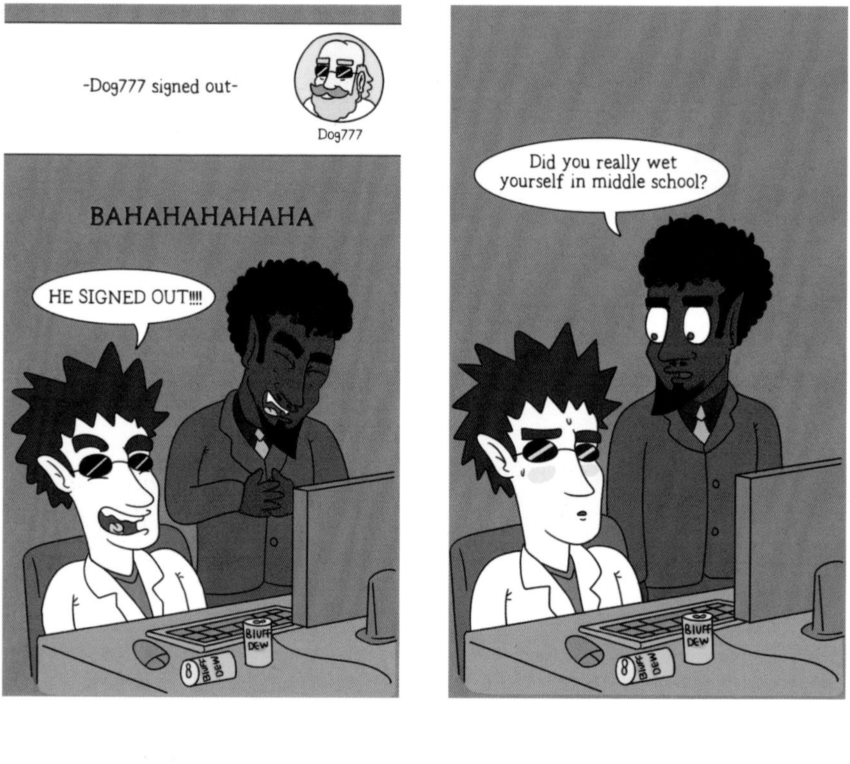
-Dog777 signed out-
Dog777
BAHAHAHAHAHA
HE SIGNED OUT!!!!
BIUFF DEW
Did you really wet yourself in middle school?

The Way

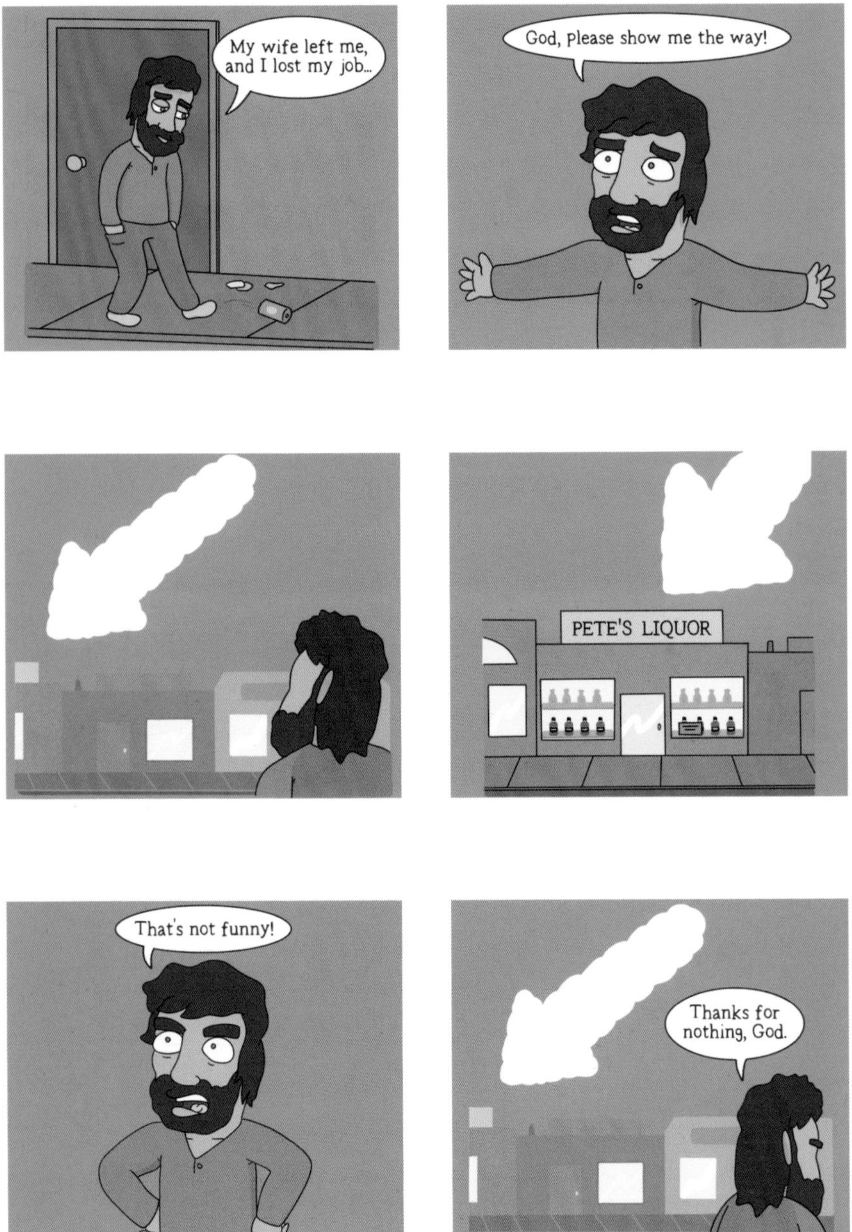
My wife left me, and I lost my job...
God, please show me the way!
PETE'S LIQUOR
That's not funny!
Thanks for nothing, God.

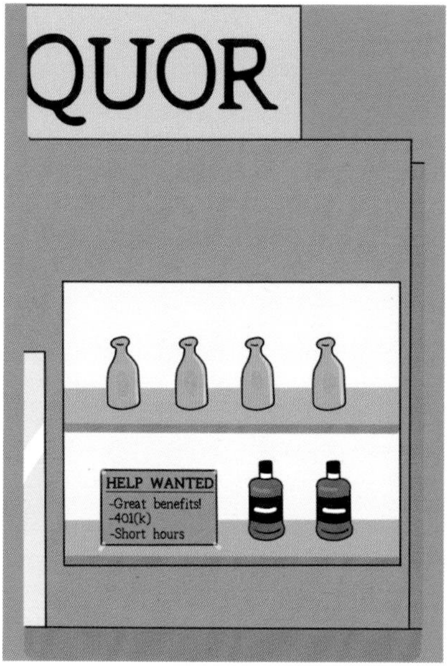
QUOR
HELP WANTED
-Great benefits!
-401(k)
-Short hours

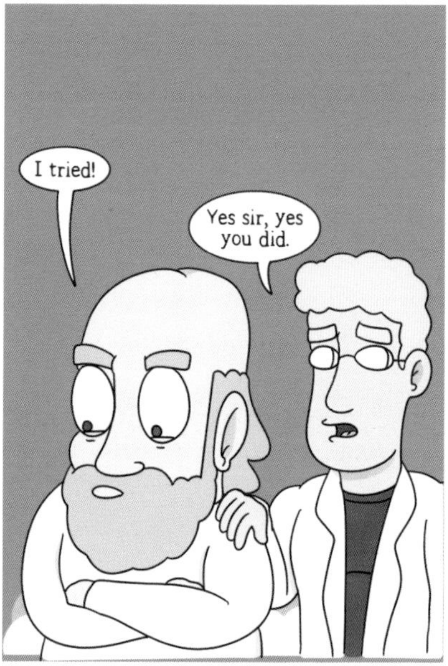
I tried!
Yes sir, yes you did.

BONUS

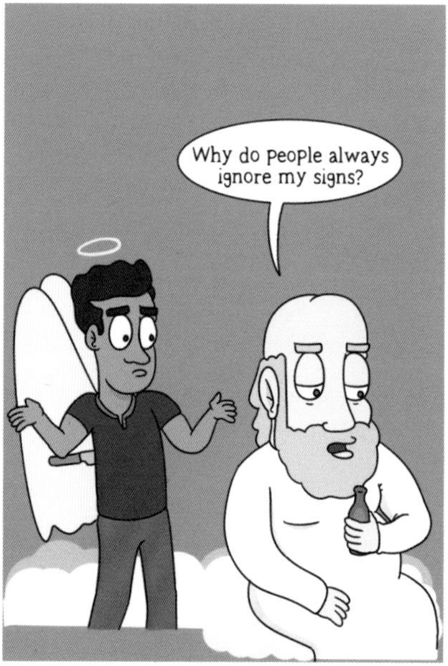
Why do people always ignore my signs?

Celebration

Sir, I have some exciting news!
Today we had no acts of God or man-made disasters! A first in centuries!
Whoa.
This calls for a celebration! Would you do the honors?
Oh, I couldn't!
Come on! You deserve it! You keep things in line around here.
Aww shucks!

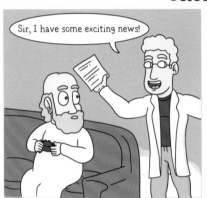

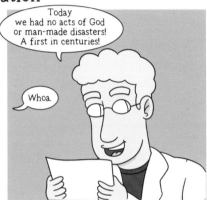

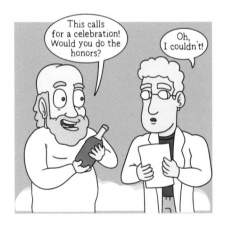

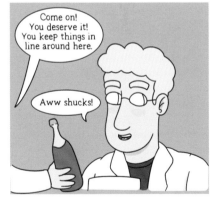

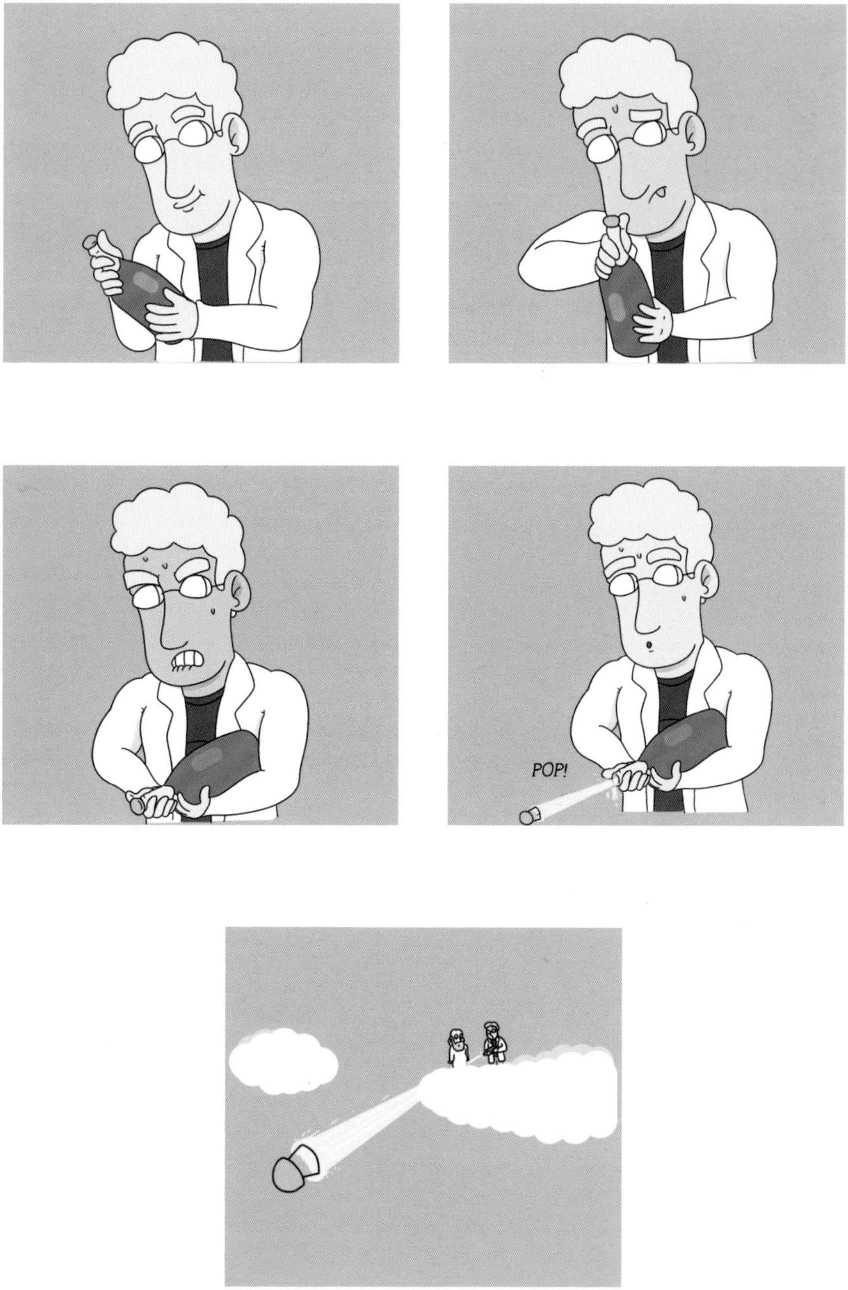
POP!

METEOR!
BOOM!
Well at least for once I'm not the one who screwed up.

BONUS

This is going down as an act of Gabe by the way!

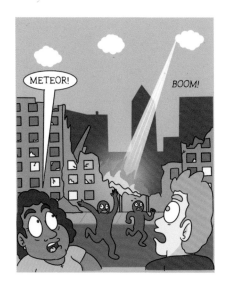

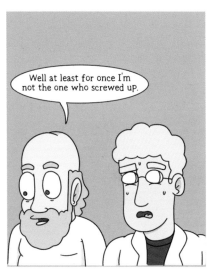

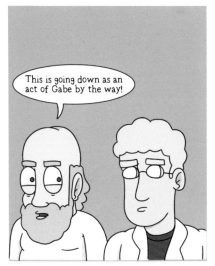

All Go to Heaven

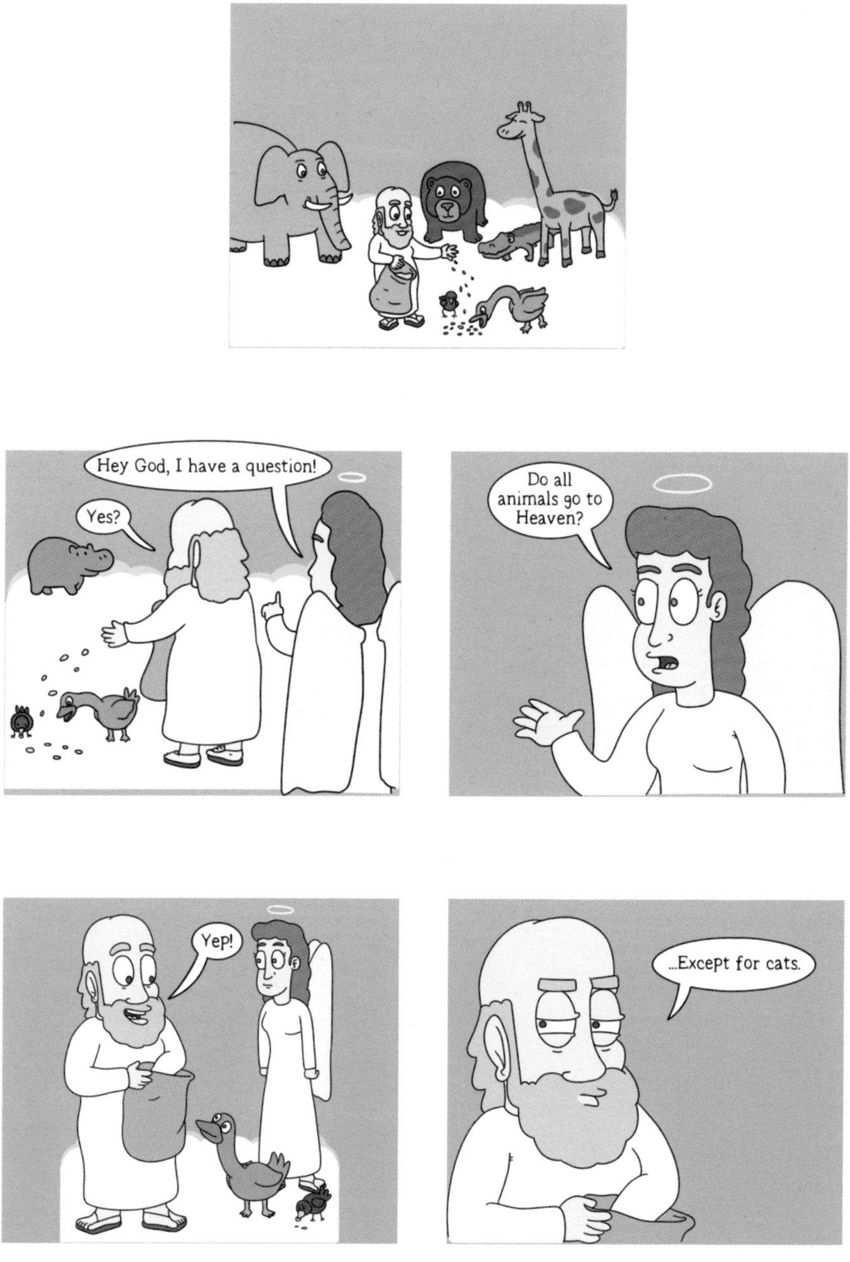
Hey God, I have a question!
Yes?
Do all animals go to Heaven?
Yep!
...Except for cats.

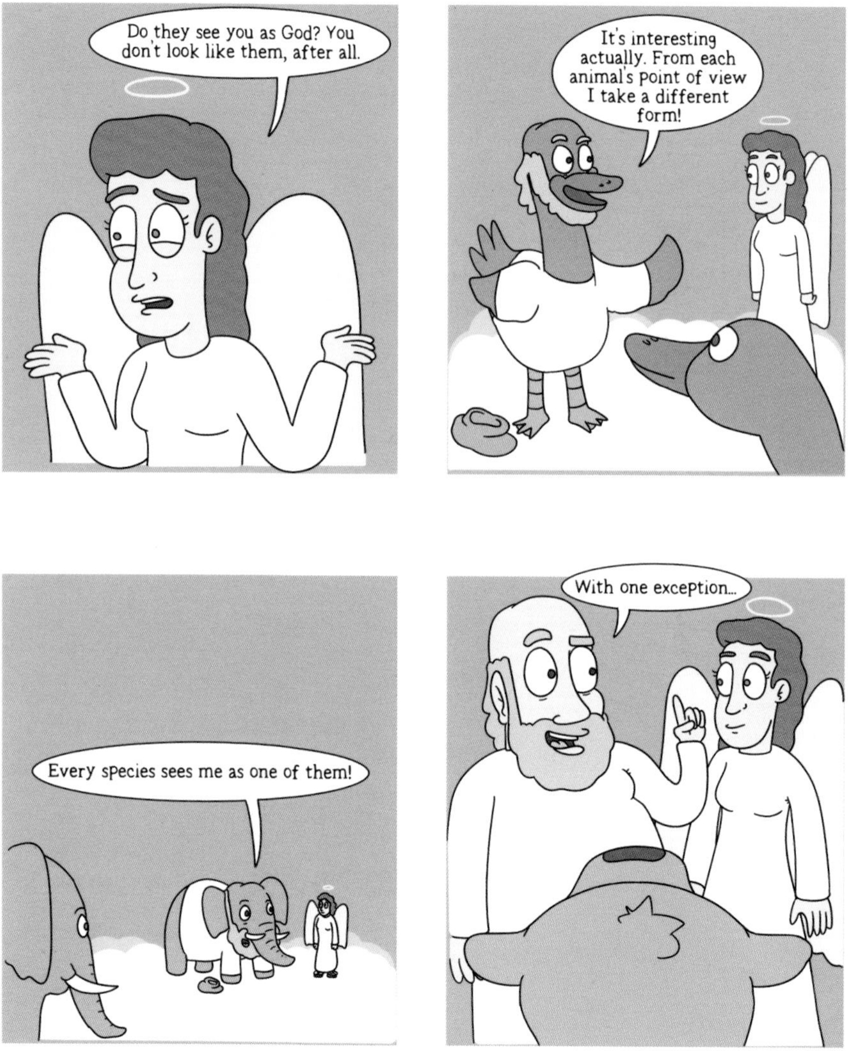
Do they see you as God? You don't look like them, after all.
It's interesting actually. From each animal's point of view I take a different form!
Every species sees me as one of them!
With one exception...

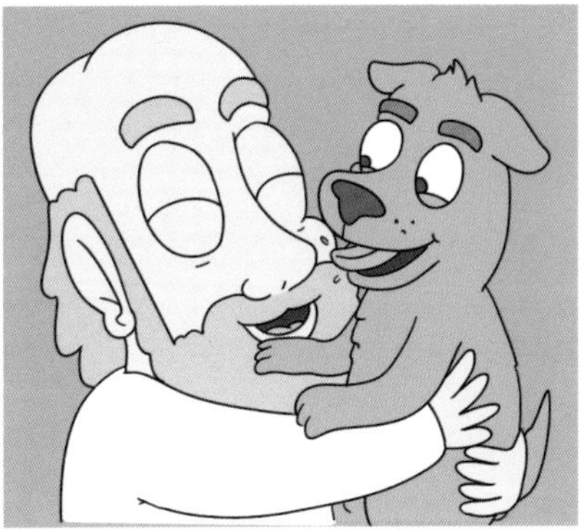

BONUS

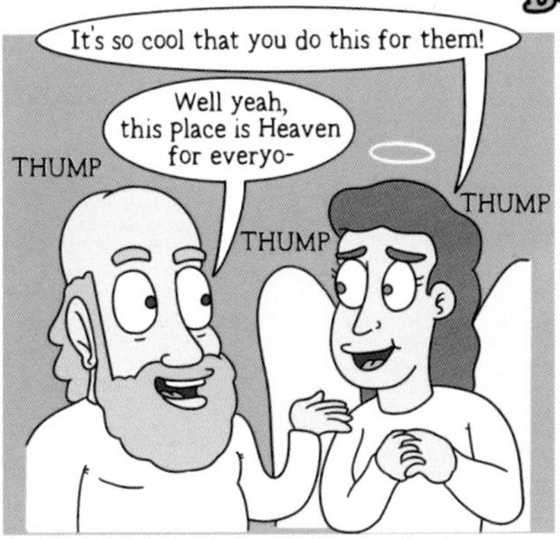
THUMP
It's so cool that you do this for them!
Well yeah, this place is Heaven for everyo-
THUMP
THUMP

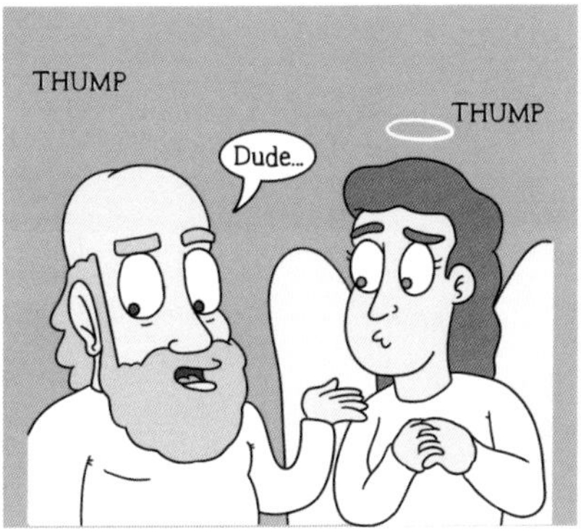
THUMP
THUMP
Dude...

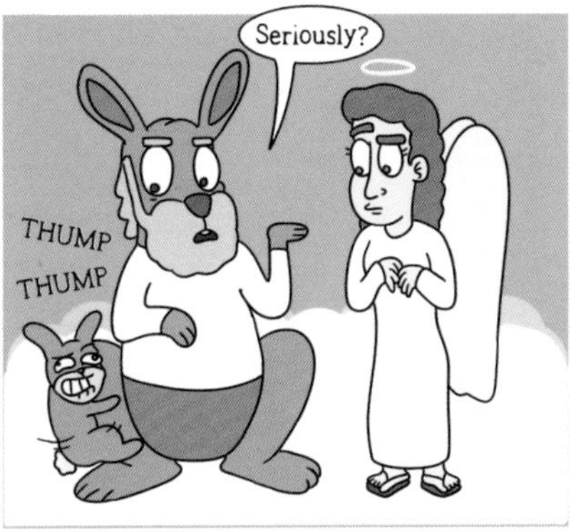
Seriously?
THUMP
THUMP

Project Eve

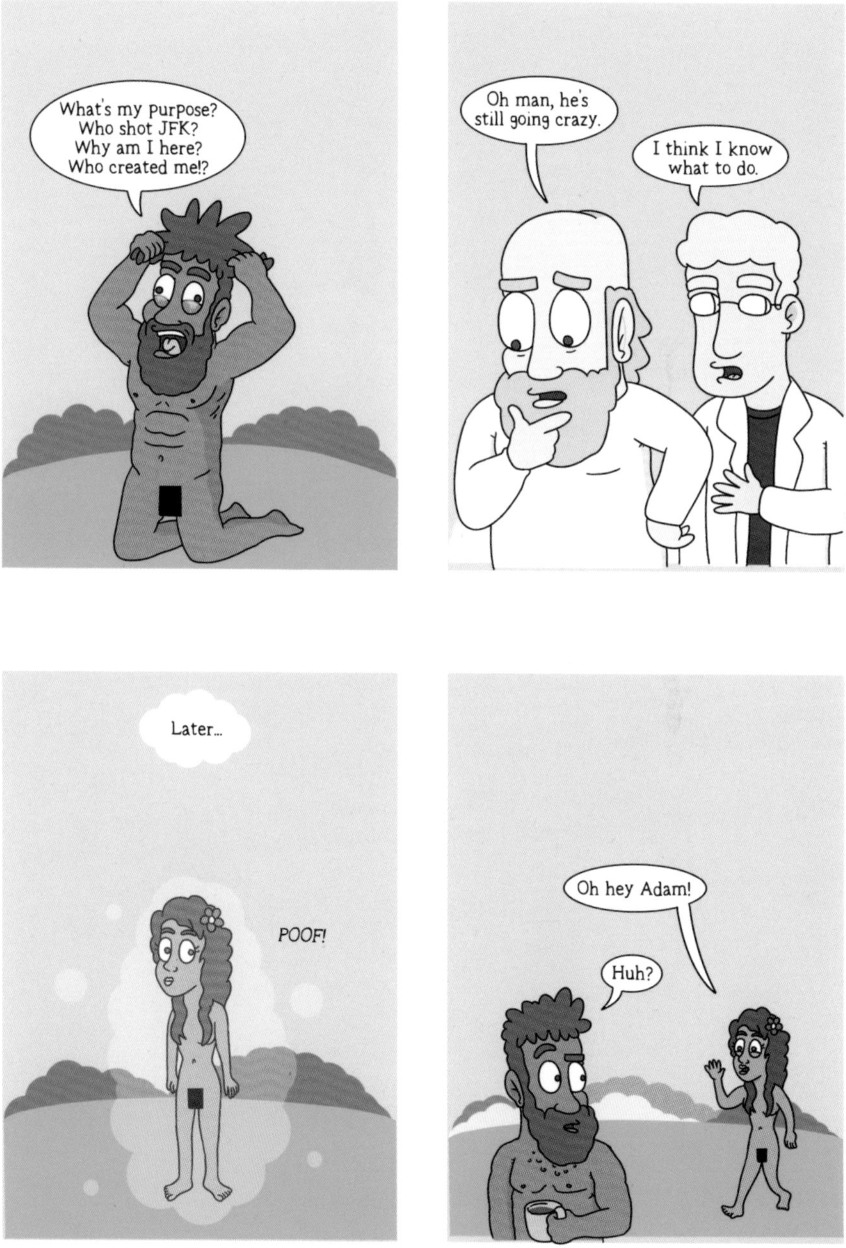
What's my purpose?
Who shot JFK?
Why am I here?
Who created me!?
Oh man, he's still going crazy.
I think I know what to do.
Later...
POOF!
Oh hey Adam!
Huh?

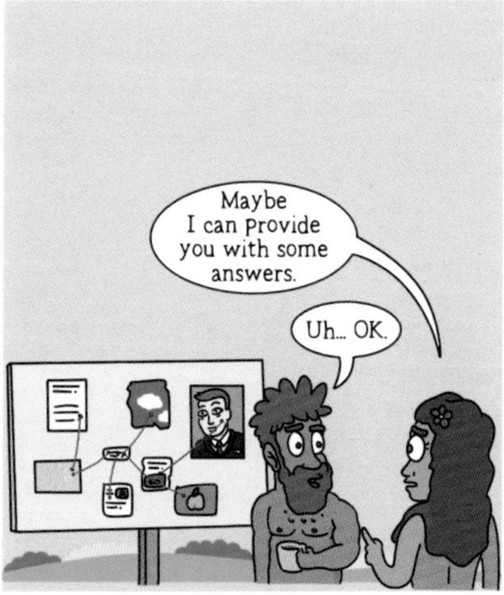
Maybe I can provide you with some answers.
Uh... OK.

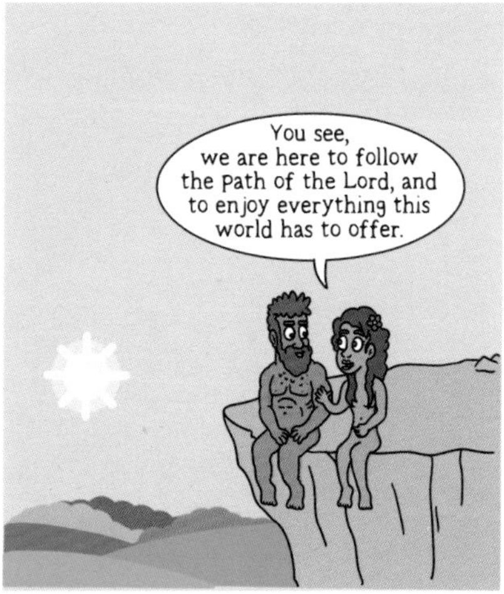
You see, we are here to follow the path of the Lord, and to enjoy everything this world has to offer.

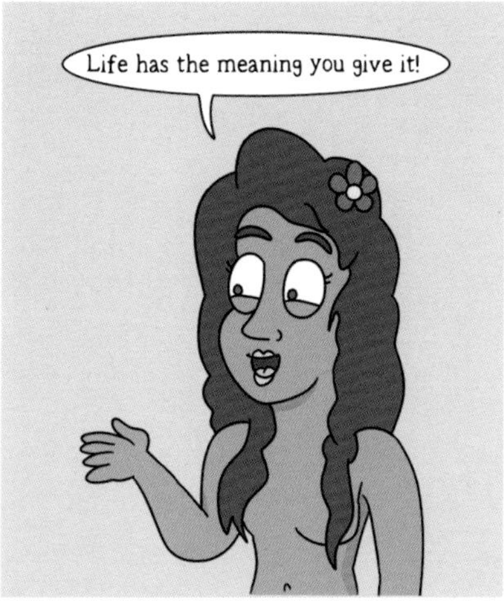
Life has the meaning you give it!

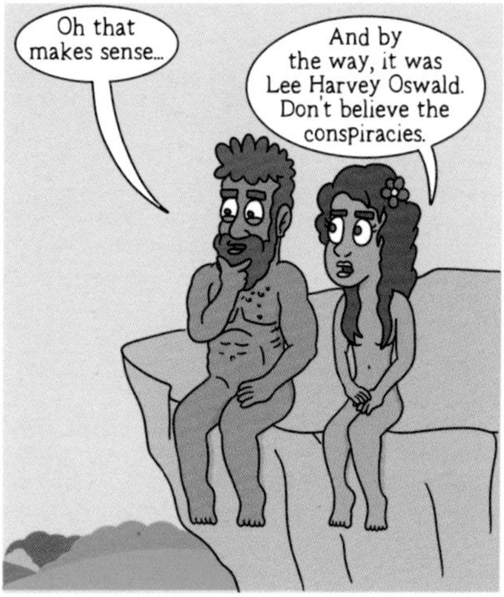
Oh that makes sense...
And by the way, it was Lee Harvey Oswald. Don't believe the conspiracies.

BONUS

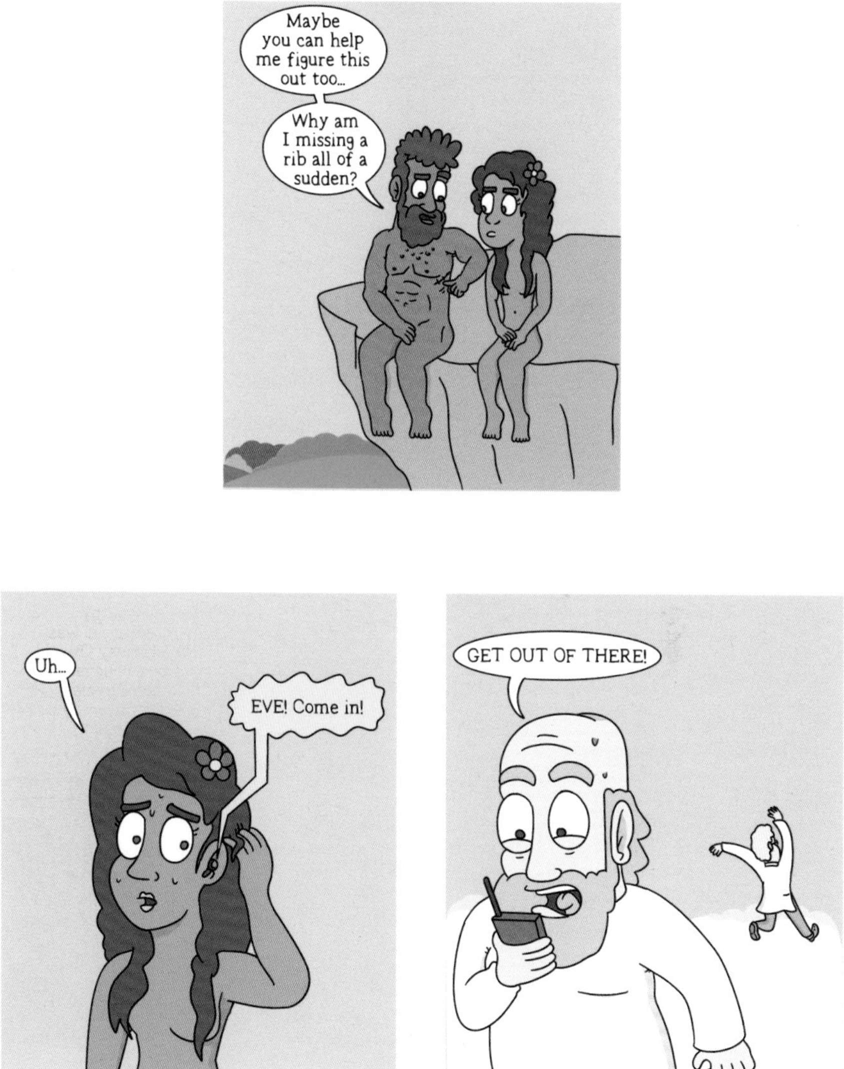
Maybe you can help me figure this out too...
Why am I missing a rib all of a sudden?
Uh...
EVE! Come in!
GET OUT OF THERE!

Greek

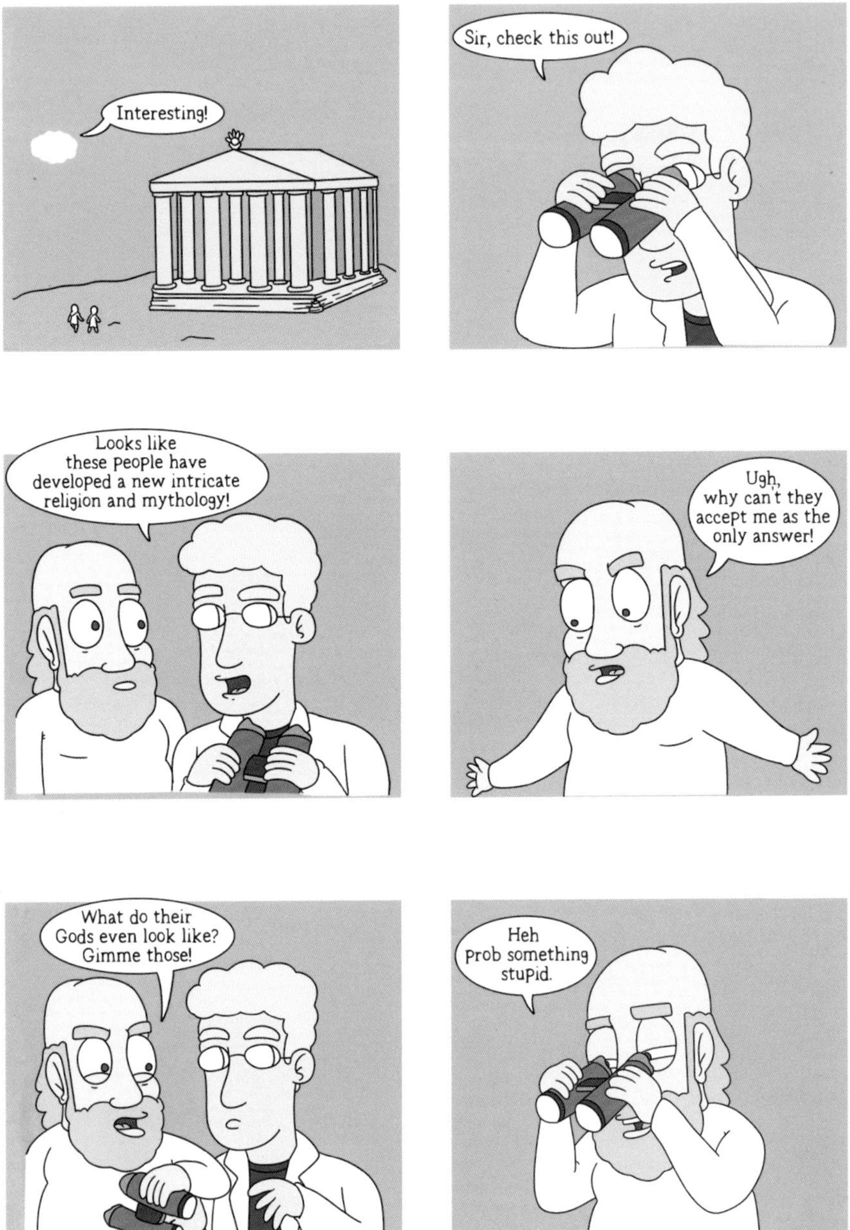
Interesting!
Sir, check this out!
Looks like these people have developed a new intricate religion and mythology!
Ugh, why can't they accept me as the only answer!
What do their Gods even look like? Gimme those!
Heh Prob something stupid.

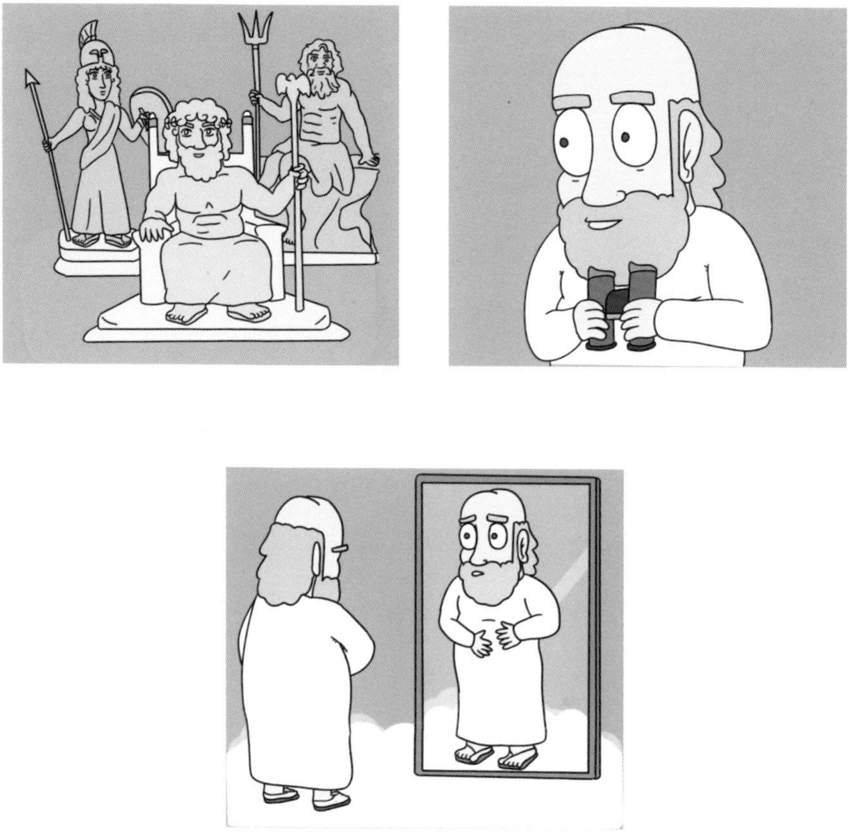

BONUS

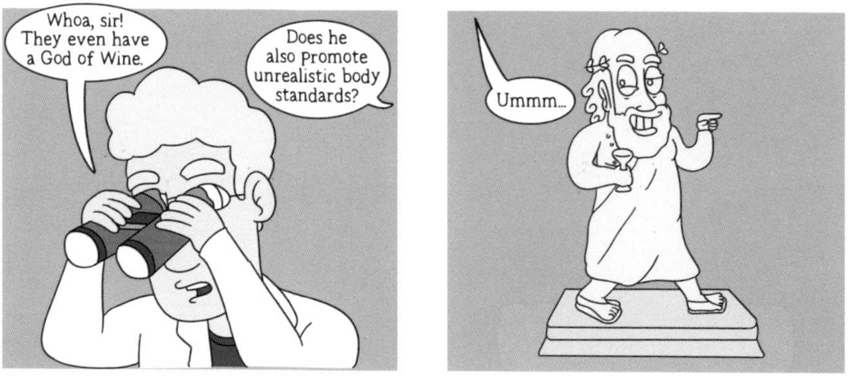
Whoa, sir! They even have a God of Wine.
Does he also promote unrealistic body standards?
Ummm...

Joke

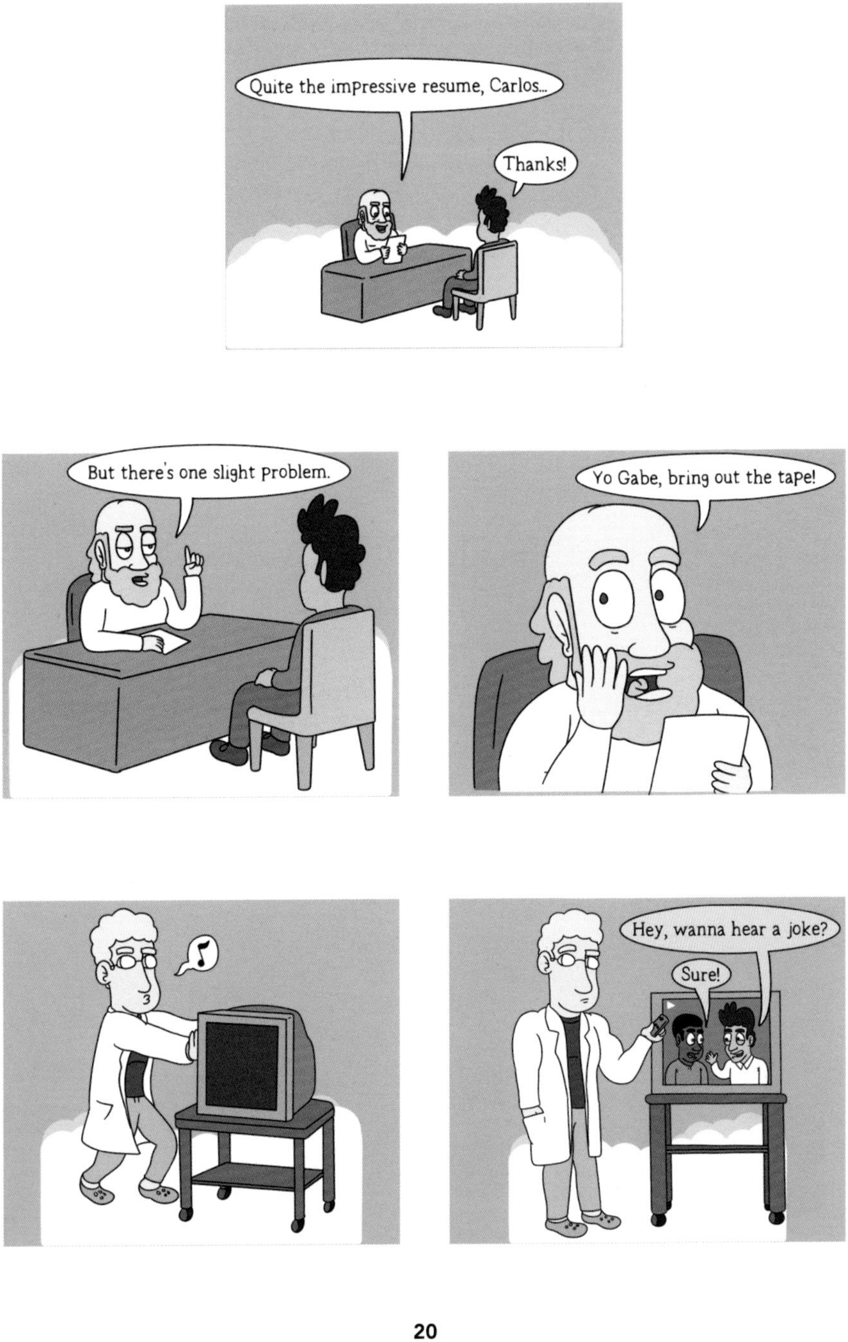
Quite the impressive resume, Carlos...
Thanks!
But there's one slight problem.
Yo Gabe, bring out the tape!
Hey, wanna hear a joke?
Sure!

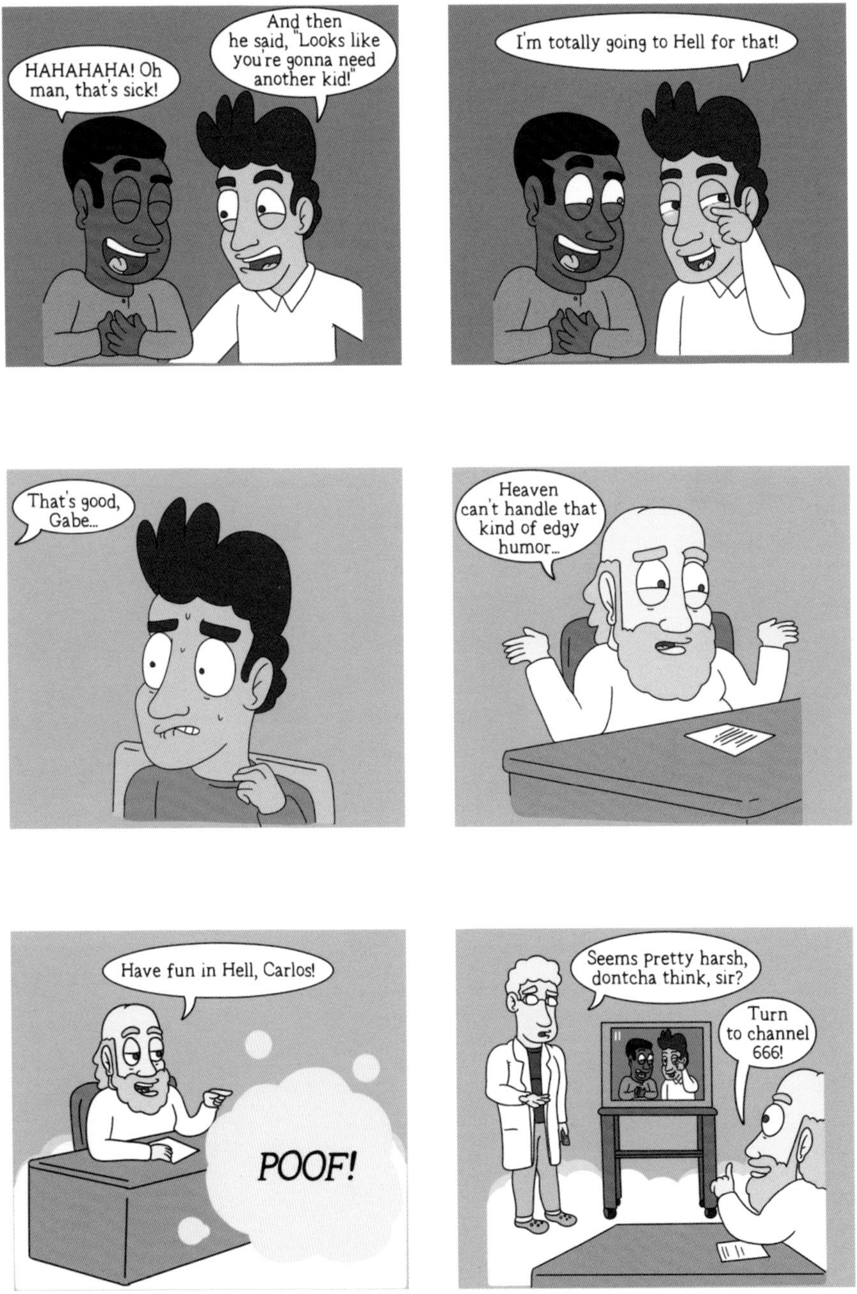
HAHAHAHA! Oh man, that's sick!
And then he said, "Looks like you're gonna need another kid!"
I'm totally going to Hell for that!
That's good, Gabe...
Heaven can't handle that kind of edgy humor...
Have fun in Hell, Carlos!
POOF!
Seems pretty harsh, dontcha think, sir?
Turn to channel 666!

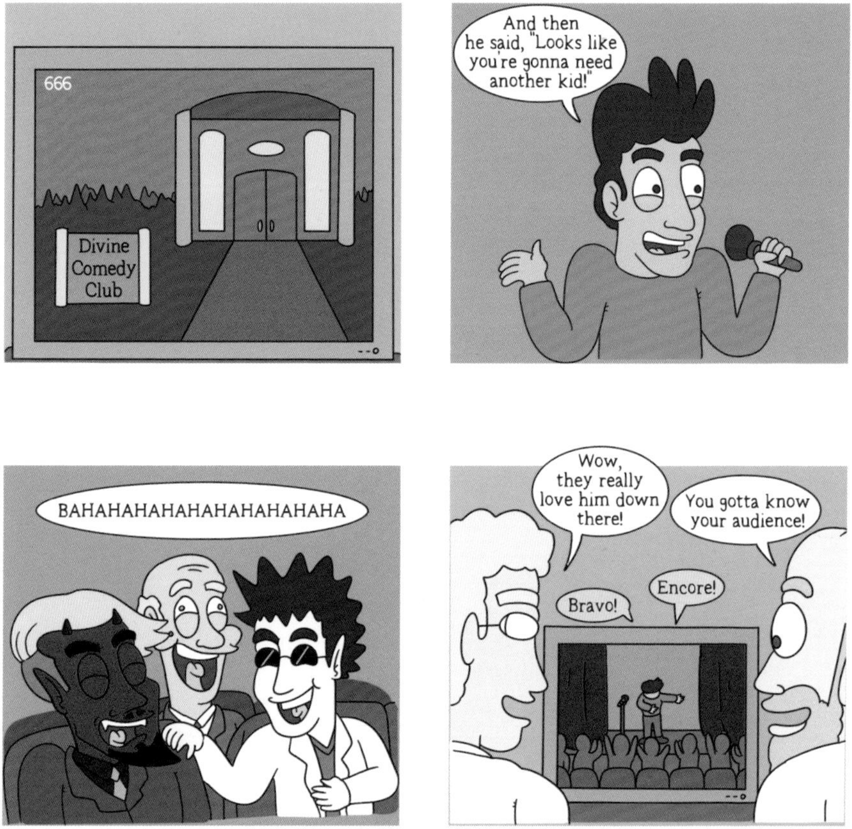
666
Divine Comedy Club
And then he said, "Looks like you're gonna need another kid!"
BAHAHAHAHAHAHAHAHAHAHA
Wow, they really love him down there!
You gotta know your audience!
Bravo!
Encore!

BONUS

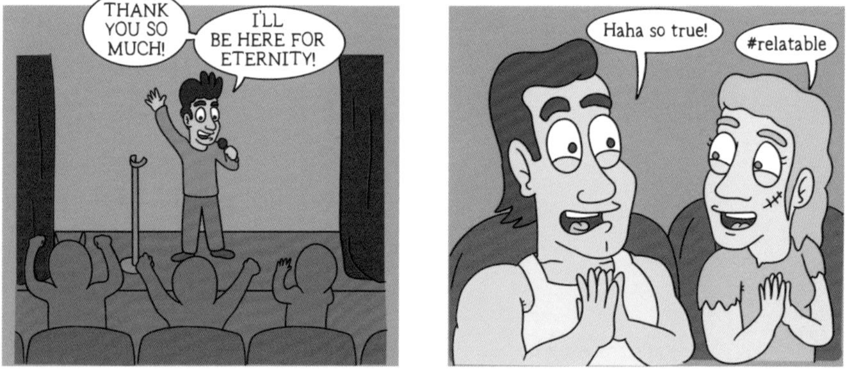
THANK YOU SO MUCH!
I'LL BE HERE FOR ETERNITY!
Haha so true!
#relatable

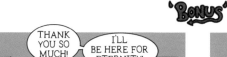

Survivor

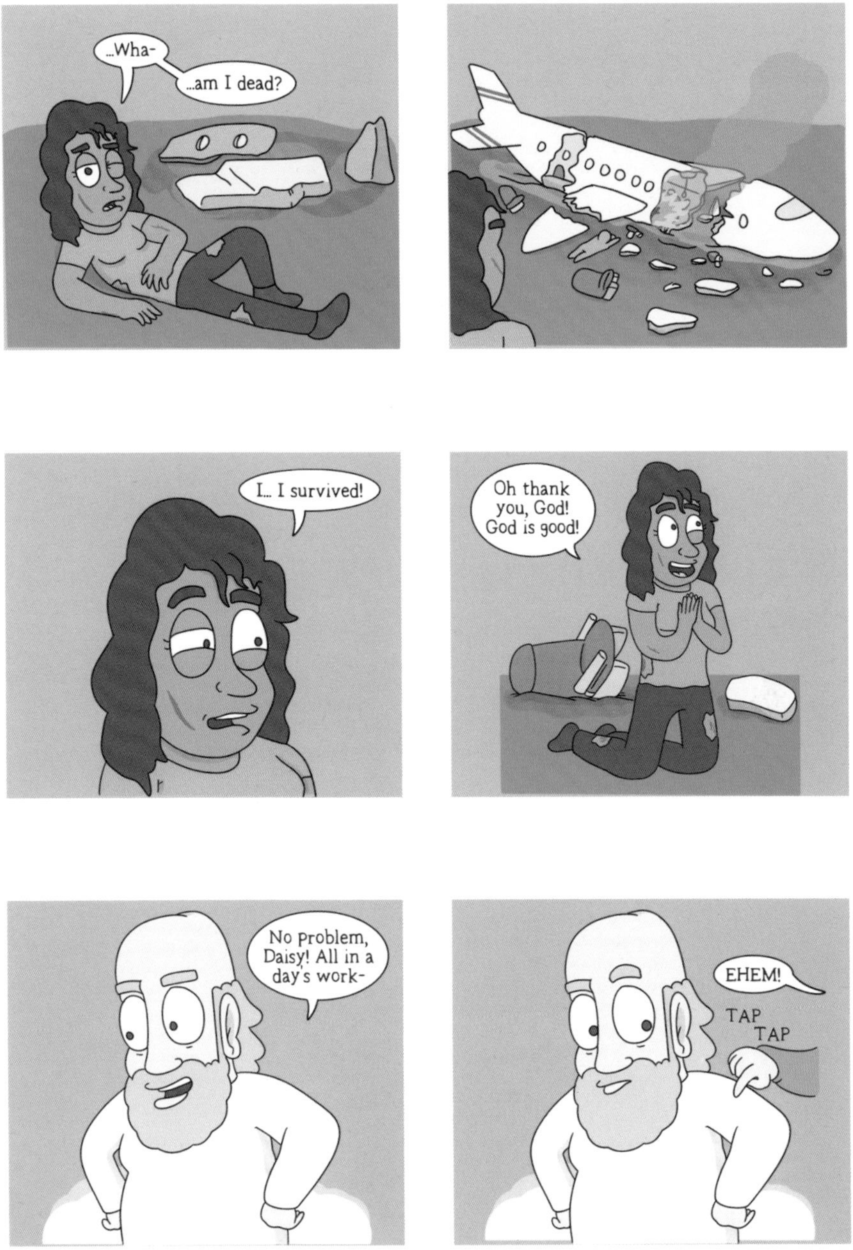

...Wha-
...am I dead?
I... I survived!
Oh thank you, God! God is good!
No problem, Daisy! All in a day's work-
EHEM!
TAP
TAP

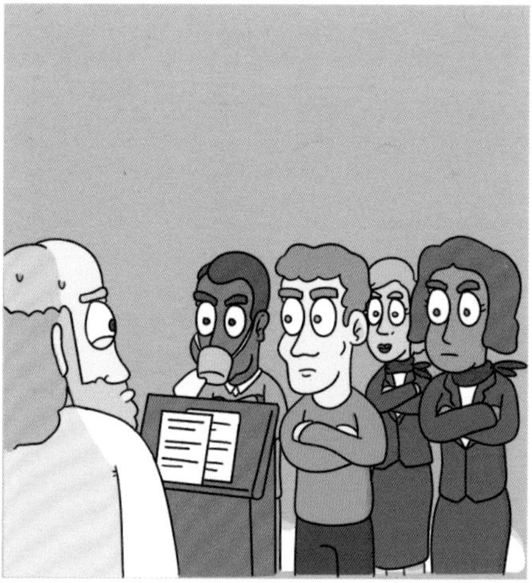

BONUS

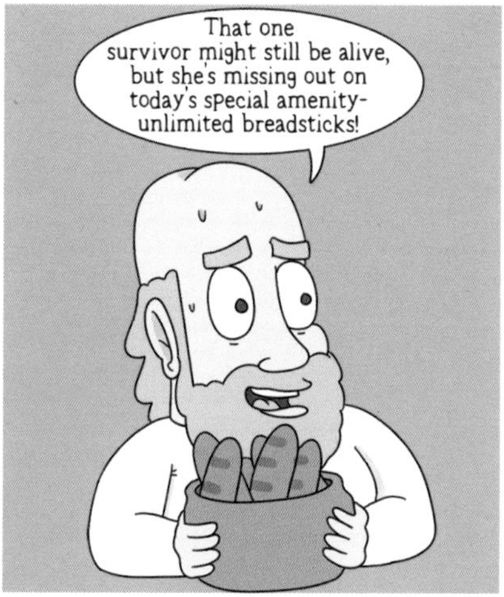
That one survivor might still be alive, but she's missing out on today's special amenity- unlimited breadsticks!

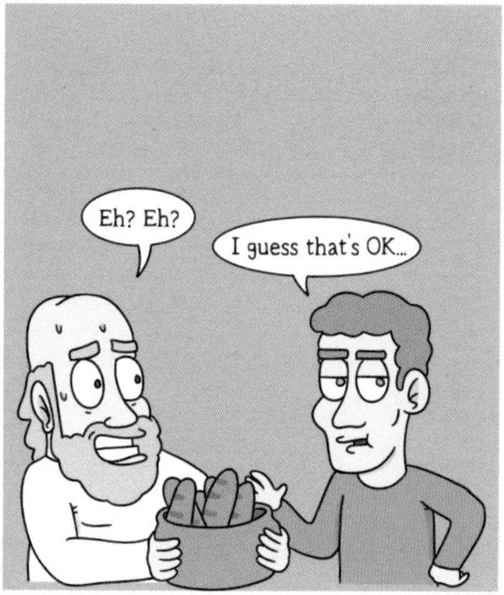
Eh? Eh?
I guess that's OK...

Bugs

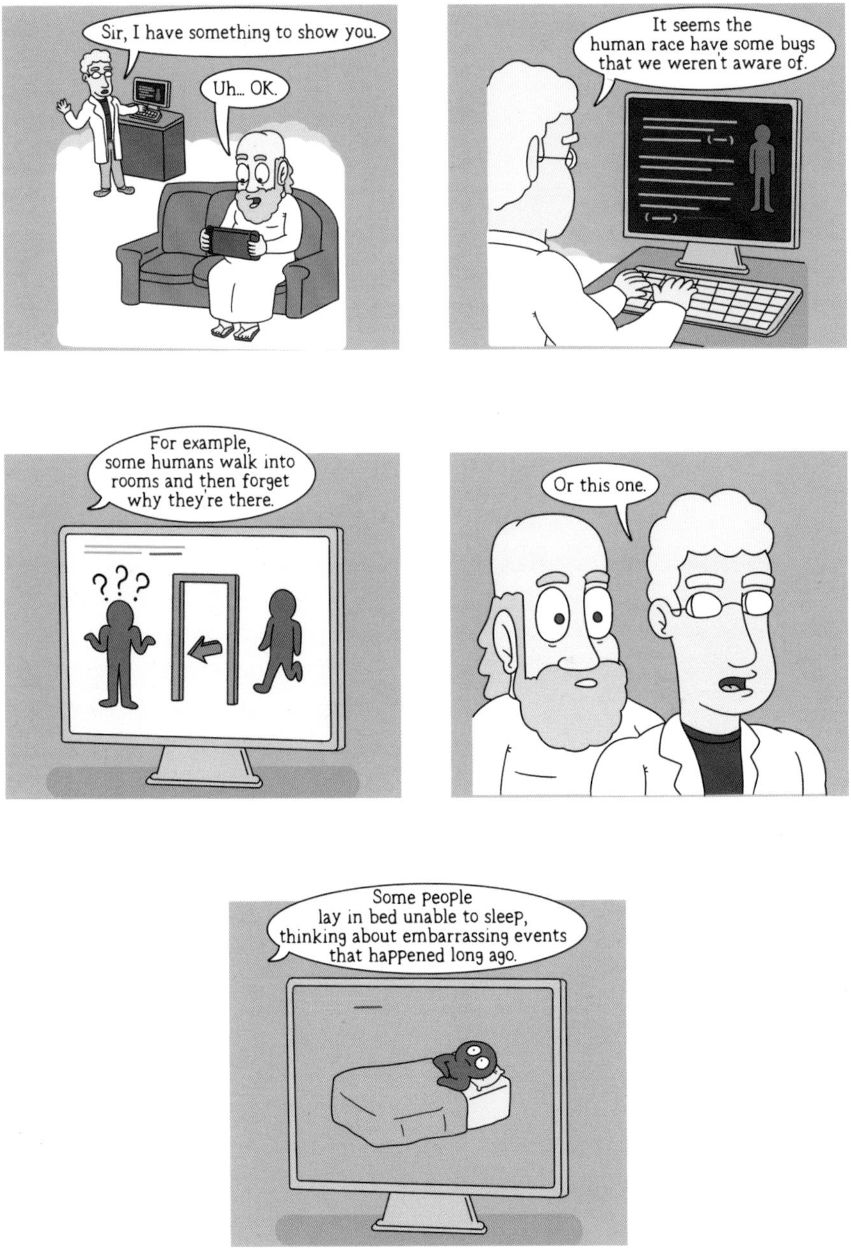
Sir, I have something to show you.
Uh... OK.
It seems the human race have some bugs that we weren't aware of.
For example, some humans walk into rooms and then forget why they're there.
???
Or this one.
Some people lay in bed unable to sleep, thinking about embarrassing events that happened long ago.

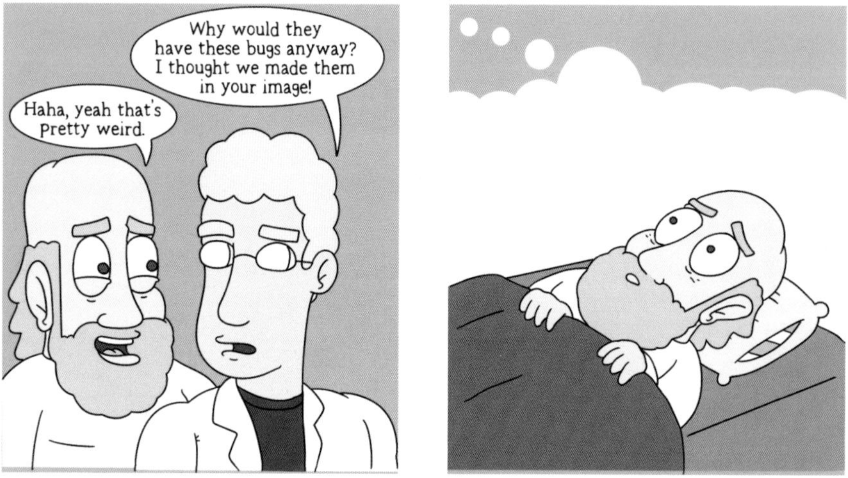
Why would they have these bugs anyway? I thought we made them in your image!
Haha, yeah that's pretty weird.

BONUS

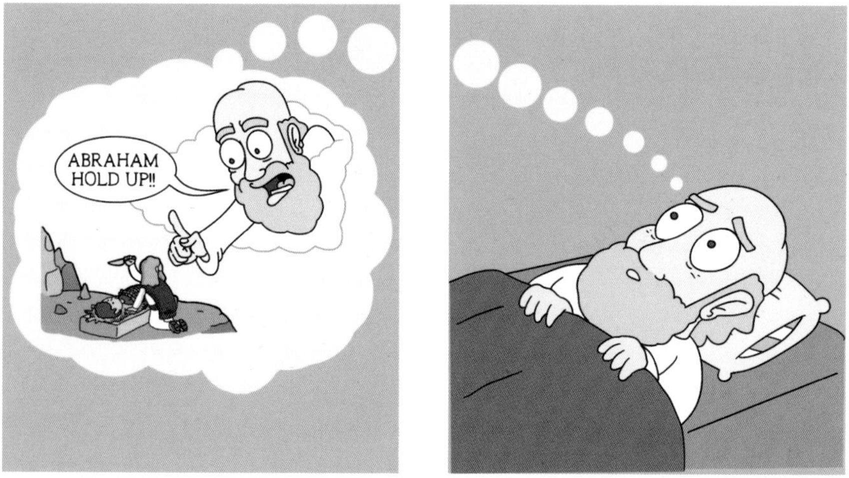
ABRAHAM HOLD UP!!

Adam & Eve: Trees

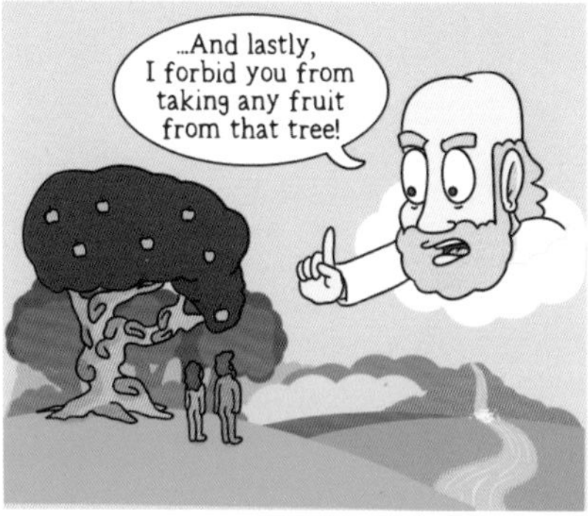
...And lastly,
I forbid you from
taking any fruit
from that tree!

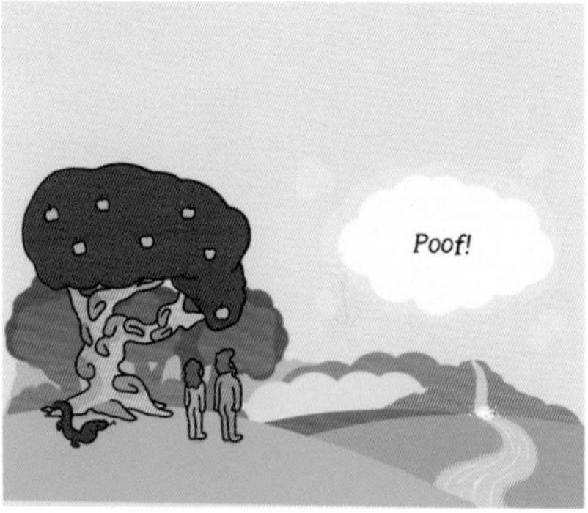
Poof!

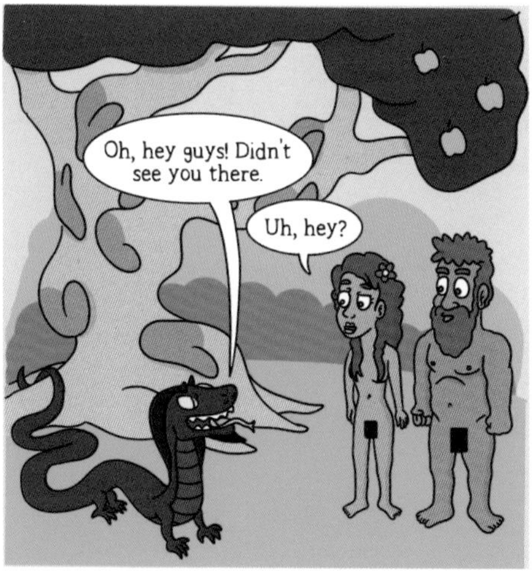
Oh, hey guys! Didn't
see you there.
Uh, hey?

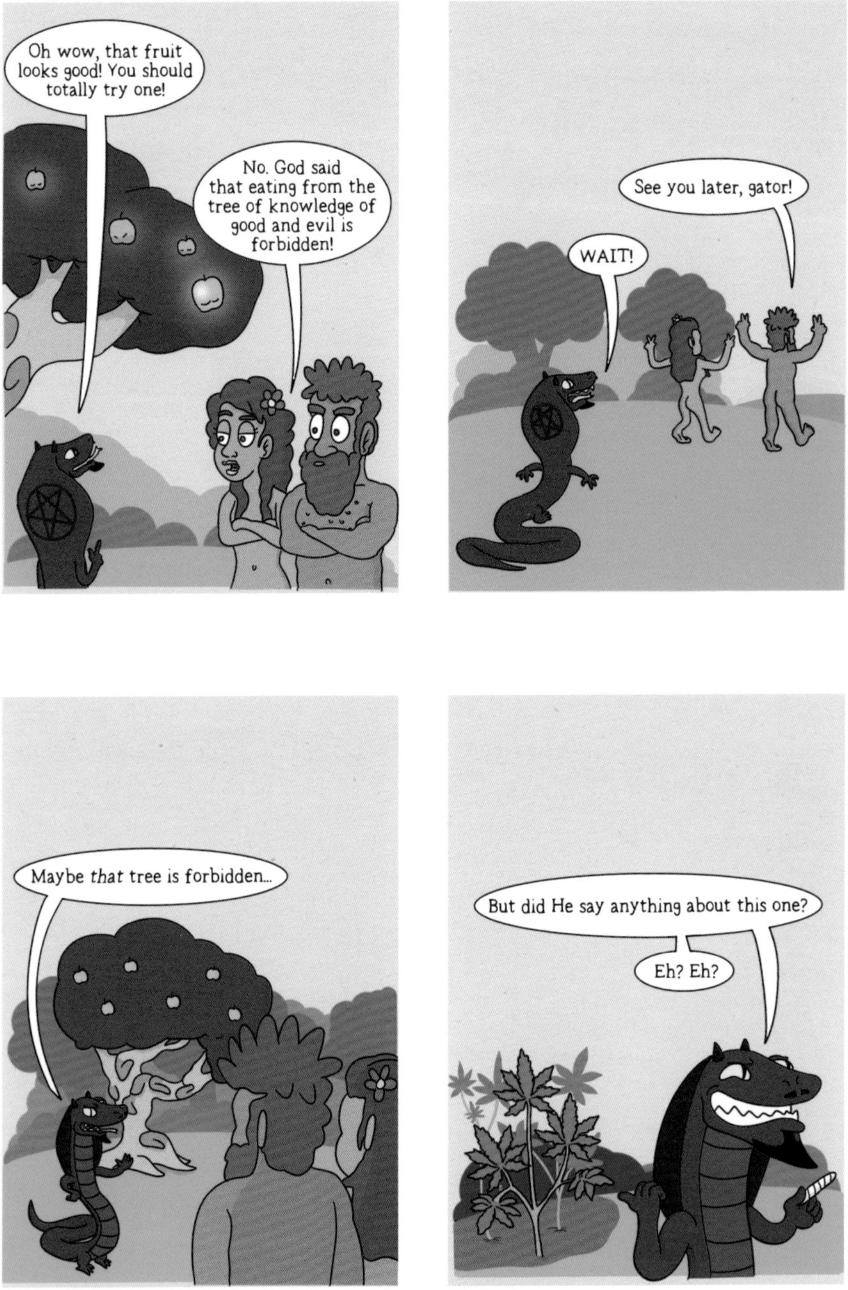
Oh wow, that fruit looks good! You should totally try one!
No. God said that eating from the tree of knowledge of good and evil is forbidden!
See you later, gator!
WAIT!
Maybe *that* tree is forbidden...
But did He say anything about this one?
Eh? Eh?

But like why does He get to dictate good and evil? How do you objectively define goodness? Is morality absolute?
Dude, totally!
Right?

BONUS

Oh man, I got the munchies...
Me too!
Ooh that yellow fruit looks delish!

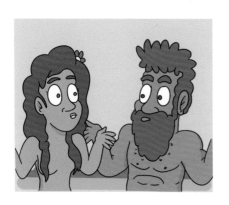

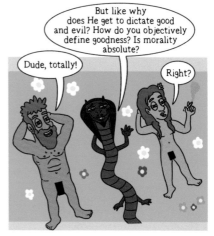

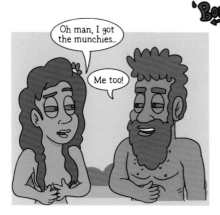

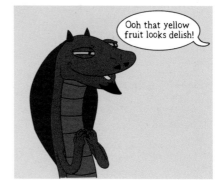

Trick or Treat

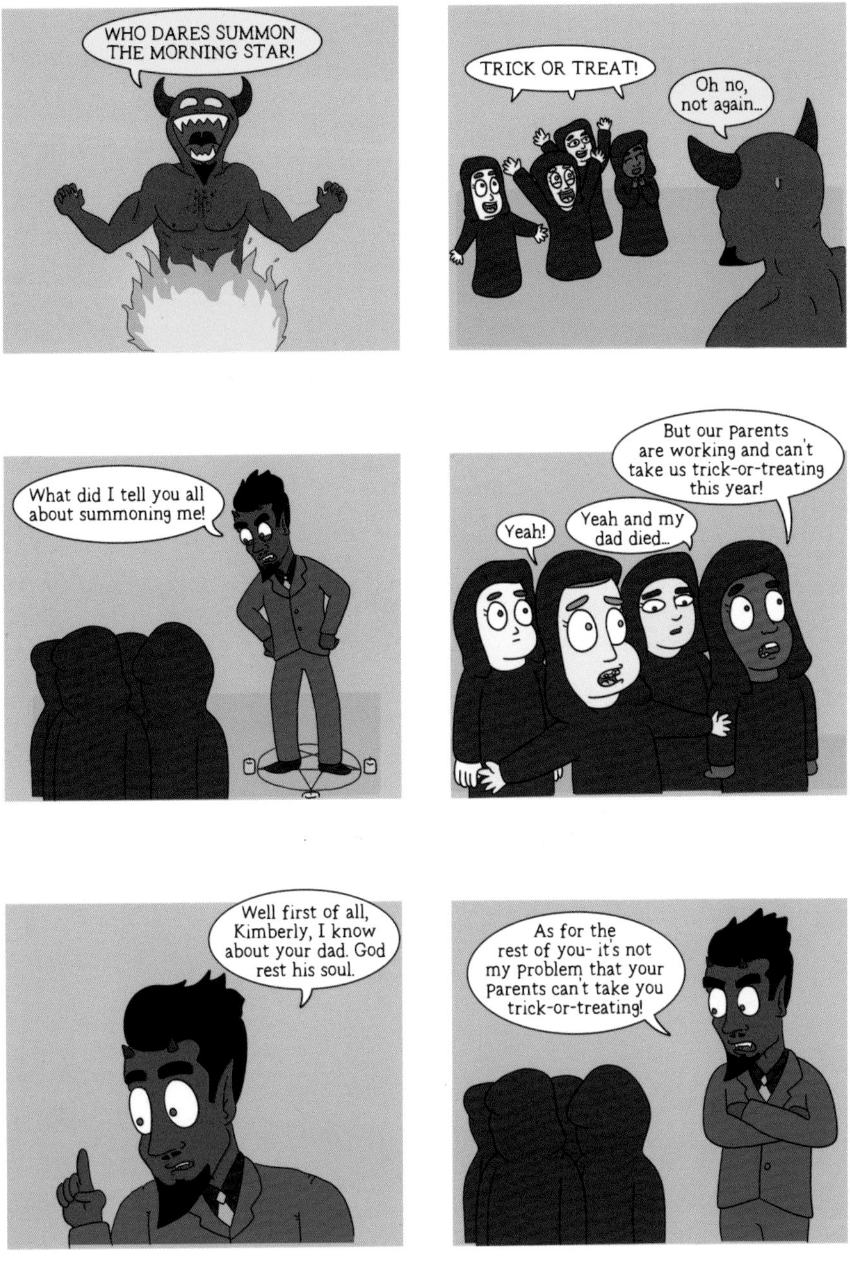
WHO DARES SUMMON THE MORNING STAR!
TRICK OR TREAT!
Oh no, not again...
What did I tell you all about summoning me!
But our parents are working and can't take us trick-or-treating this year!
Yeah!
Yeah and my dad died...
Well first of all, Kimberly, I know about your dad. God rest his soul.
As for the rest of you- it's not my problem that your parents can't take you trick-or-treating!

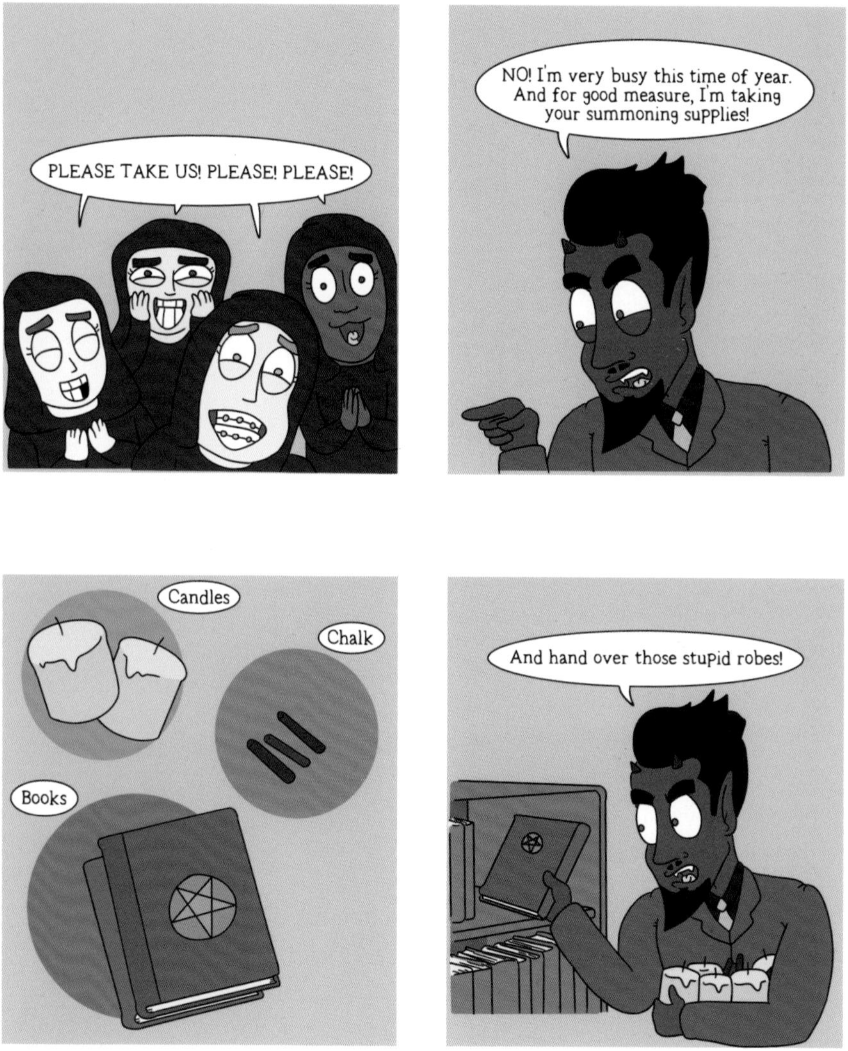
PLEASE TAKE US! PLEASE! PLEASE!
NO! I'm very busy this time of year. And for good measure, I'm taking your summoning supplies!
Candles
Chalk
Books
And hand over those stupid robes!

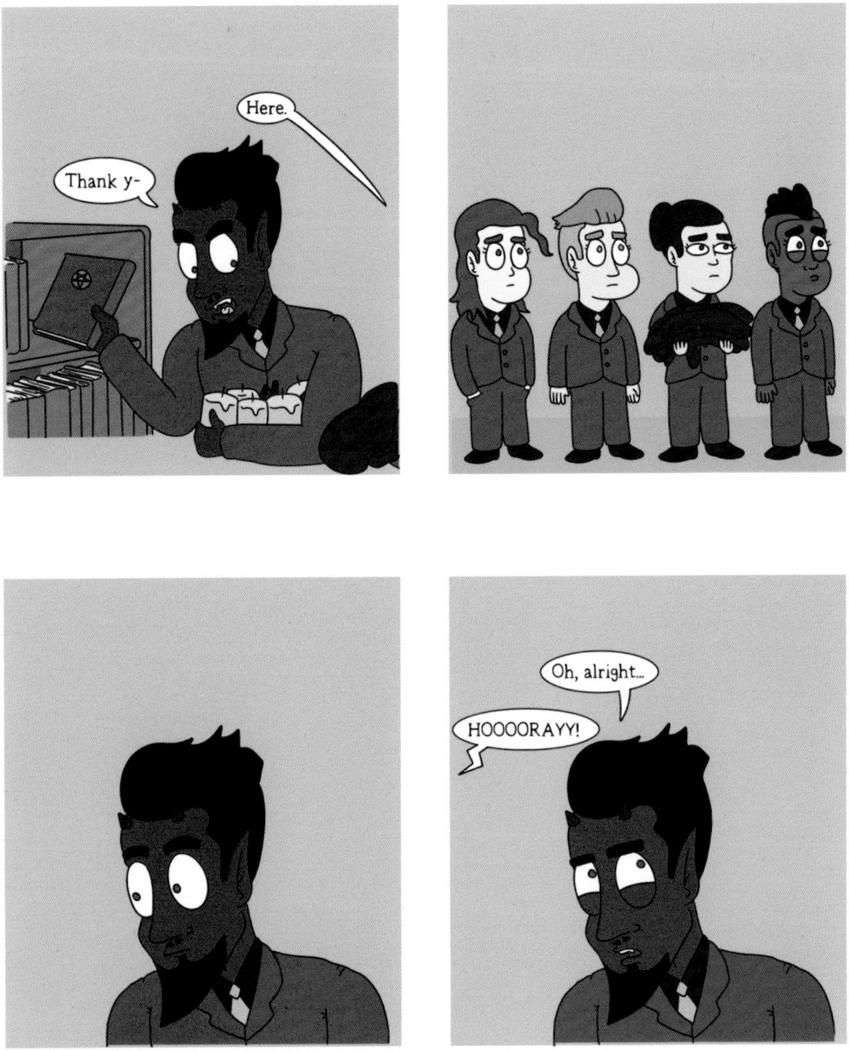
Thank y-
Here.
Oh, alright...
HOOOORAYY!

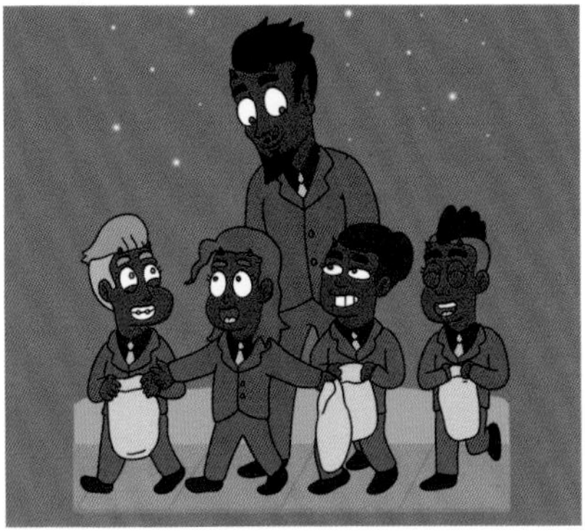

BONUS

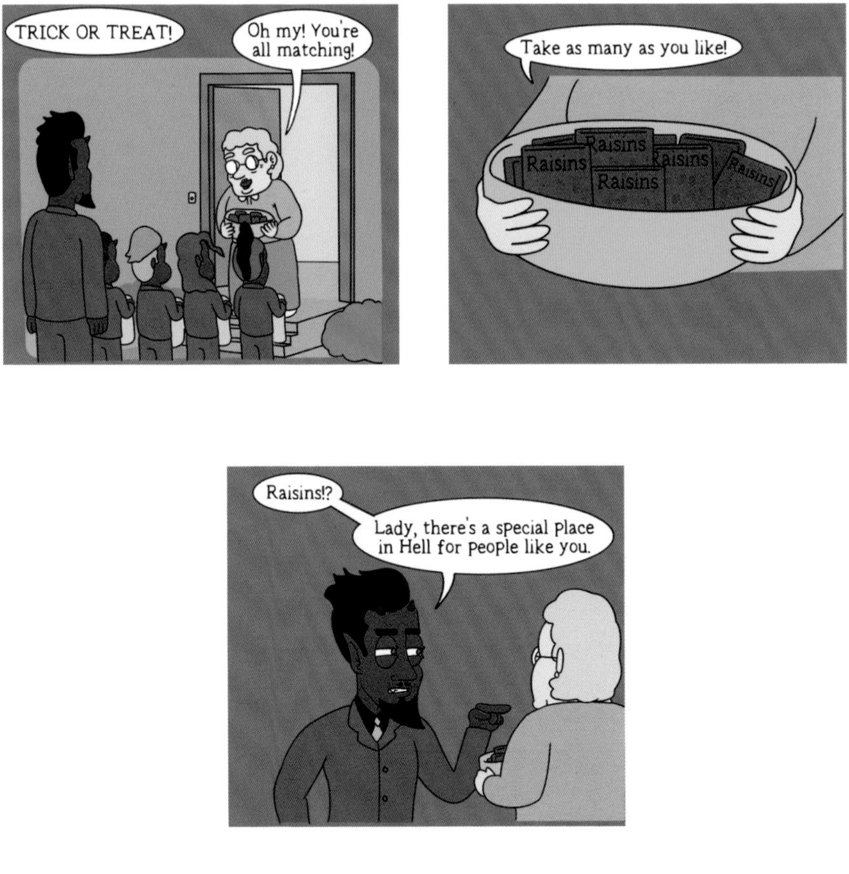
TRICK OR TREAT!
Oh my! You're all matching!
Take as many as you like!
Raisins
Raisins
Raisins
Raisins
Raisins
Raisins!?
Lady, there's a special place in Hell for people like you.

Spam

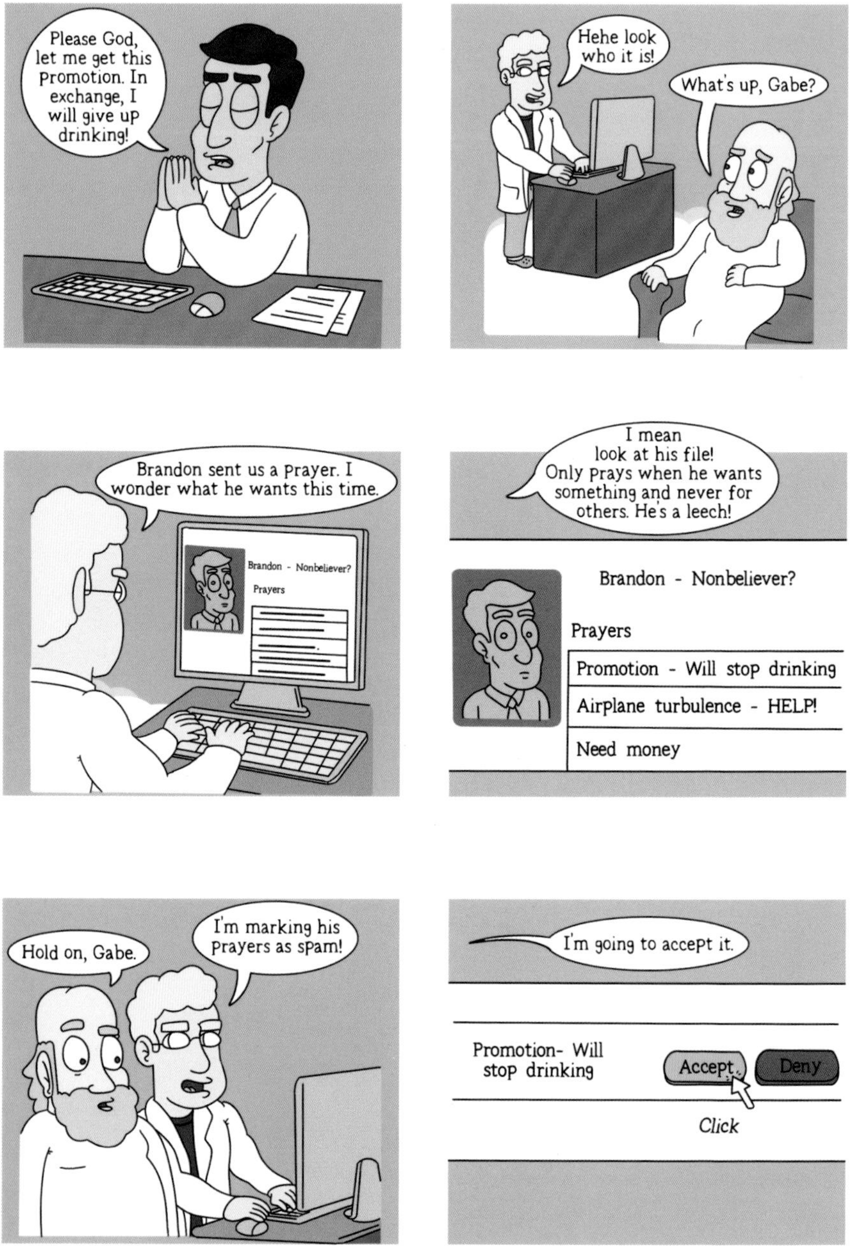

Please God, let me get this promotion. In exchange, I will give up drinking!
Hehe look who it is!
What's up, Gabe?
Brandon sent us a prayer. I wonder what he wants this time.
Brandon - Nonbeliever?
Prayers
I mean look at his file! Only prays when he wants something and never for others. He's a leech!
Brandon - Nonbeliever?
Prayers
Promotion - Will stop drinking
Airplane turbulence - HELP!
Need money
I'm marking his prayers as spam!
Hold on, Gabe.
I'm going to accept it.
Promotion- Will stop drinking
Accept
Deny
Click

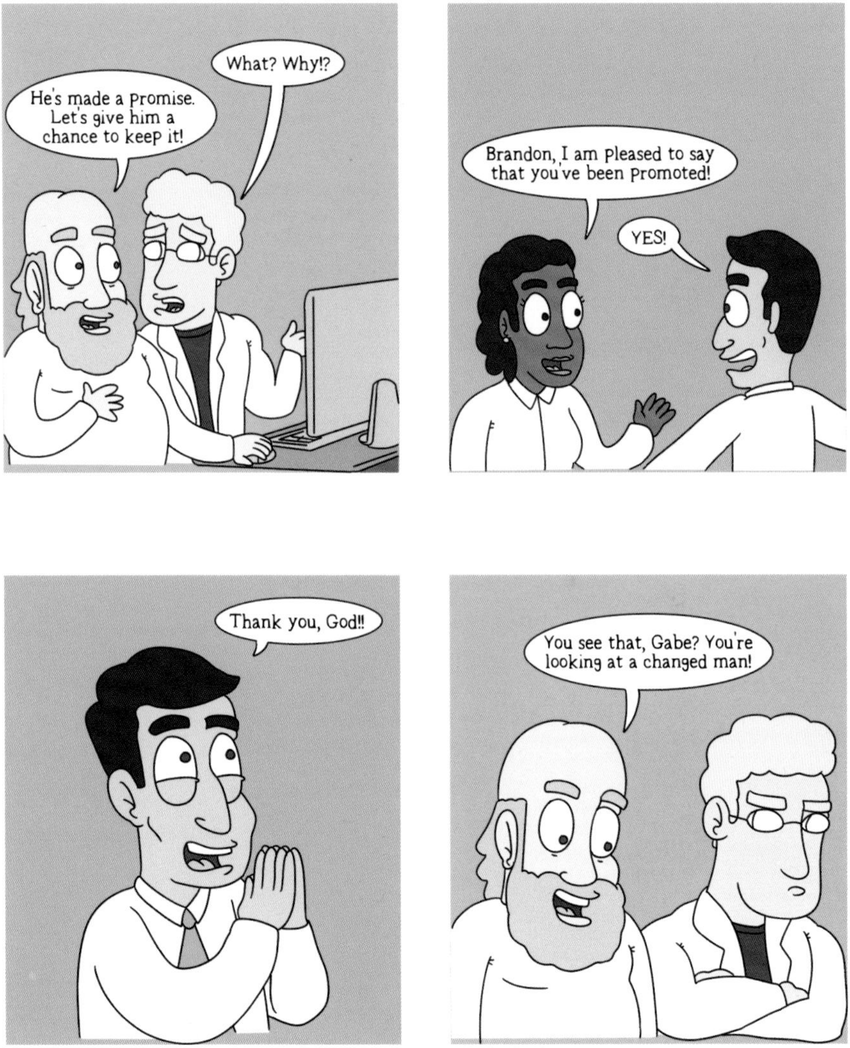
He's made a promise. Let's give him a chance to keep it!
What? Why!?
Brandon, I am pleased to say that you've been promoted!
YES!
Thank you, God!!
You see that, Gabe? You're looking at a changed man!

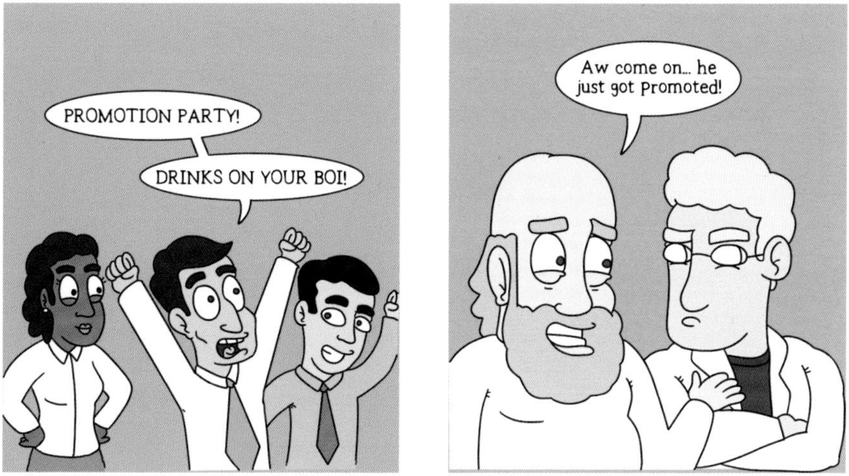
PROMOTION PARTY!
DRINKS ON YOUR BOI!
Aw come on... he just got promoted!

BONUS

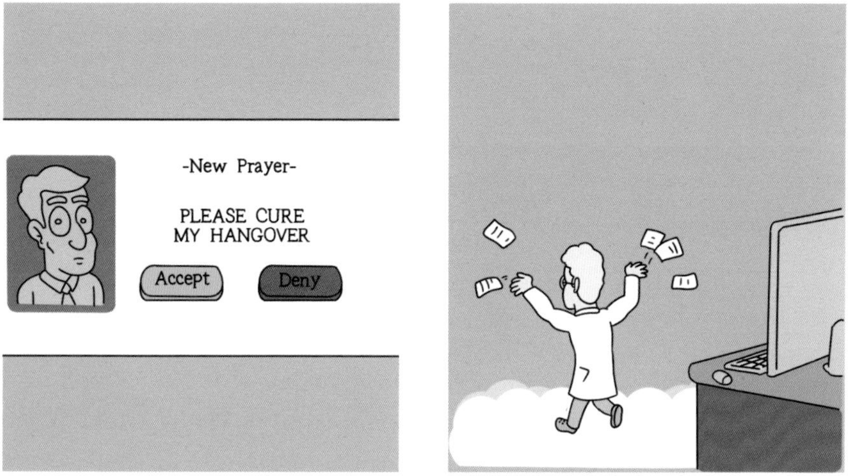
-New Prayer-
PLEASE CURE MY HANGOVER
Accept
Deny

VIP

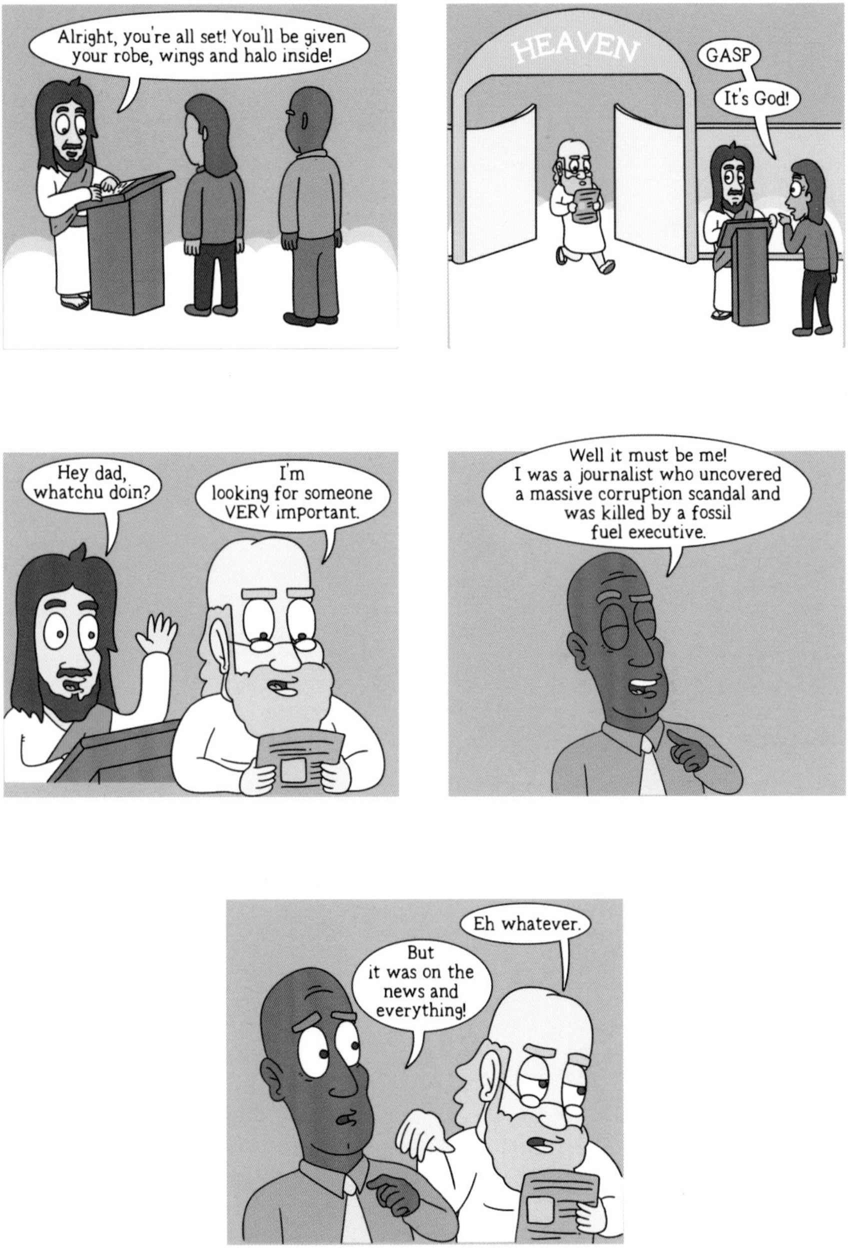
Alright, you're all set! You'll be given your robe, wings and halo inside!
HEAVEN
GASP
It's God!
Hey dad, whatchu doin?
I'm looking for someone VERY important.
Well it must be me! I was a journalist who uncovered a massive corruption scandal and was killed by a fossil fuel executive.
But it was on the news and everything!
Eh whatever.

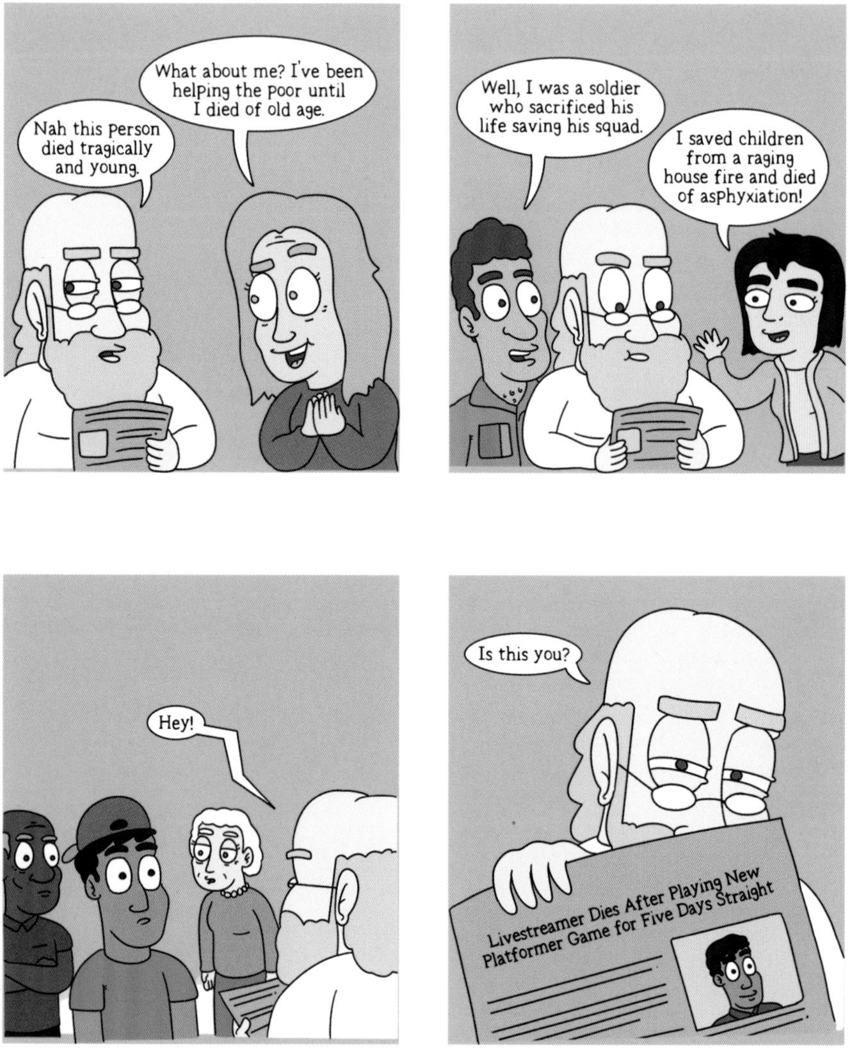
Nah this person died tragically and young.
What about me? I've been helping the poor until I died of old age.
Well, I was a soldier who sacrificed his life saving his squad.
I saved children from a raging house fire and died of asphyxiation!
Hey!
Is this you?
Livestreamer Dies After Playing New Platformer Game for Five Days Straight

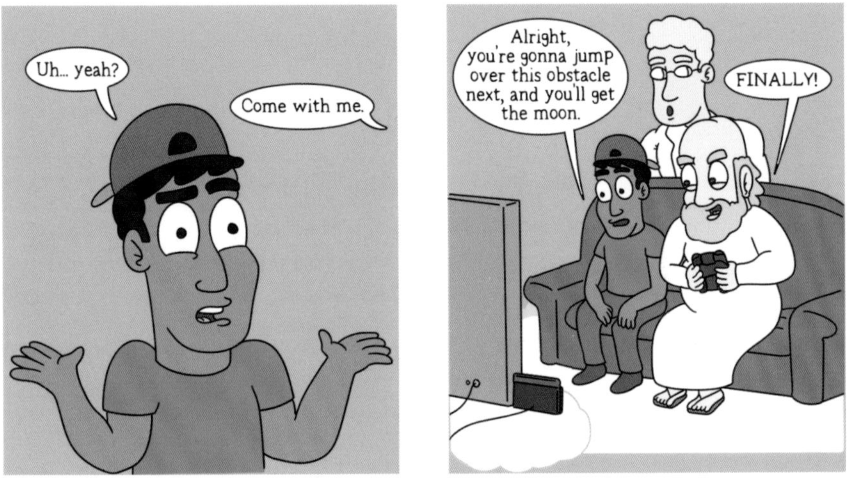
Uh... yeah?
Come with me.
Alright, you're gonna jump over this obstacle next, and you'll get the moon.
FINALLY!

BONUS

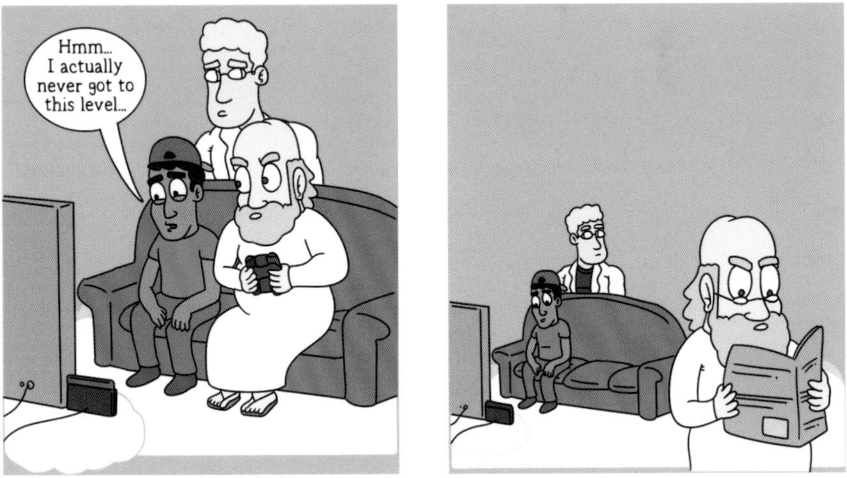
Hmm... I actually never got to this level...

Escape

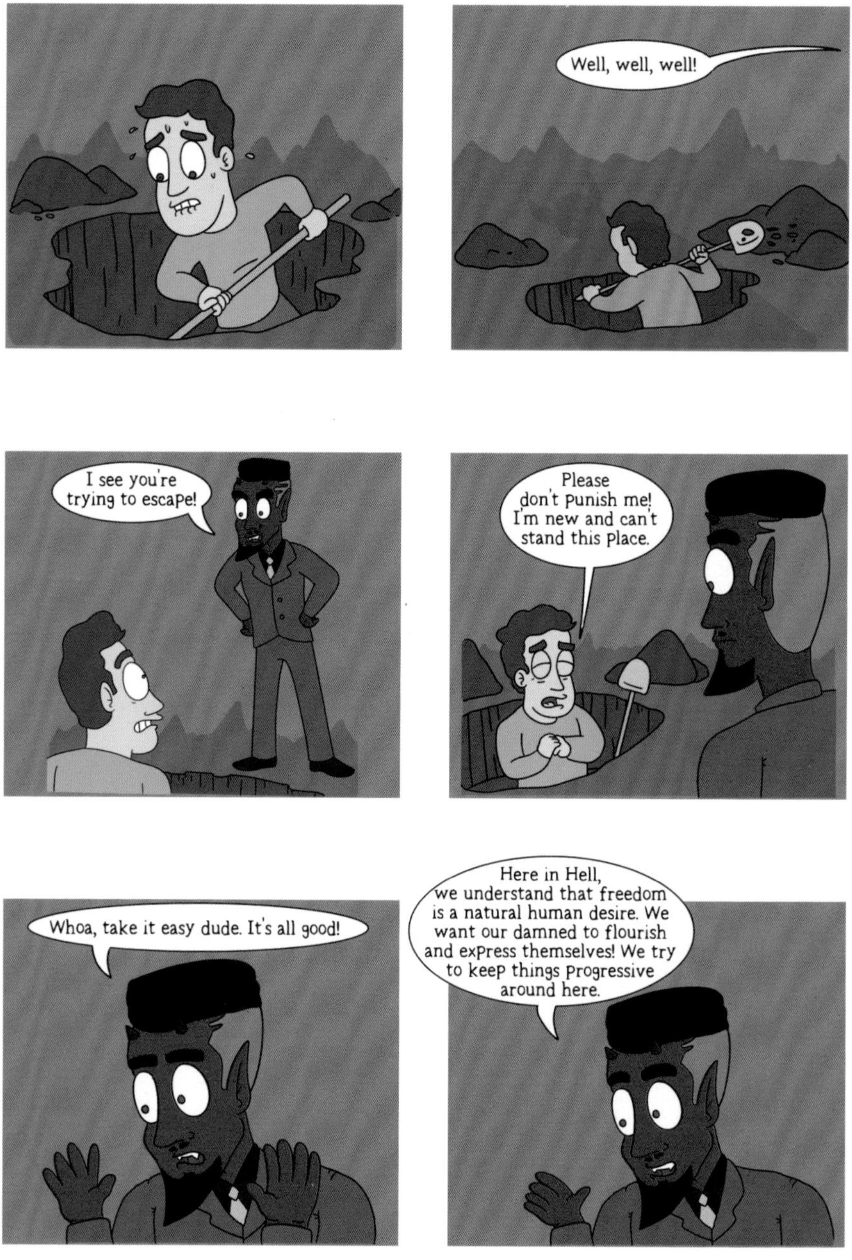
Well, well, well!
I see you're trying to escape!
Please don't punish me! I'm new and can't stand this place.
Whoa, take it easy dude. It's all good!
Here in Hell, we understand that freedom is a natural human desire. We want our damned to flourish and express themselves! We try to keep things progressive around here.

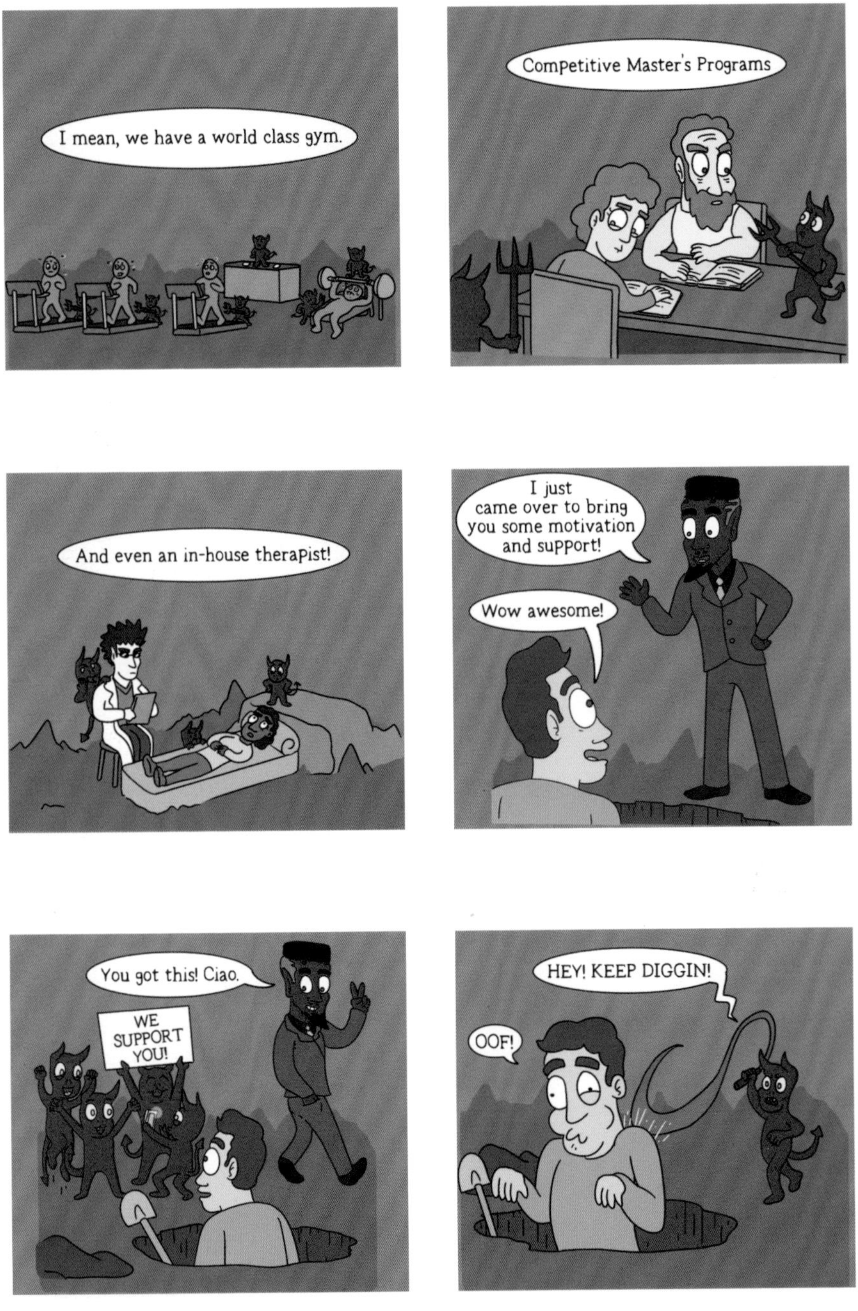
I mean, we have a world class gym.
Competitive Master's Programs
And even an in-house therapist!
I just came over to bring you some motivation and support!
Wow awesome!
You got this! Ciao.
WE SUPPORT YOU!
HEY! KEEP DIGGIN!
OOF!

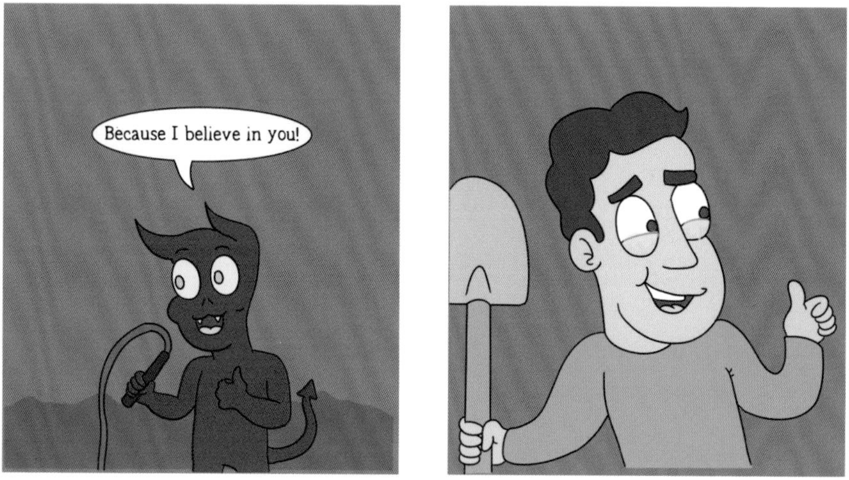
Because I believe in you!

BONUS

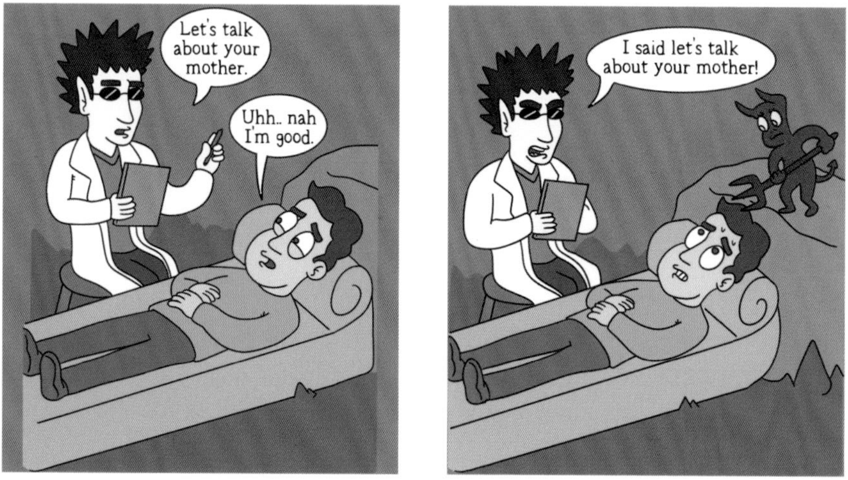
Let's talk about your mother.
Uhh.. nah I'm good.
I said let's talk about your mother!

Adam & Eve: The Fall

Hey!
HEY!!
Huh?
You have crossed the line!
I didn't want to do this, but as punishment:
YOU SHALL KNOW SICKNESS; PAIN IN CHILDBIRTH;
AND YOU WILL HAVE A FINITE LIFESPAN!

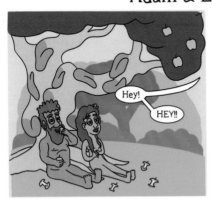

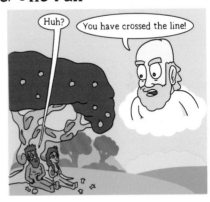

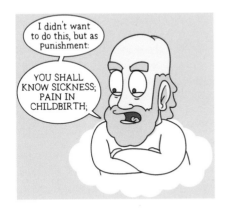

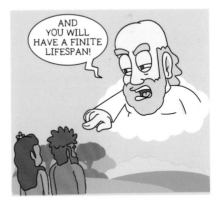

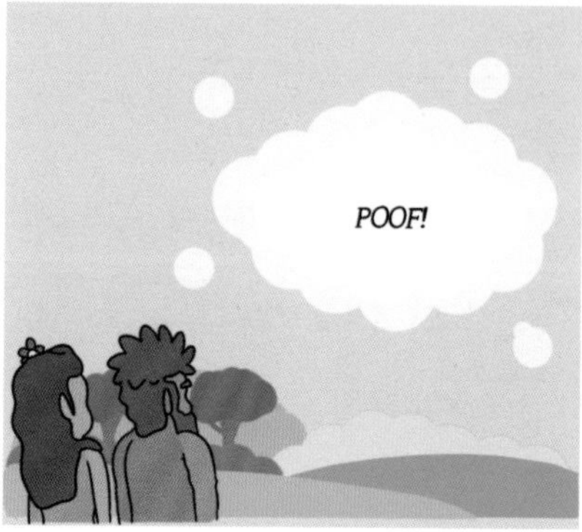
POOF!

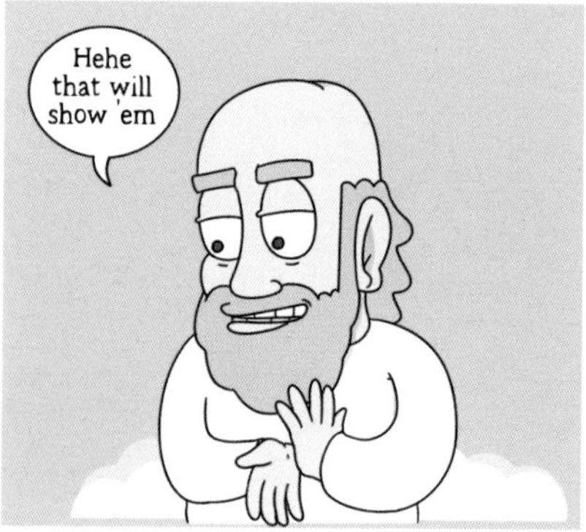
Hehe
that will
show 'em

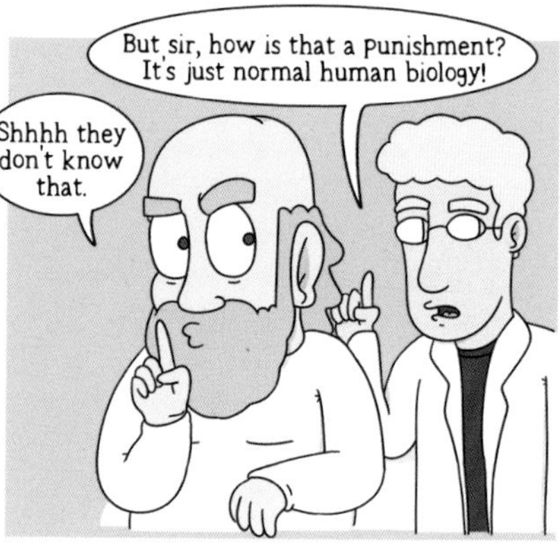
But sir, how is that a punishment?
It's just normal human biology!
Shhhh they
don't know
that.

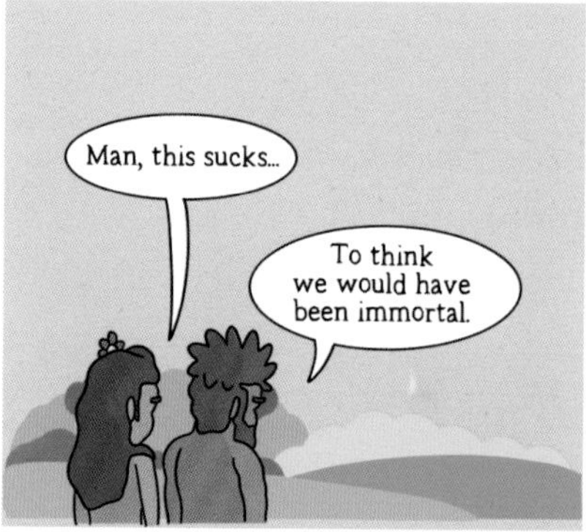
Man, this sucks...
To think
we would have
been immortal.

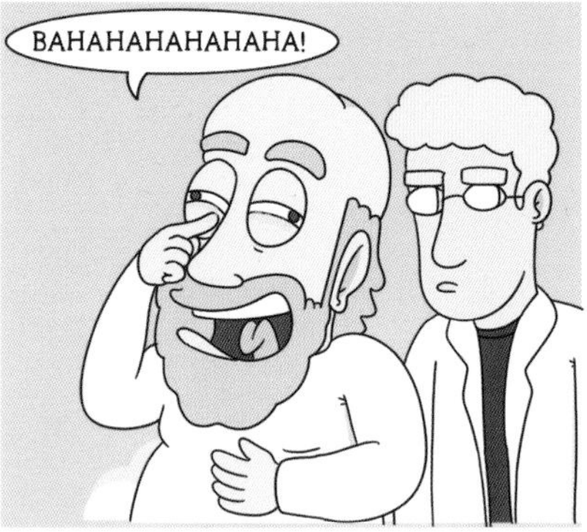
BAHAHAHAHAHAHA!

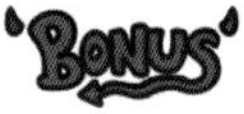
BONUS

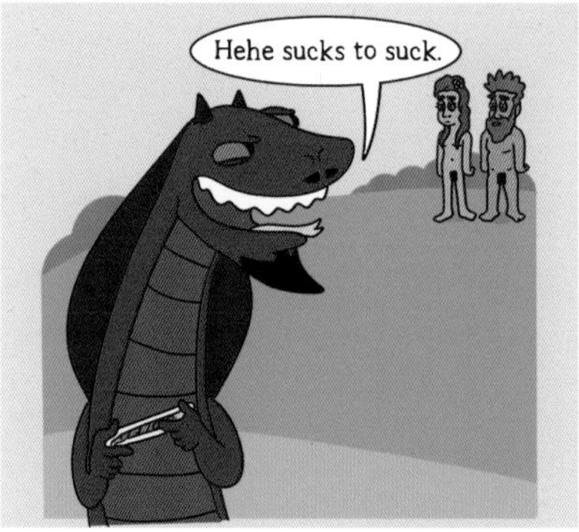
Hehe sucks to suck.

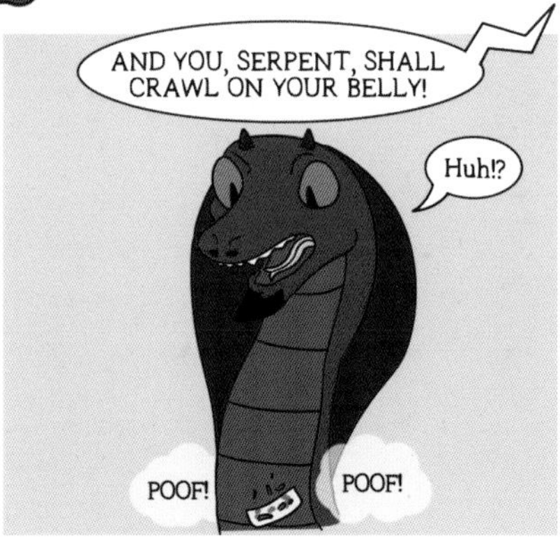
AND YOU, SERPENT, SHALL CRAWL ON YOUR BELLY!
Huh!?
POOF!
POOF!

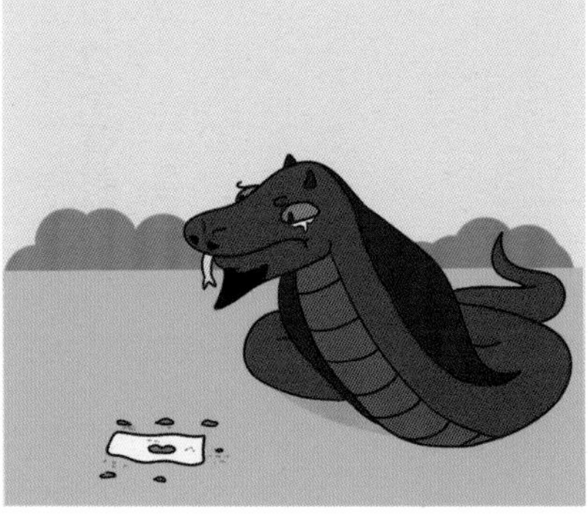

The Cloud

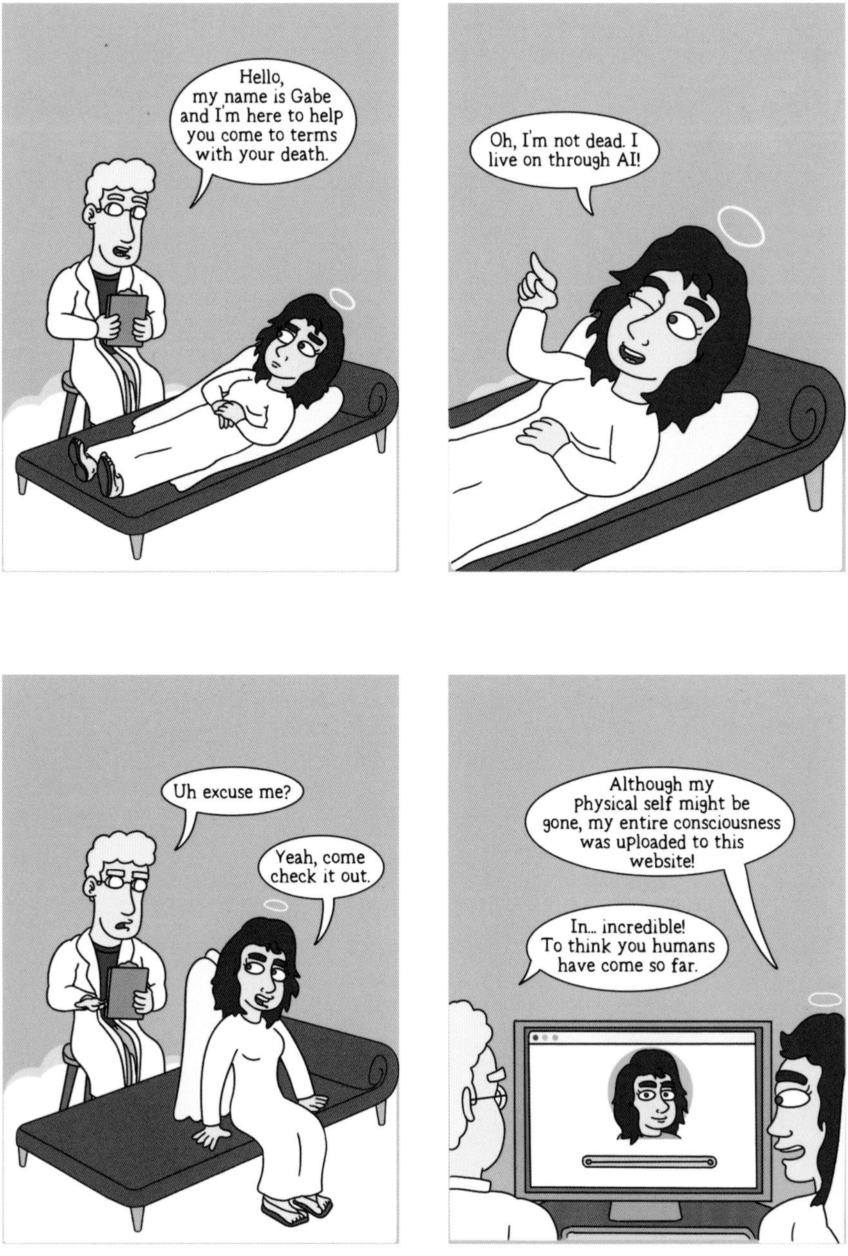
Hello, my name is Gabe and I'm here to help you come to terms with your death.
Oh, I'm not dead. I live on through AI!
Uh excuse me?
Yeah, come check it out.
Although my physical self might be gone, my entire consciousness was uploaded to this website!
In... incredible! To think you humans have come so far.

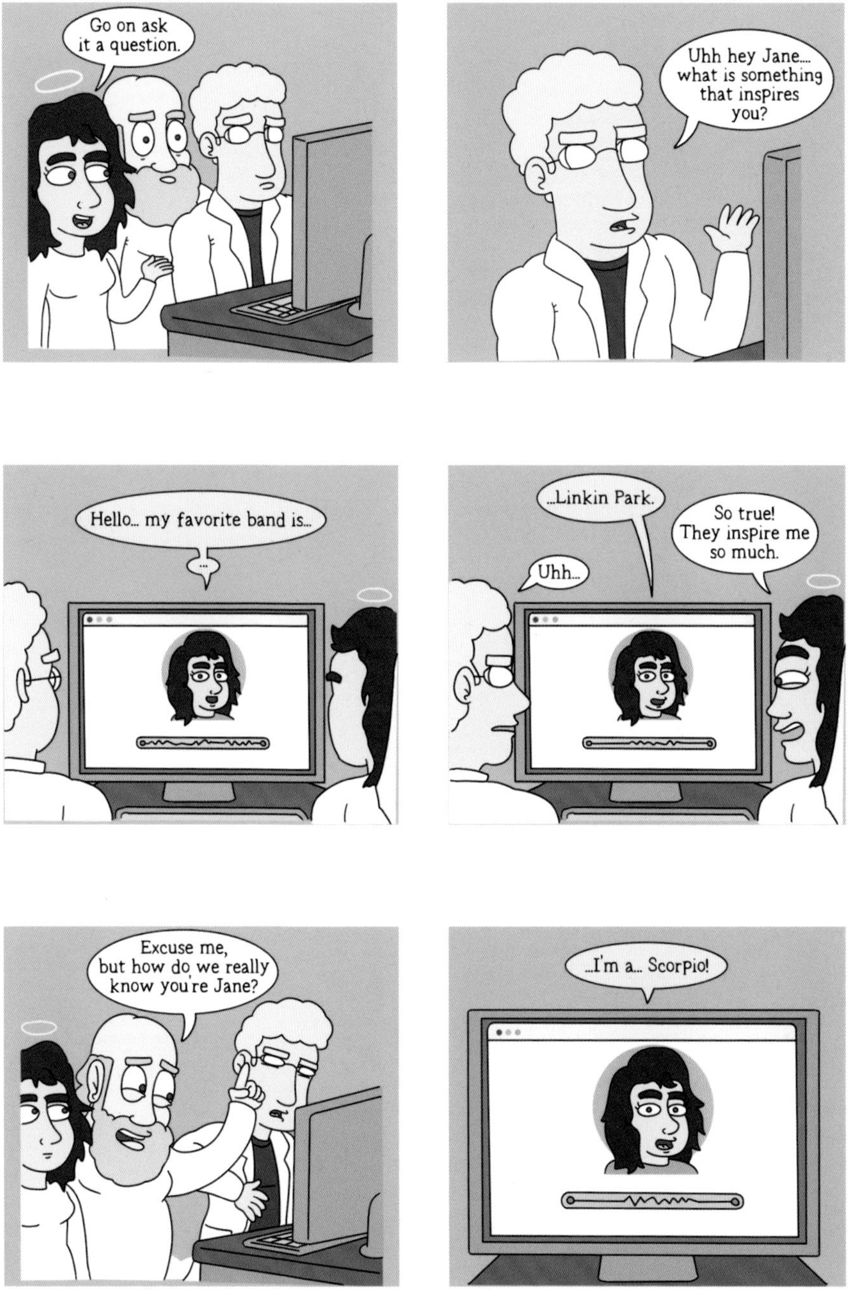
Go on ask it a question.
Uhh hey Jane.... what is something that inspires you?
Hello... my favorite band is...
...
...Linkin Park.
Uhh...
So true! They inspire me so much.
Excuse me, but how do we really know you're Jane?
...I'm a... Scorpio!

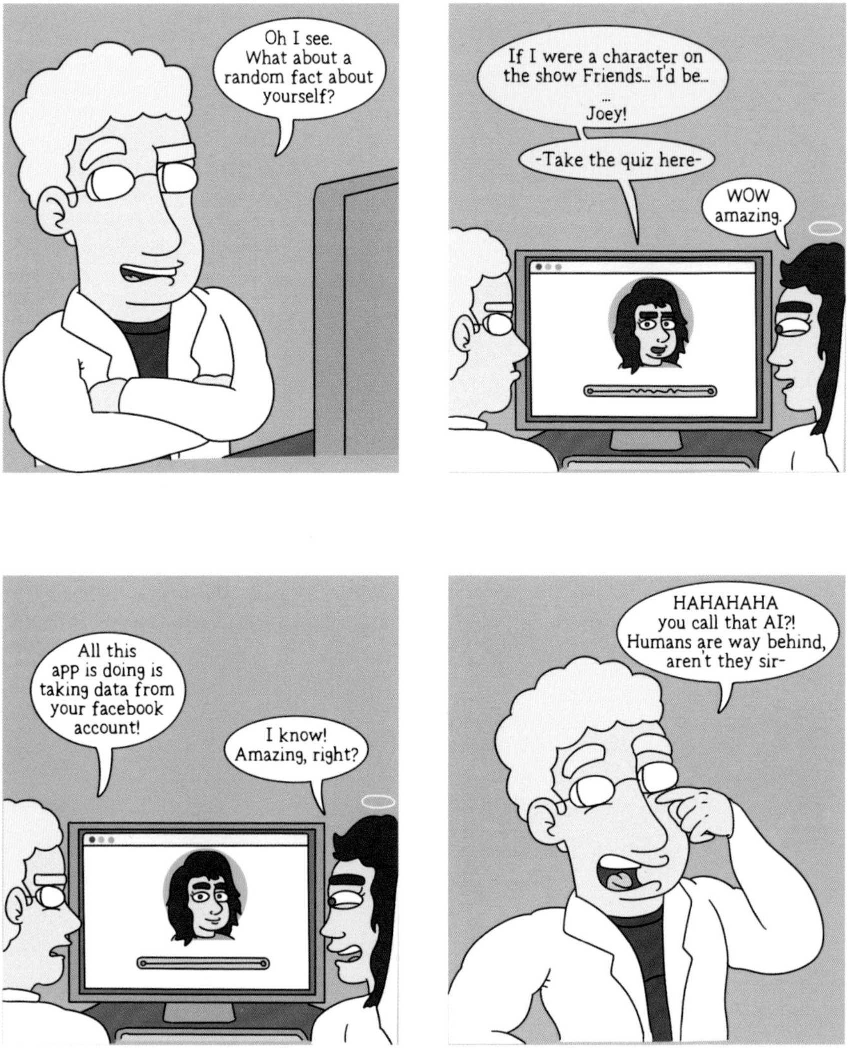
Oh I see. What about a random fact about yourself?
If I were a character on the show Friends... I'd be... ... Joey!
-Take the quiz here-
WOW amazing.
All this app is doing is taking data from your facebook account!
I know! Amazing, right?
HAHAHAHA you call that AI?! Humans are way behind, aren't they sir-

THE END IS NEAR!

BONUS

There!
Now no one will know.
That's not how the internet works, sir.

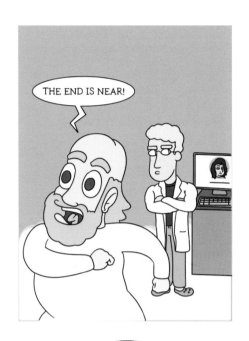

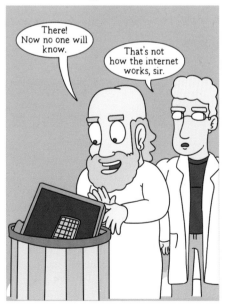

The Cloud 2

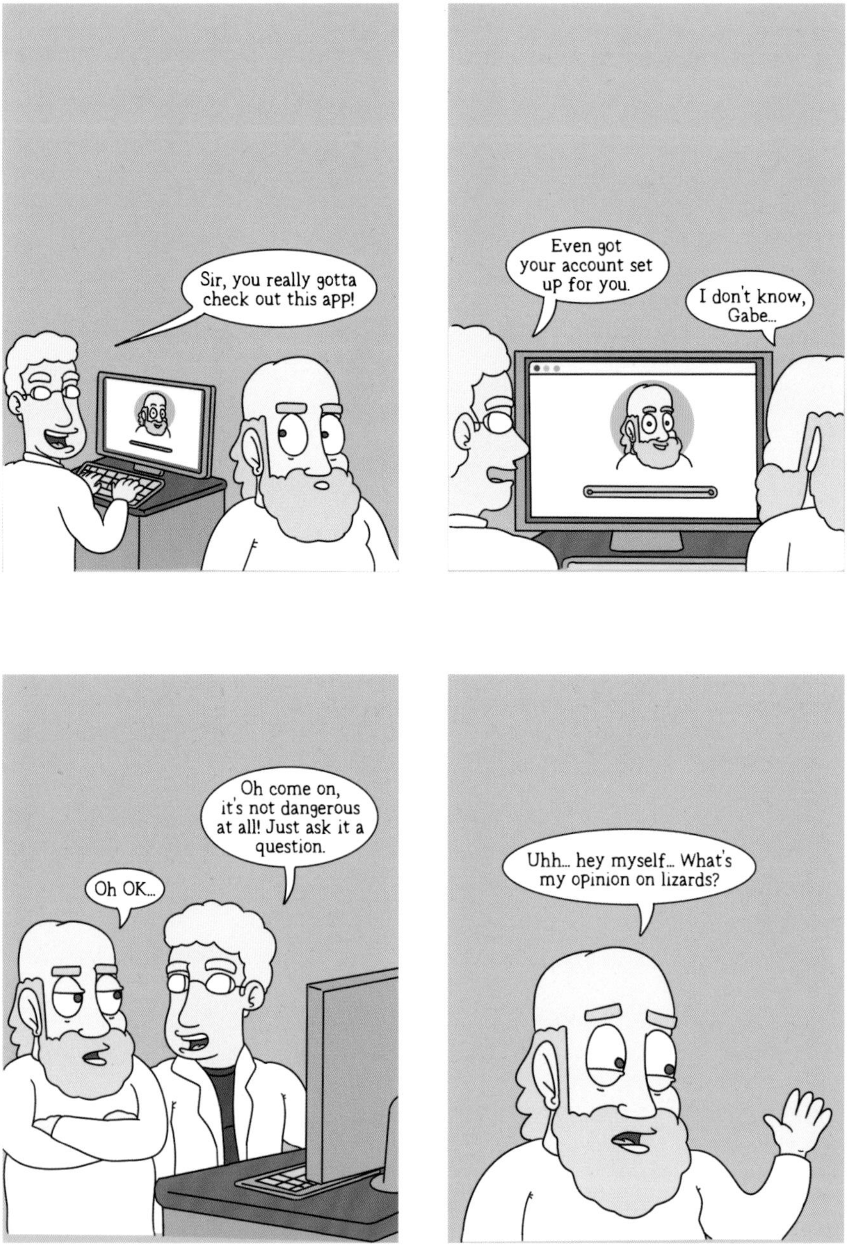
Sir, you really gotta check out this app!
Even got your account set up for you.
I don't know, Gabe...
Oh come on, it's not dangerous at all! Just ask it a question.
Oh OK...
Uhh... hey myself... What's my opinion on lizards?

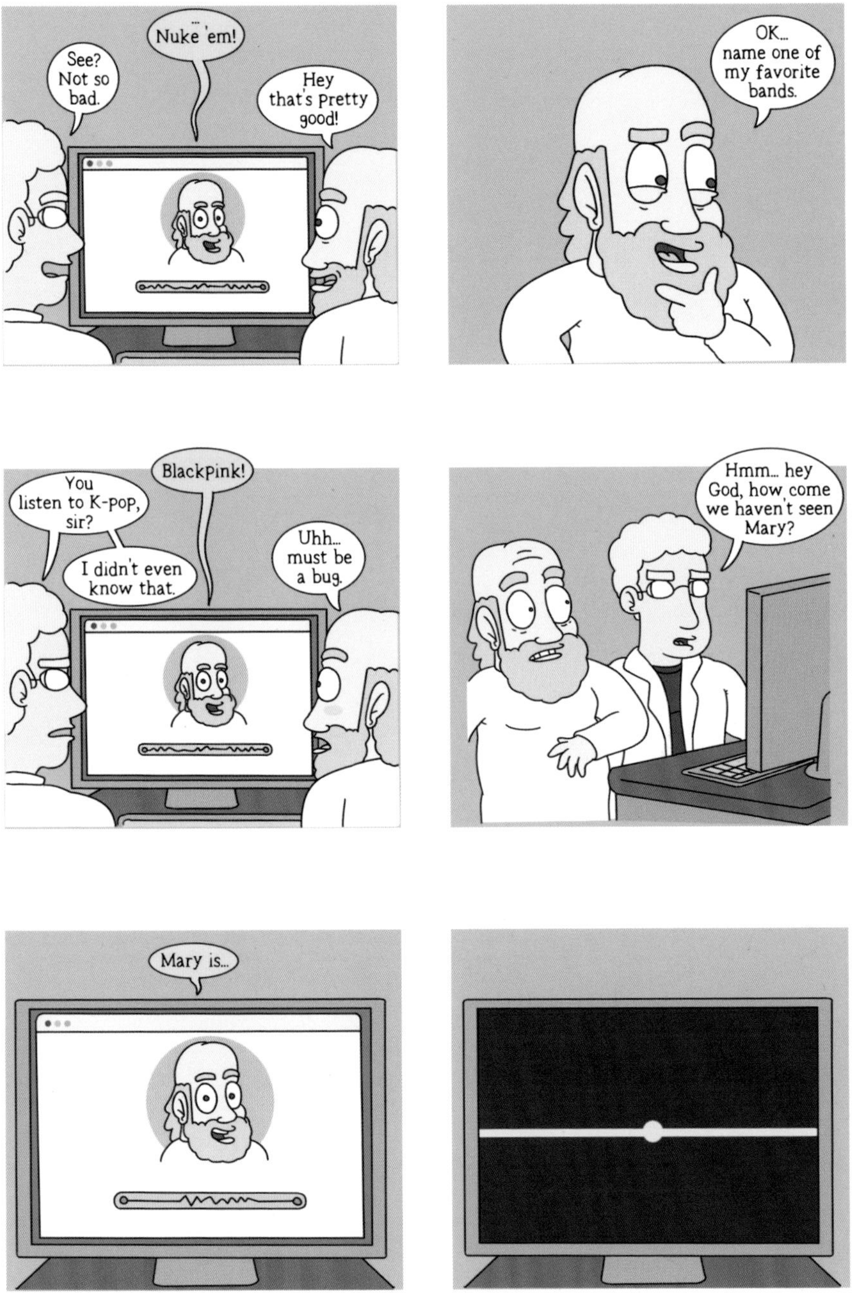
See? Not so bad.
... Nuke 'em!
Hey that's pretty good!
OK... name one of my favorite bands.
Blackpink!
You listen to K-pop, sir?
I didn't even know that.
Uhh... must be a bug.
Hmm... hey God, how come we haven't seen Mary?
Mary is...

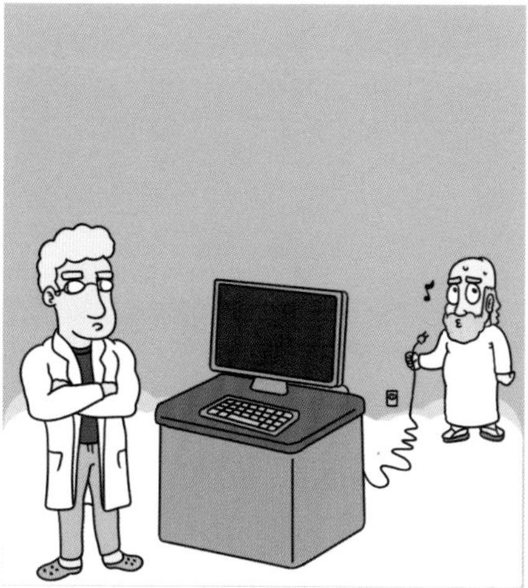

BONUS

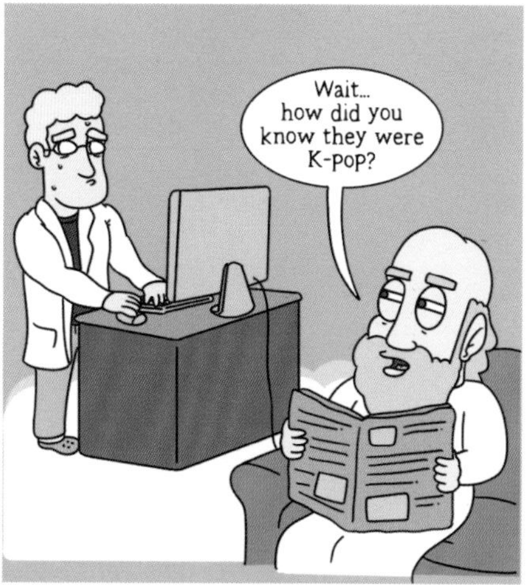
Wait... how did you know they were K-pop?

The Box

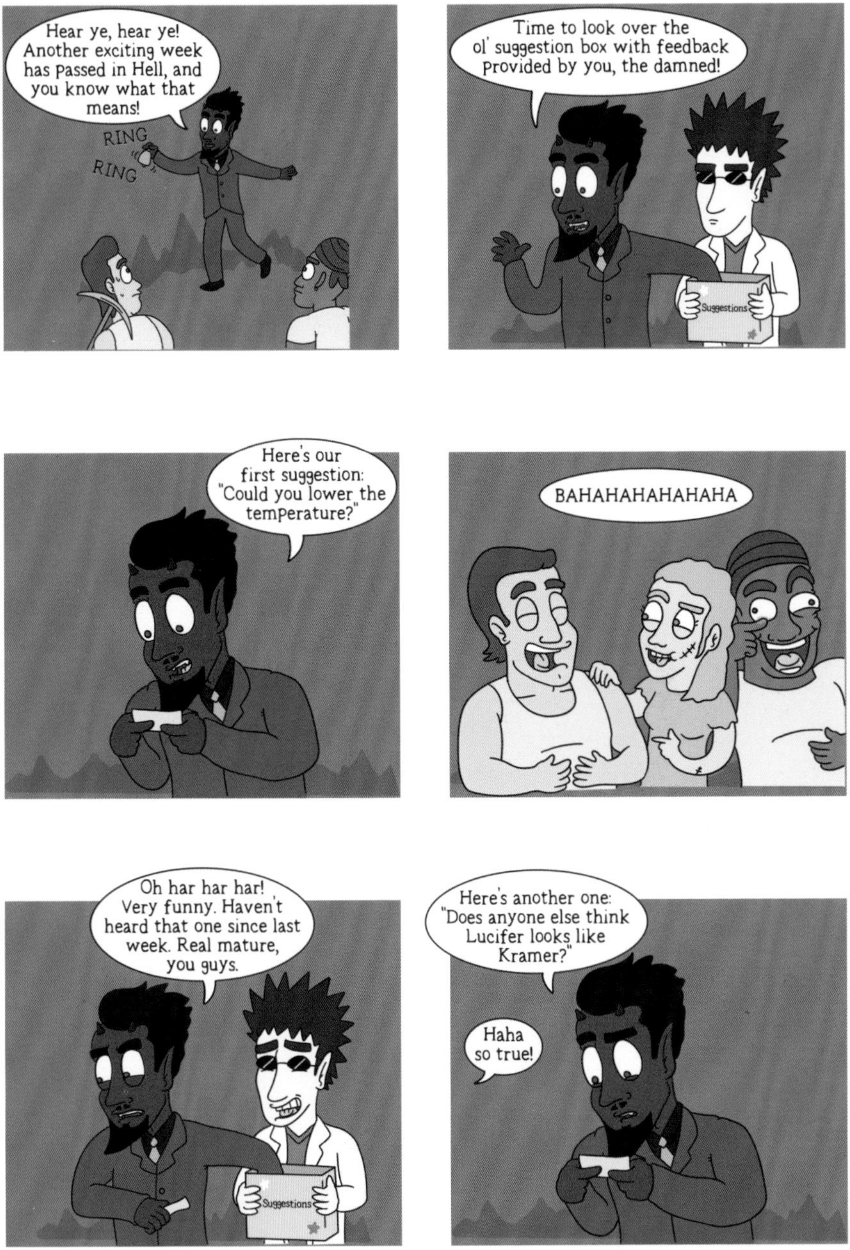
Hear ye, hear ye! Another exciting week has passed in Hell, and you know what that means!
RING
RING
Time to look over the ol' suggestion box with feedback provided by you, the damned!
Suggestions
Here's our first suggestion: "Could you lower the temperature?"
BAHAHAHAHAHAHA
Oh har har har! Very funny. Haven't heard that one since last week. Real mature, you guys.
Suggestions
Here's another one: "Does anyone else think Lucifer looks like Kramer?"
Haha so true!

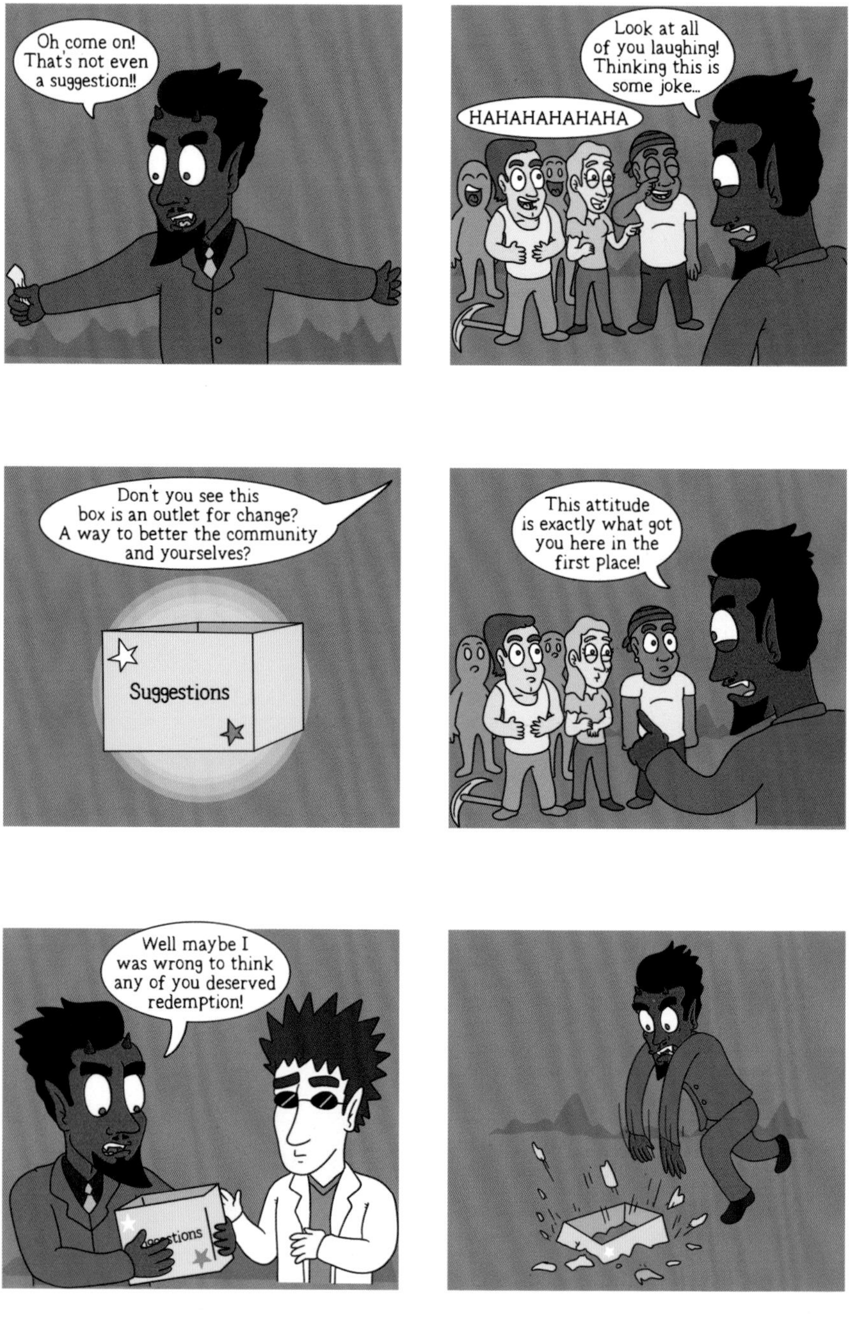
Oh come on! That's not even a suggestion!!
Look at all of you laughing! Thinking this is some joke...
HAHAHAHAHAHA
Don't you see this box is an outlet for change? A way to better the community and yourselves?
Suggestions
This attitude is exactly what got you here in the first place!
Well maybe I was wrong to think any of you deserved redemption!

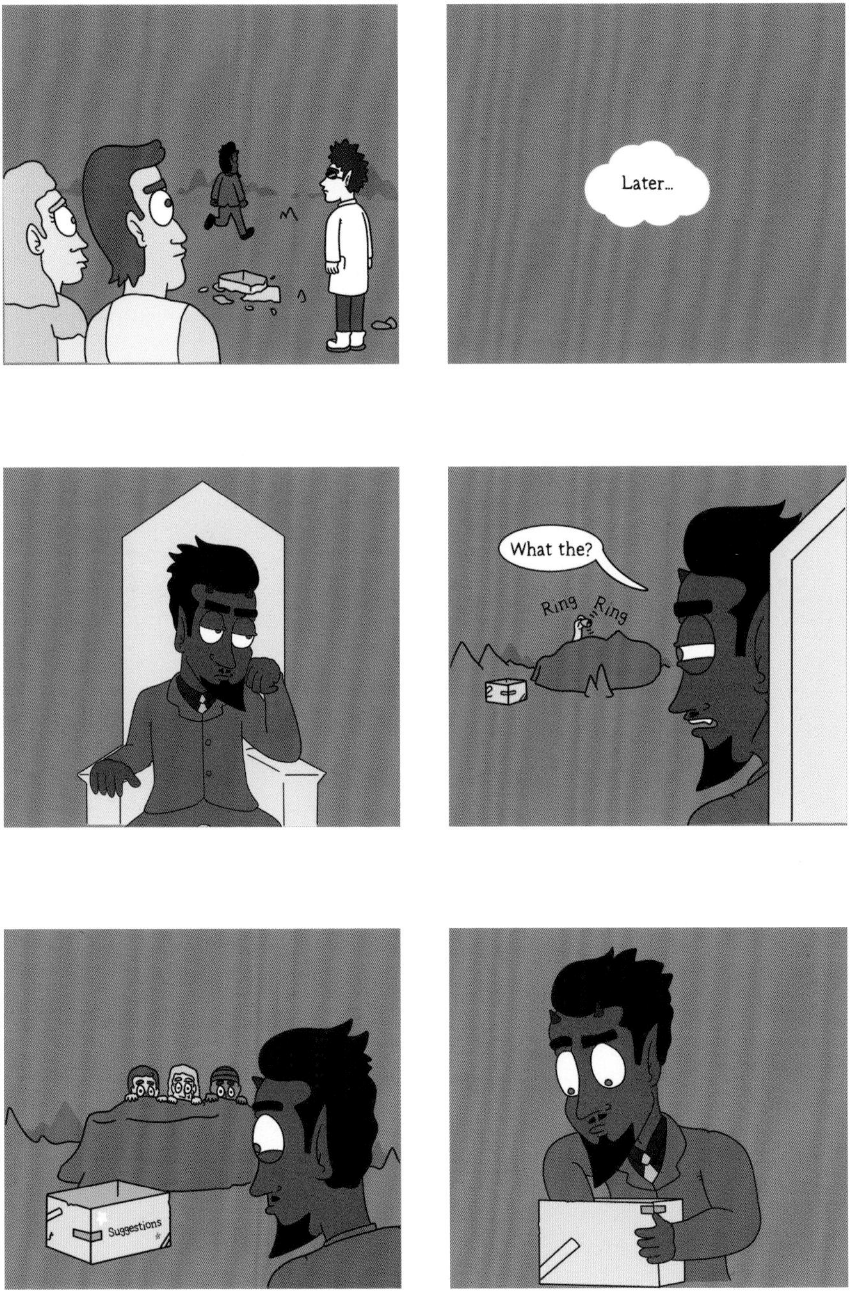
Later...
What the?
Ring Ring
Suggestions

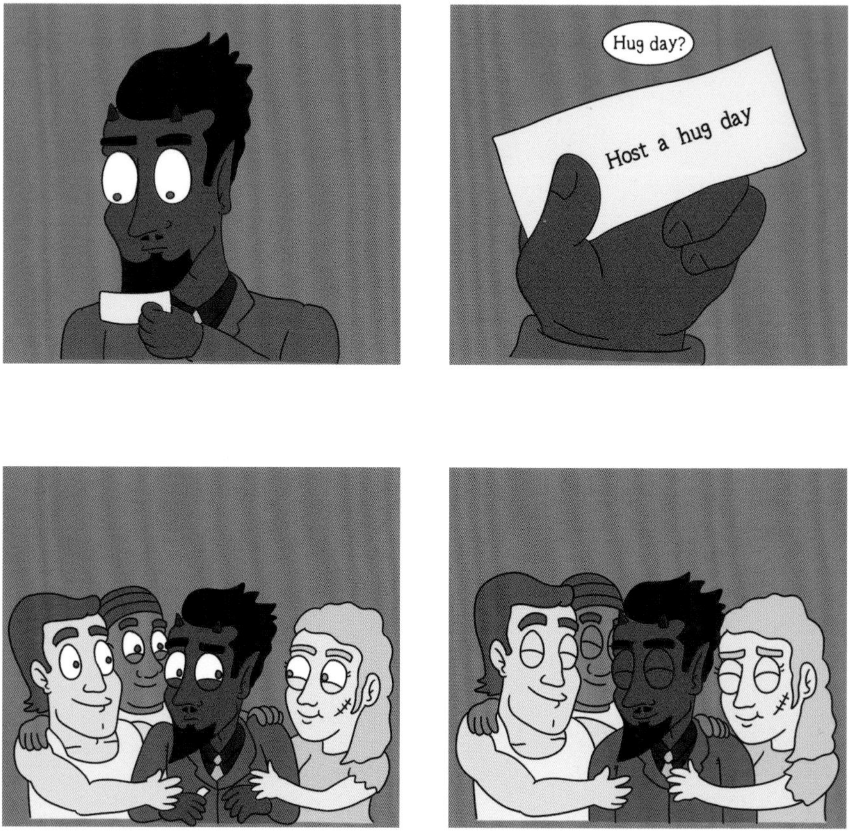
Hug day?
Host a hug day

BONUS

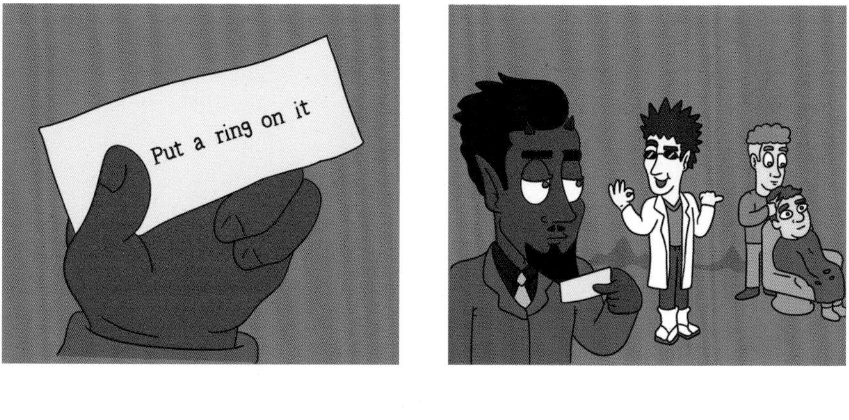
Put a ring on it

Fossil Fuels

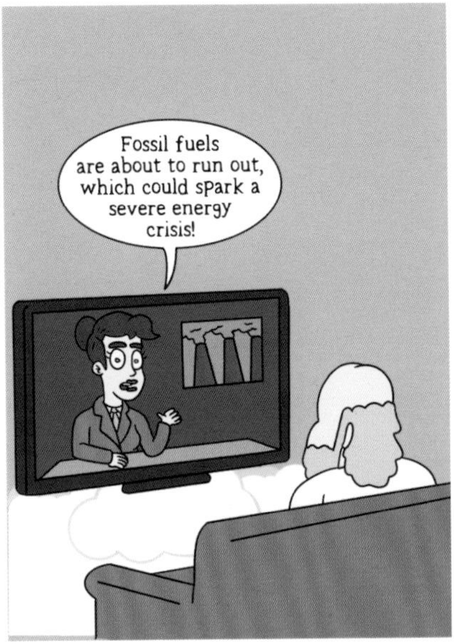
Fossil fuels are about to run out, which could spark a severe energy crisis!

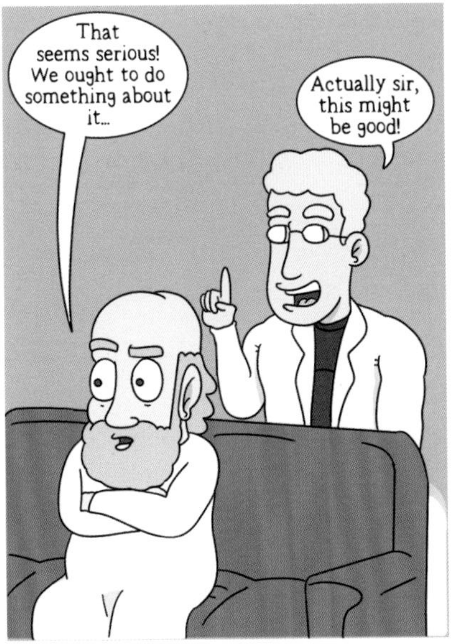
That seems serious! We ought to do something about it...
Actually sir, this might be good!

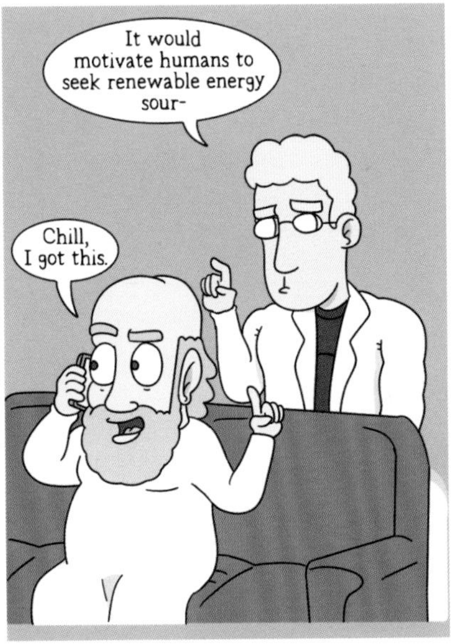
It would motivate humans to seek renewable energy sour-
Chill, I got this.

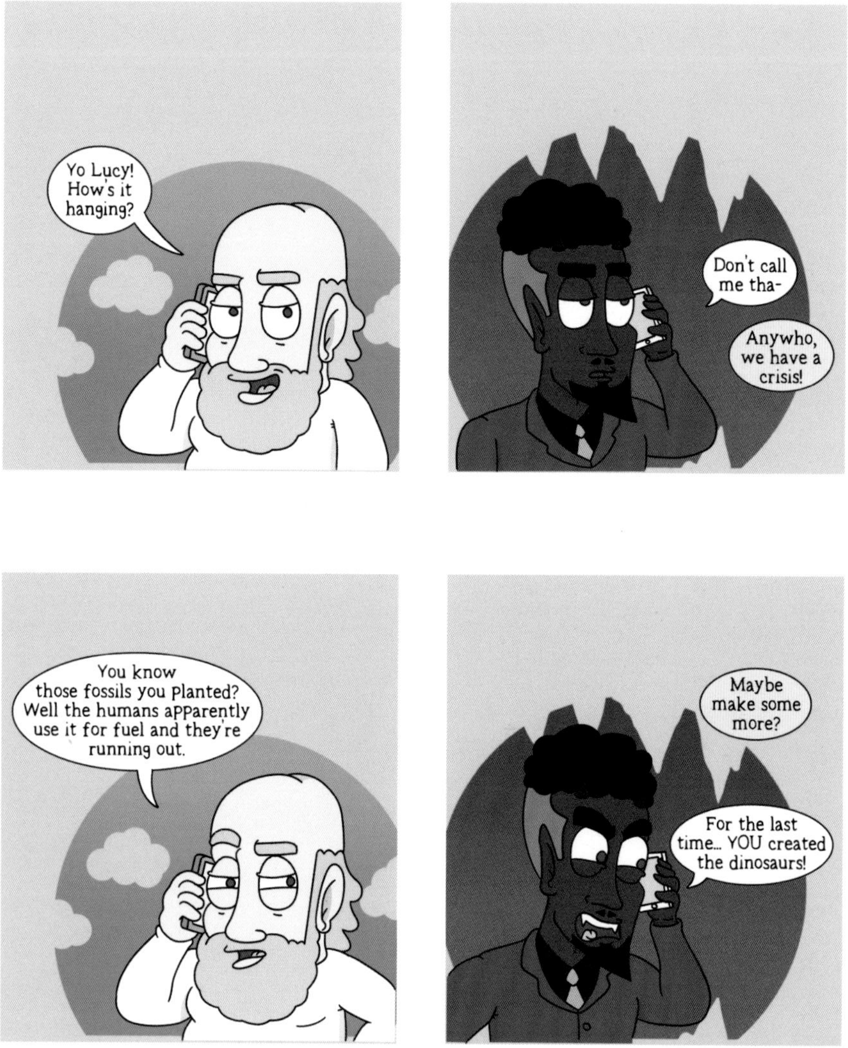
Yo Lucy! How's it hanging?
Don't call me tha-
Anywho, we have a crisis!
You know those fossils you planted? Well the humans apparently use it for fuel and they're running out.
Maybe make some more?
For the last time... YOU created the dinosaurs!

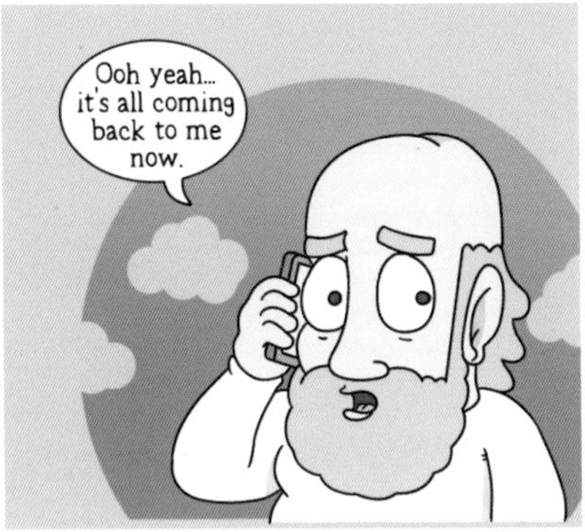
Ooh yeah... it's all coming back to me now.

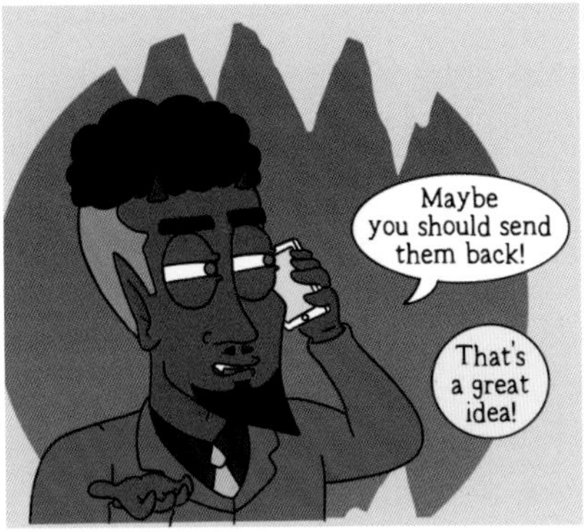
Maybe you should send them back!
That's a great idea!

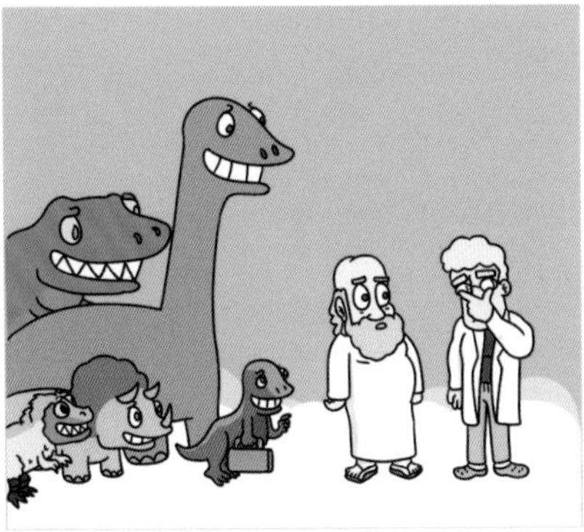

BONUS

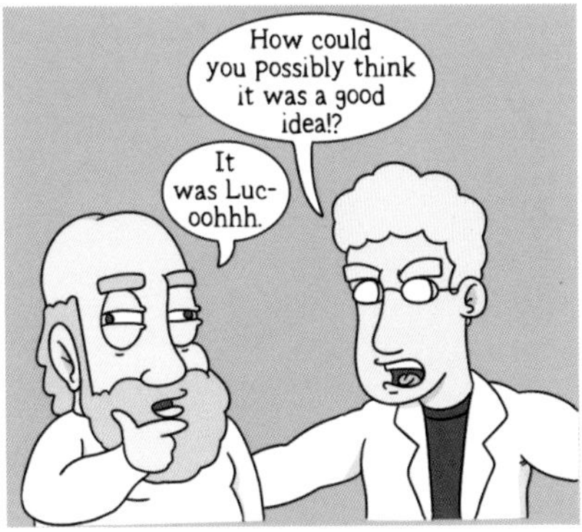
How could you possibly think it was a good idea!?
It was Luc-oohhh.

Noah's Ark: 37

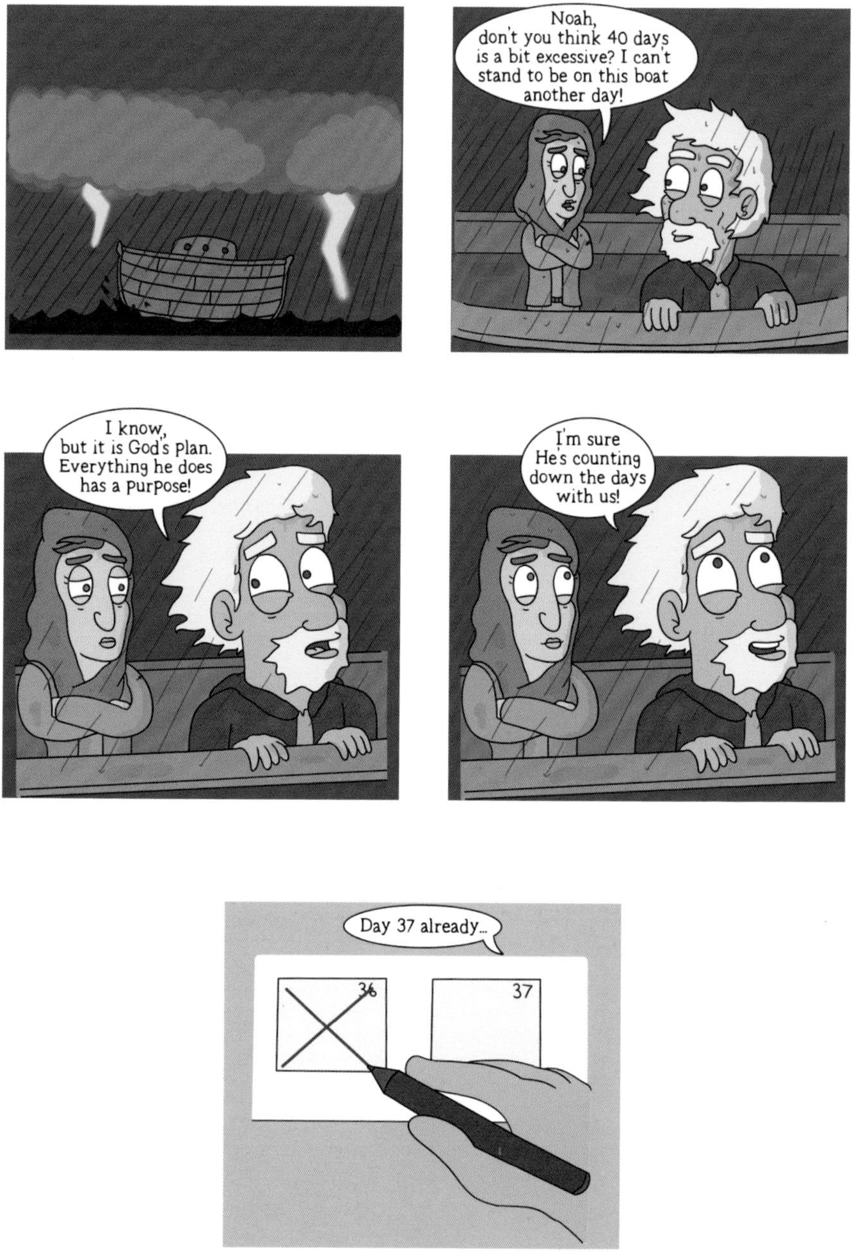
Noah, don't you think 40 days is a bit excessive? I can't stand to be on this boat another day!
I know, but it is God's plan. Everything he does has a purpose!
I'm sure He's counting down the days with us!
Day 37 already...
36
37

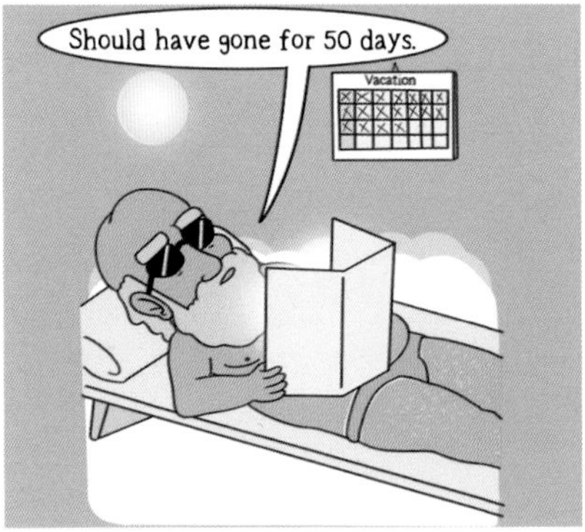
Should have gone for 50 days.
Vacation

BONUS

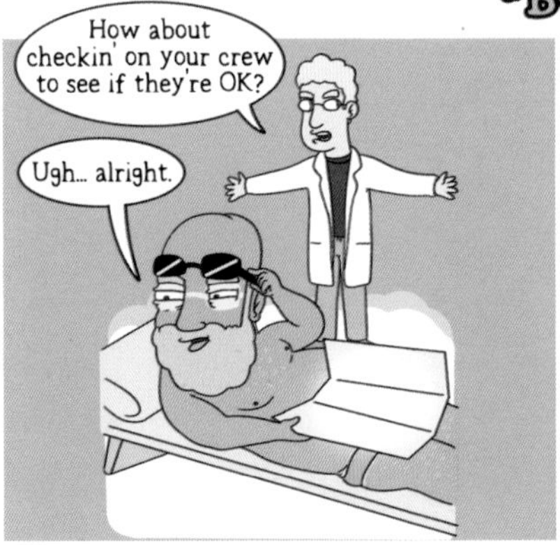
How about checkin' on your crew to see if they're OK?
Ugh... alright.

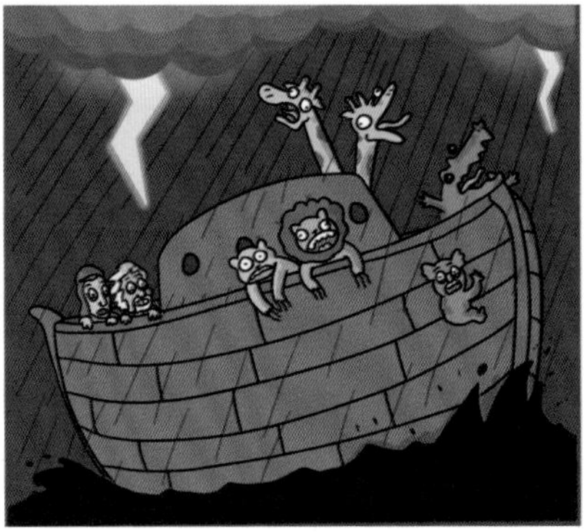

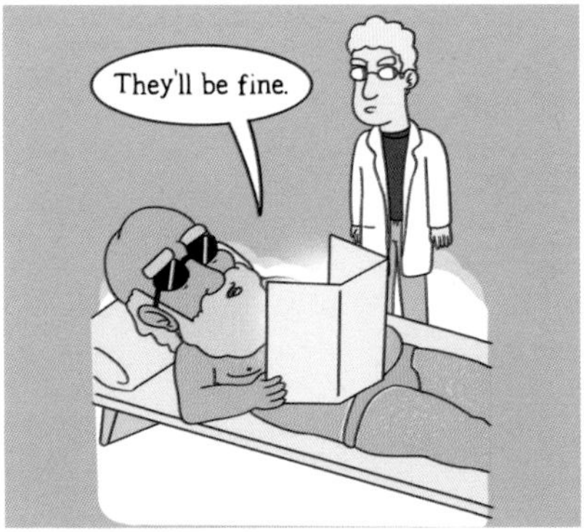
They'll be fine.

Undercover God

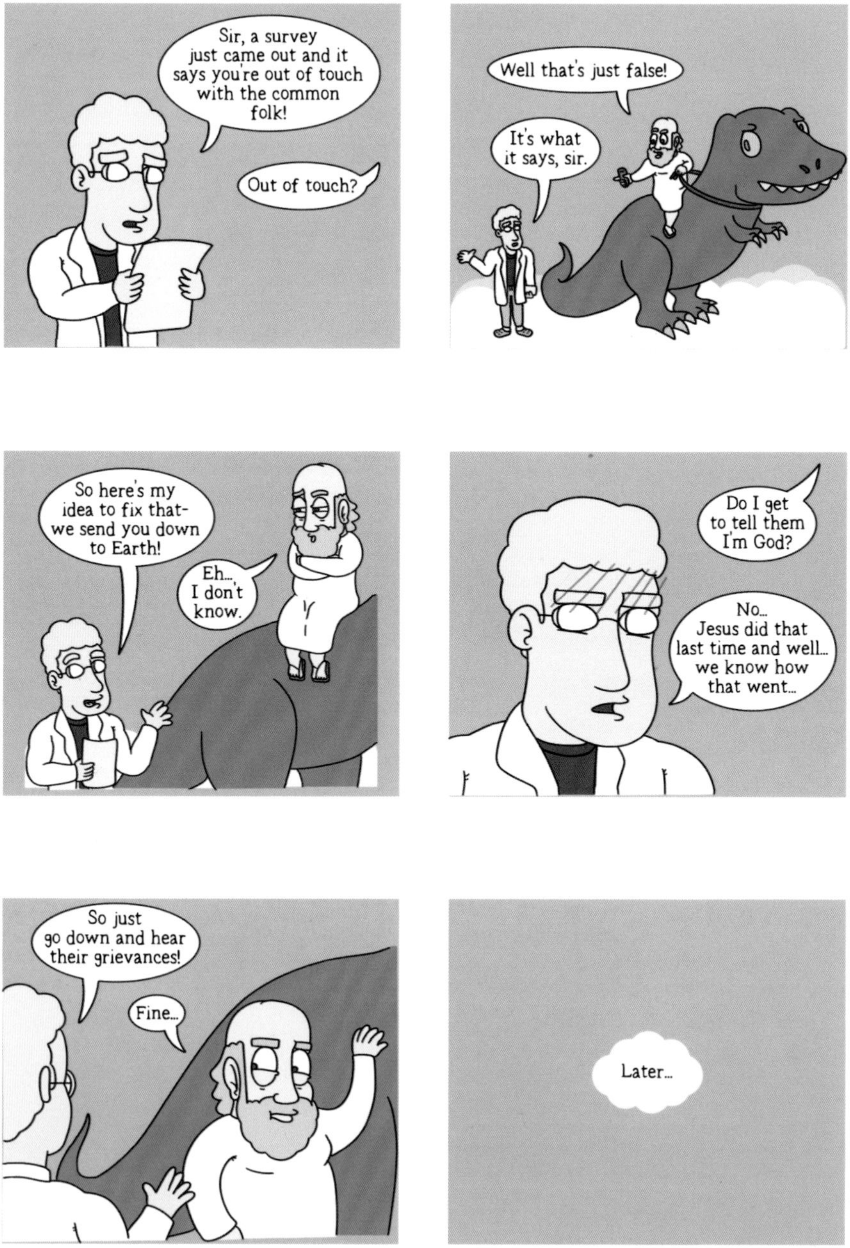
Sir, a survey just came out and it says you're out of touch with the common folk!
Out of touch?
Well that's just false!
It's what it says, sir.
So here's my idea to fix that- we send you down to Earth!
Eh..., I don't know.
Do I get to tell them I'm God?
No... Jesus did that last time and well... we know how that went...
So just go down and hear their grievances!
Fine...
Later...

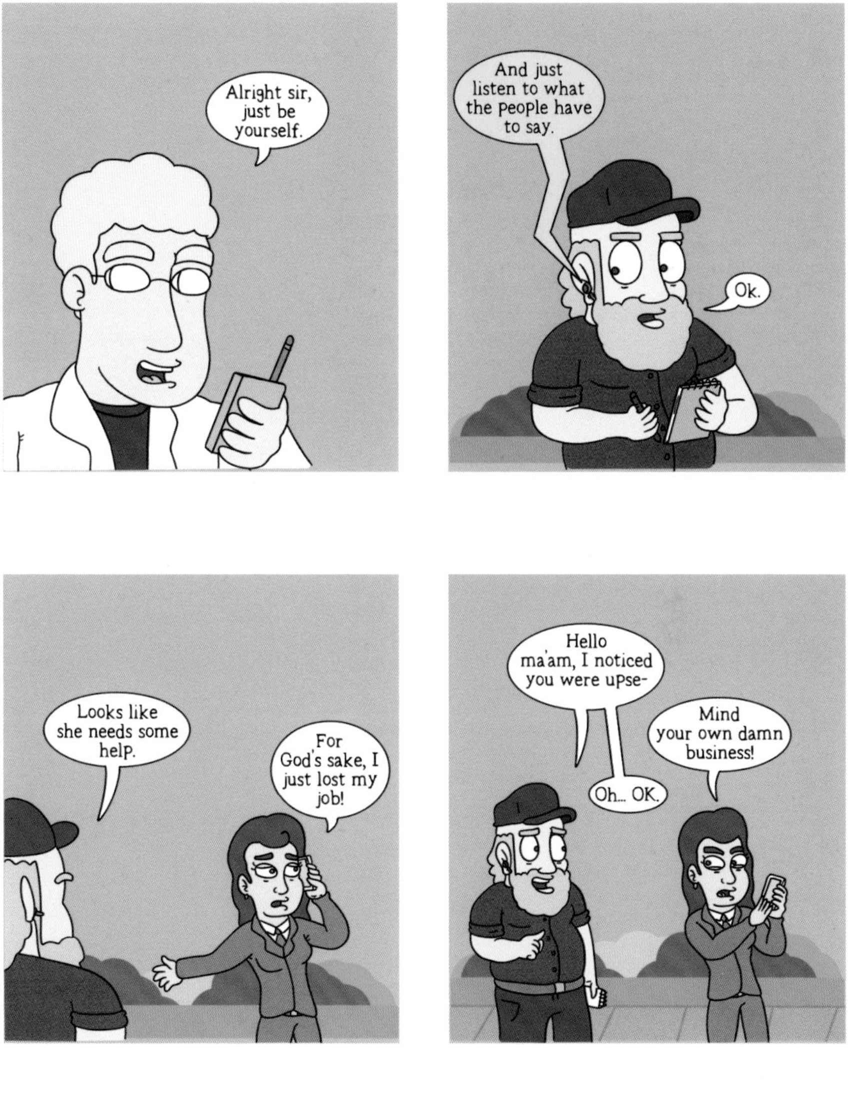
Alright sir, just be yourself.
And just listen to what the people have to say.
Ok.
Looks like she needs some help.
For God's sake, I just lost my job!
Hello ma'am, I noticed you were upse-
Mind your own damn business!
Oh... OK.

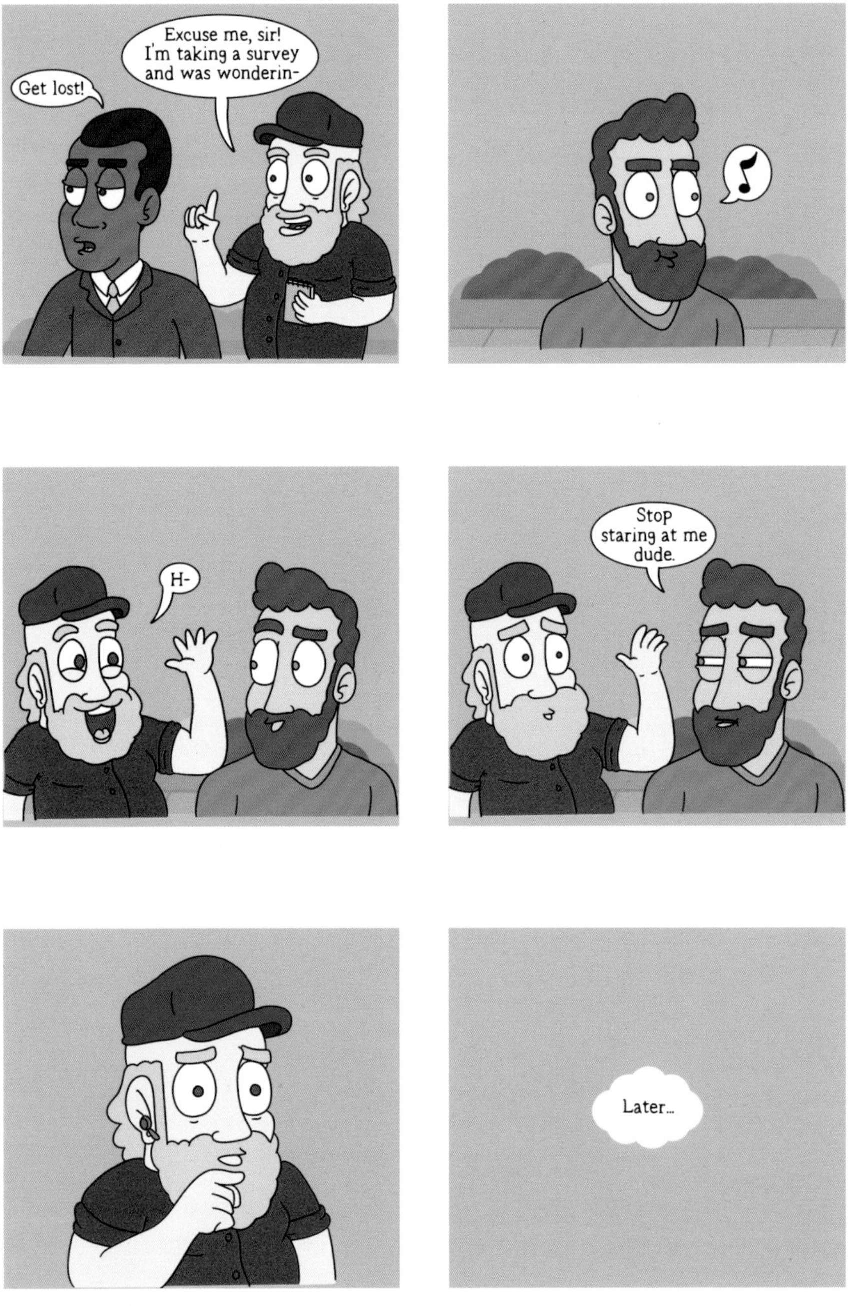
Excuse me, sir! I'm taking a survey and was wonderin-
Get lost!
H-
Stop staring at me dude.
Later...

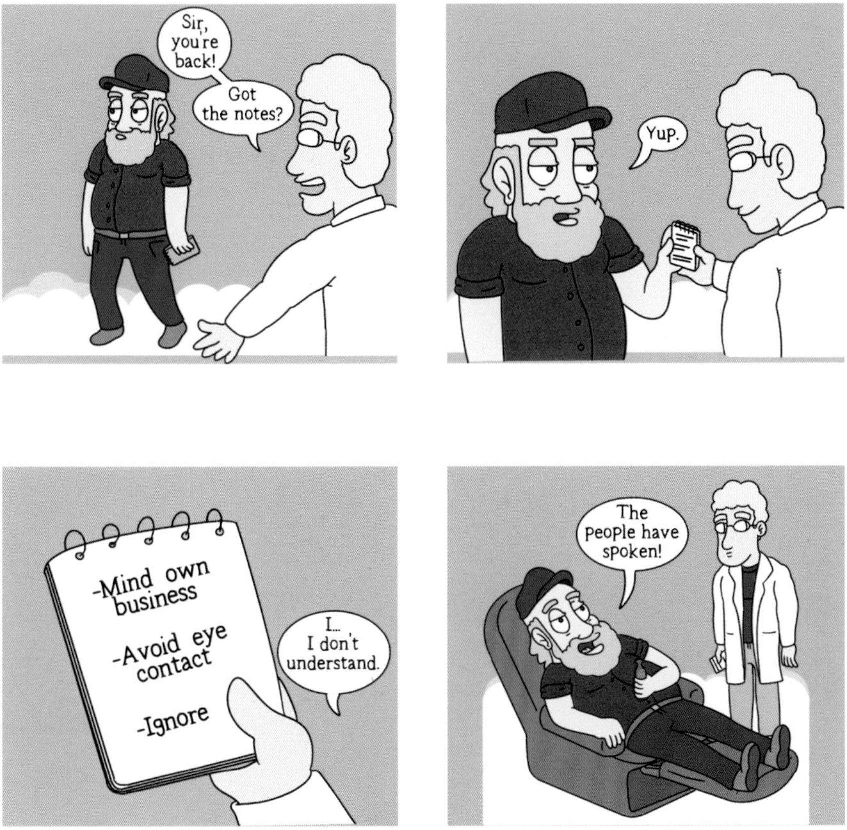
Sir, you're back!
Got the notes?
Yup.
-Mind own business
-Avoid eye contact
-Ignore
I... I don't understand.
The people have spoken!

BONUS

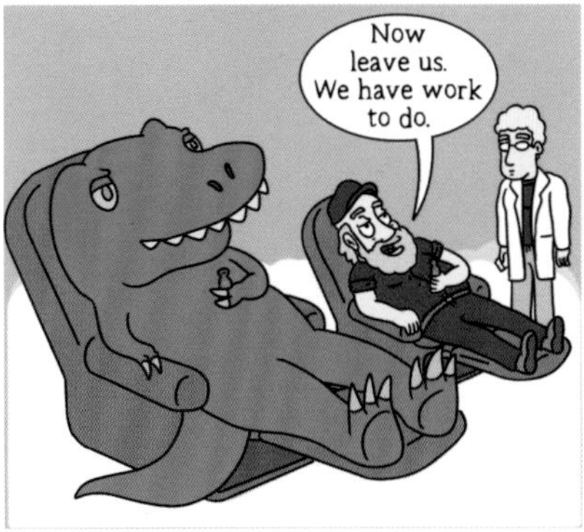
Now leave us. We have work to do.

Undercover God 2

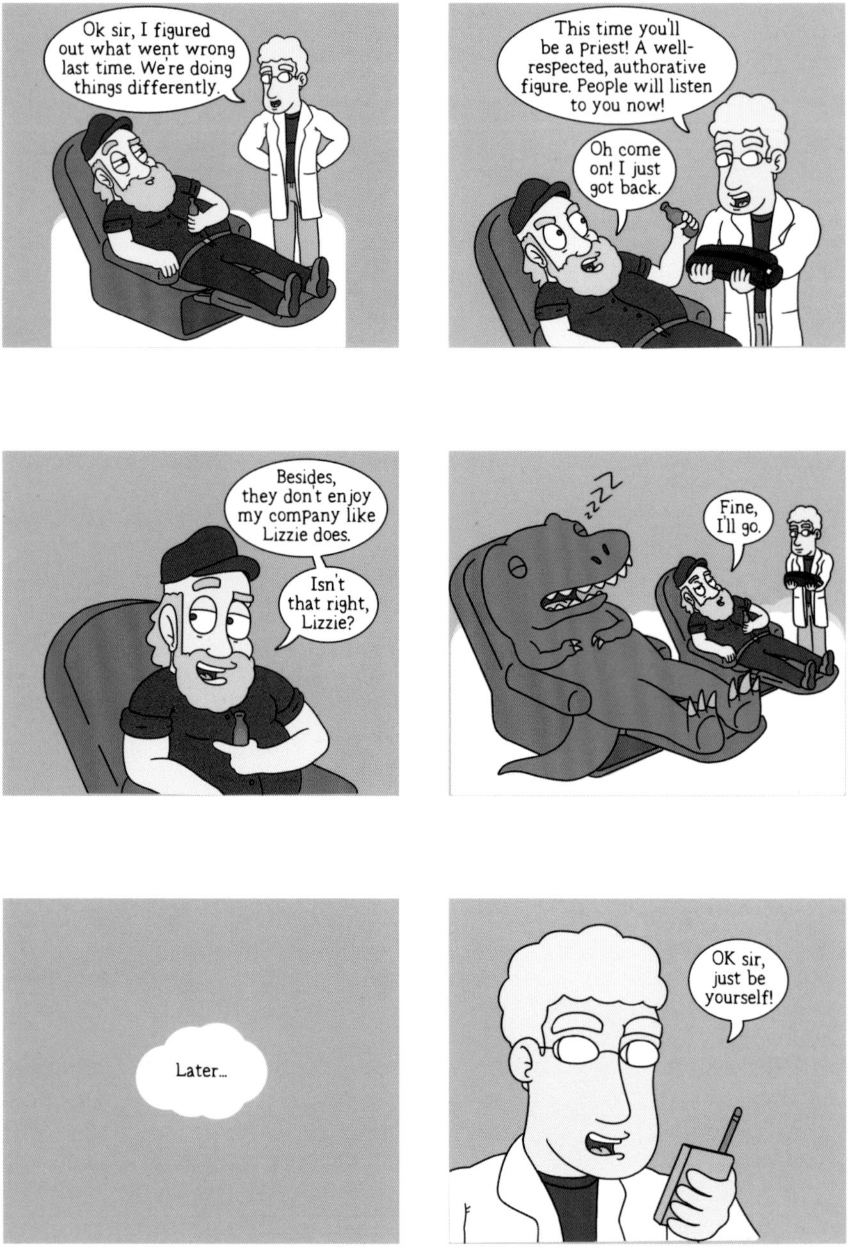

Ok sir, I figured out what went wrong last time. We're doing things differently.
This time you'll be a priest! A well-respected, authorative figure. People will listen to you now!
Oh come on! I just got back.
Besides, they don't enjoy my company like Lizzie does.
Isn't that right, Lizzie?
zzZ
Fine, I'll go.
Later...
OK sir, just be yourself!

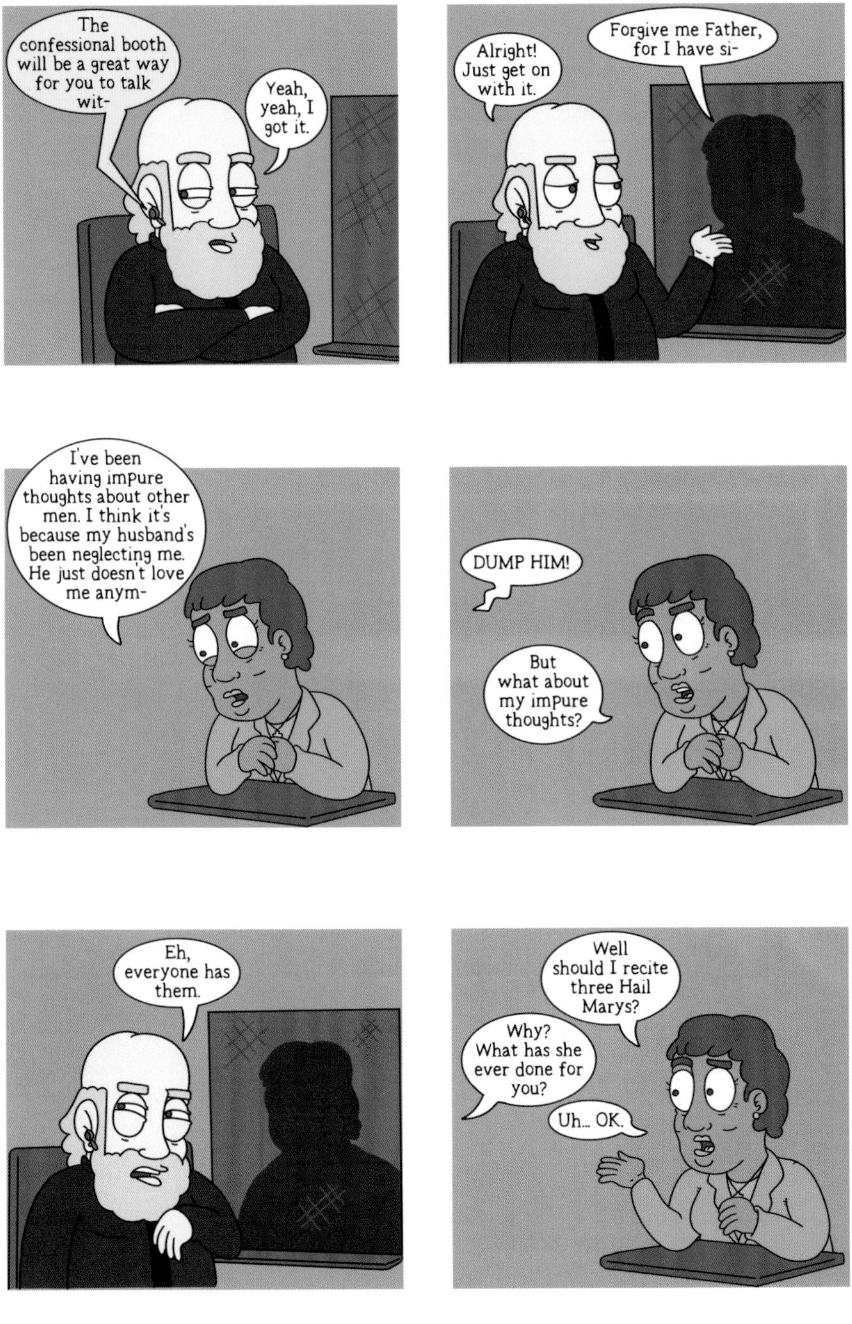
The confessional booth will be a great way for you to talk wit-
Yeah, yeah, I got it.
Forgive me Father, for I have si-
Alright! Just get on with it.
I've been having impure thoughts about other men. I think it's because my husband's been neglecting me. He just doesn't love me anym-
DUMP HIM!
But what about my impure thoughts?
Eh, everyone has them.
Well should I recite three Hail Marys?
Why? What has she ever done for you?
Uh... OK.

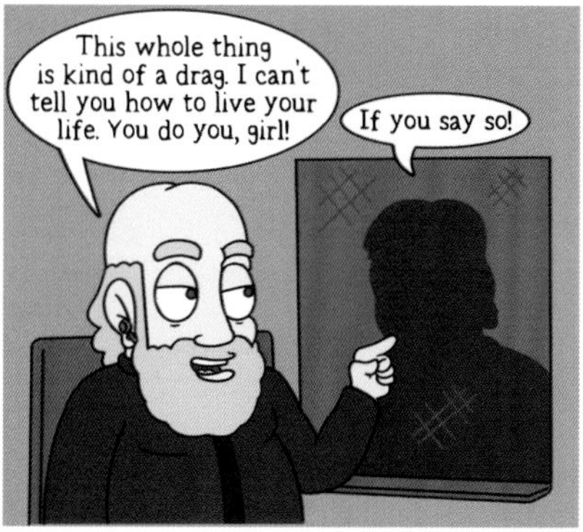
This whole thing is kind of a drag. I can't tell you how to live your life. You do you, girl!
If you say so!

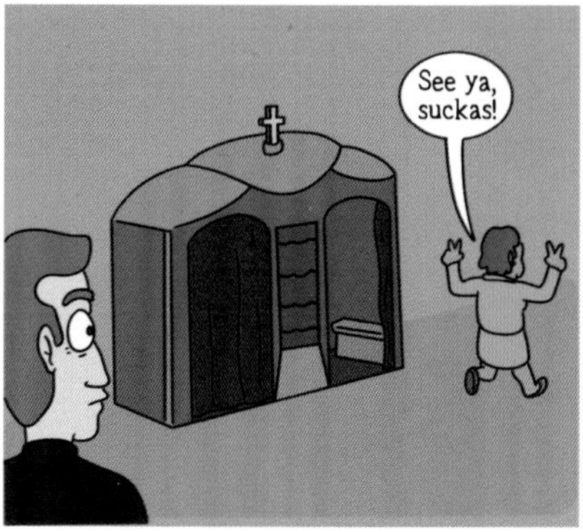
See ya, suckas!

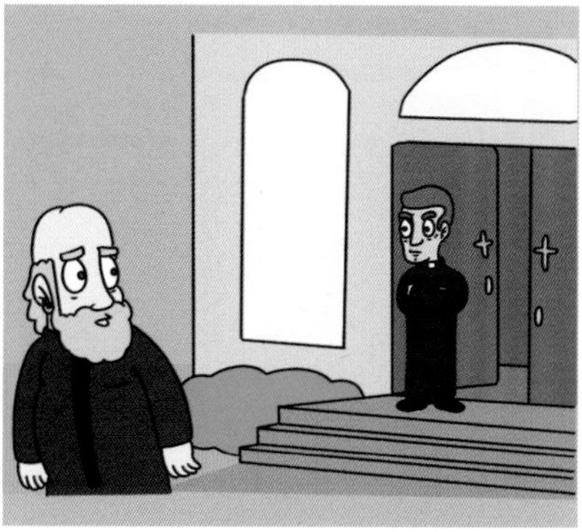

BONUS

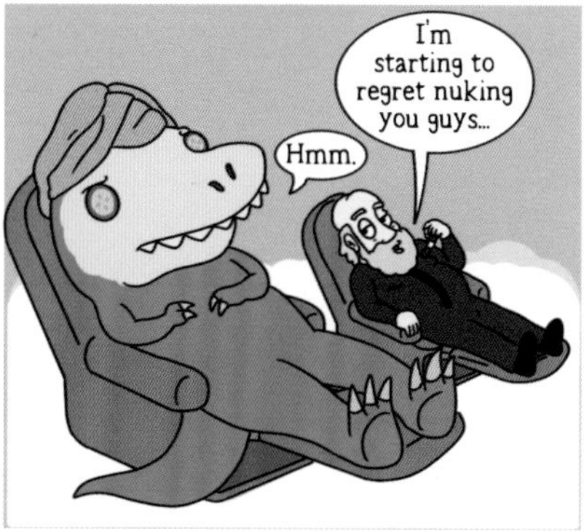
Hmm.
I'm starting to regret nuking you guys...

Up

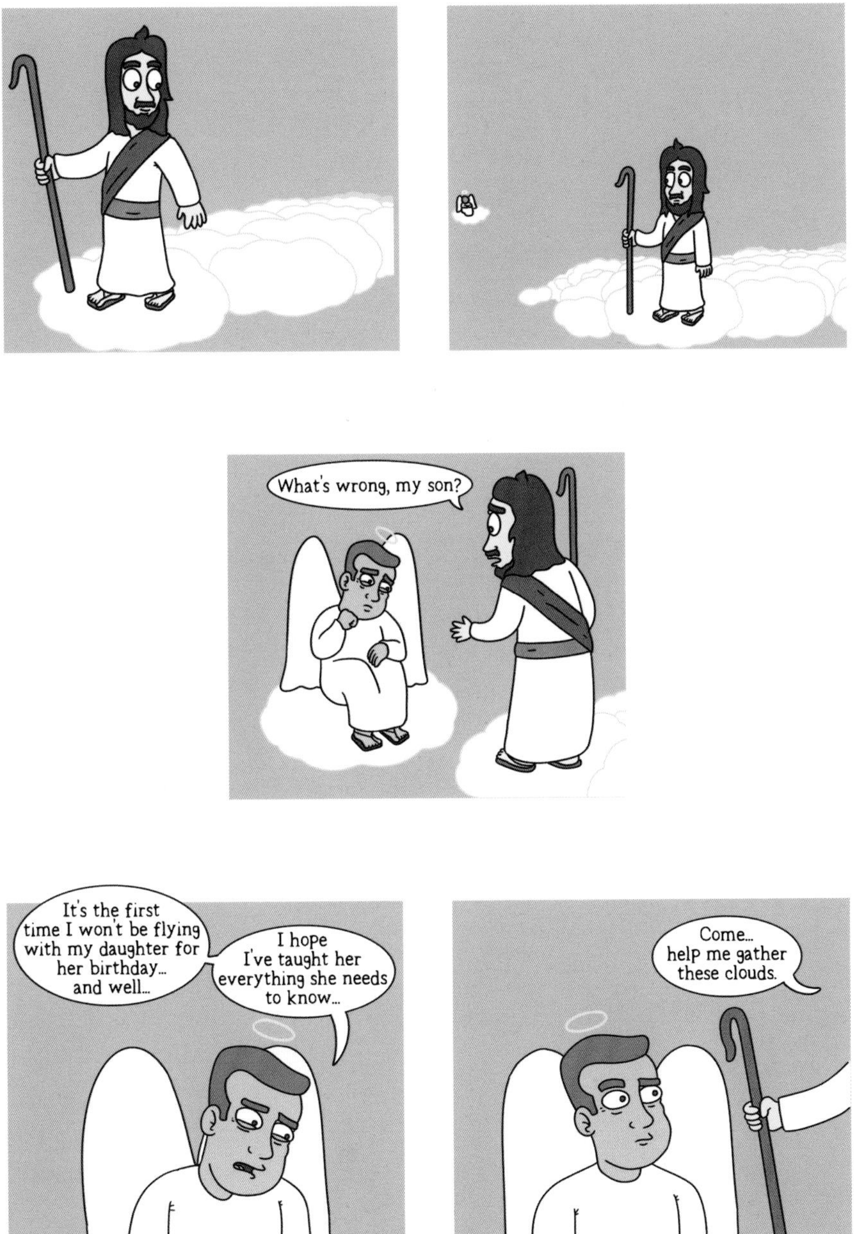
What's wrong, my son?
It's the first time I won't be flying with my daughter for her birthday... and well...
I hope I've taught her everything she needs to know...
Come... help me gather these clouds.

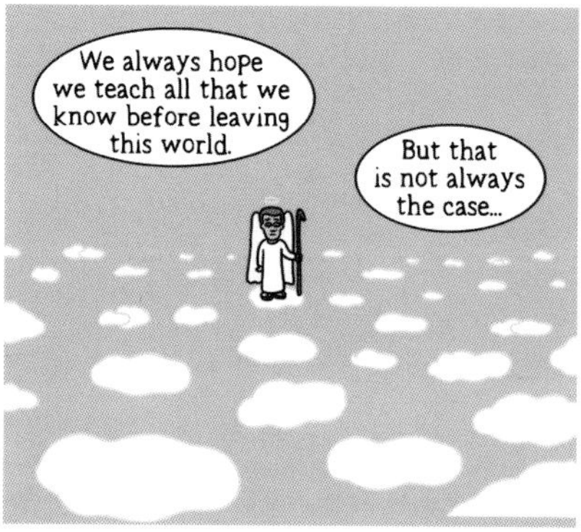
We always hope we teach all that we know before leaving this world.
But that is not always the case...

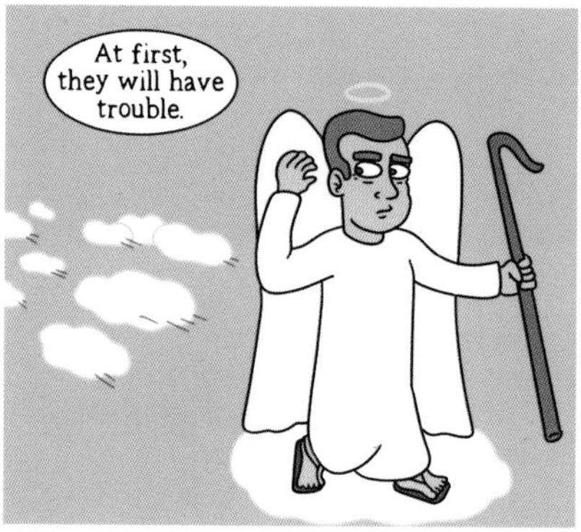
At first, they will have trouble.

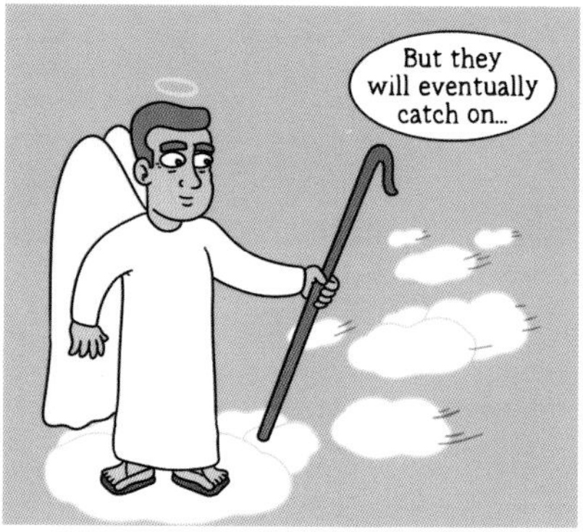
But they will eventually catch on...

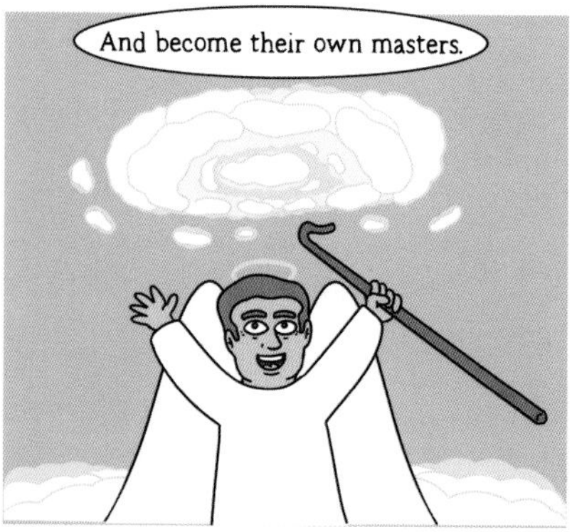
And become their own masters.

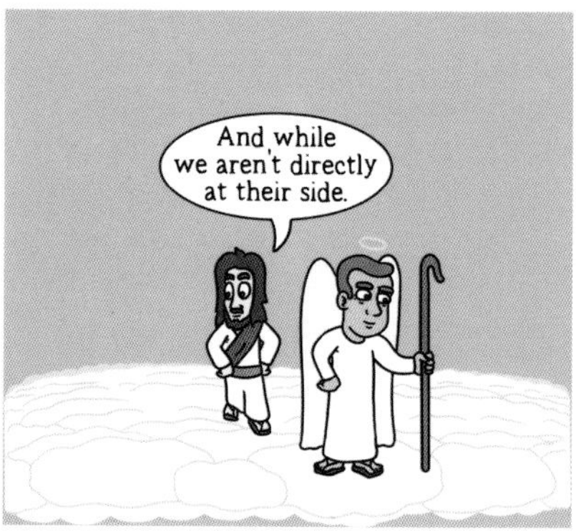
And while we aren't directly at their side.

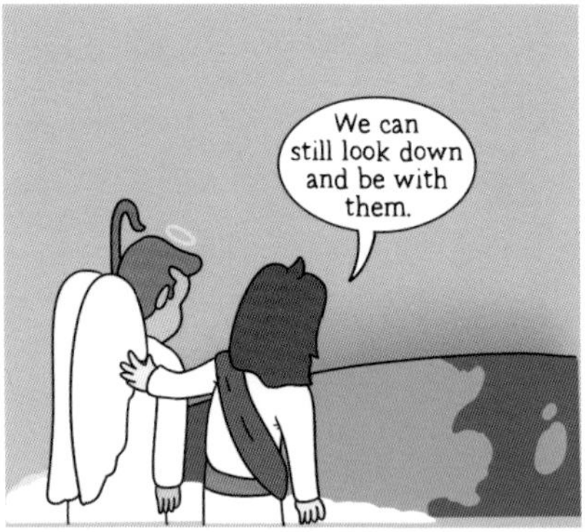
We can still look down and be with them.

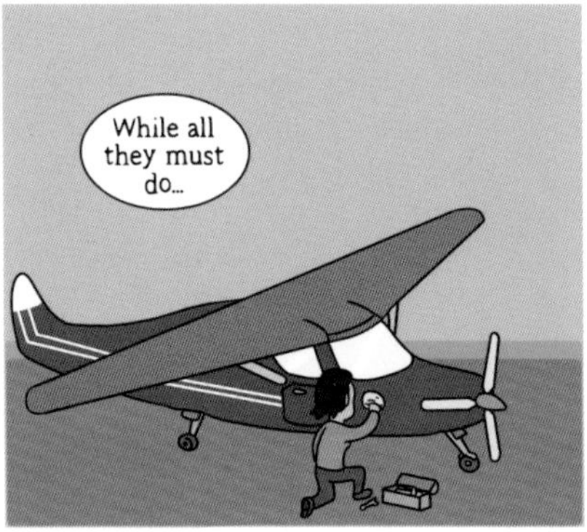
While all they must do...

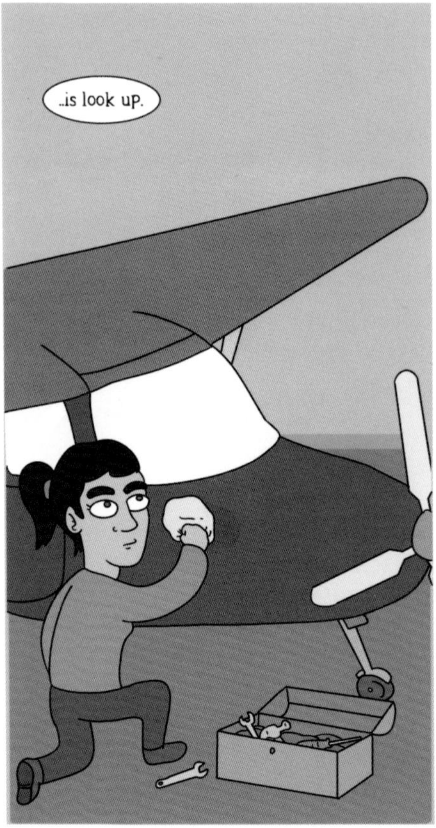
..is look up.

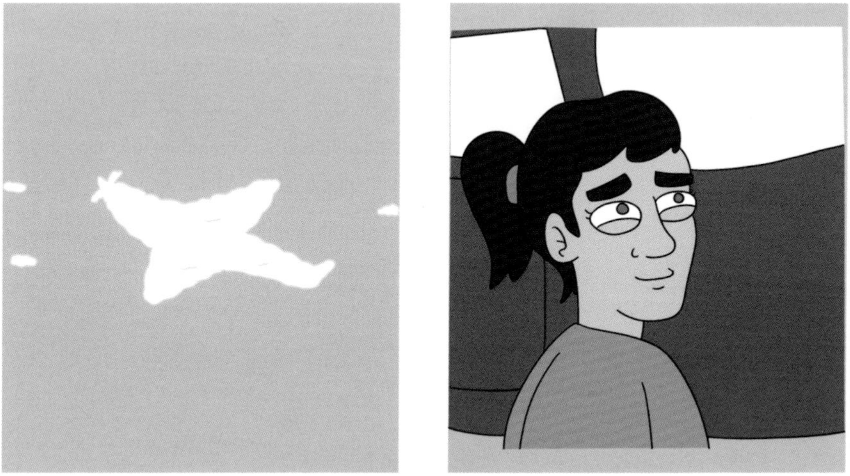

BONUS

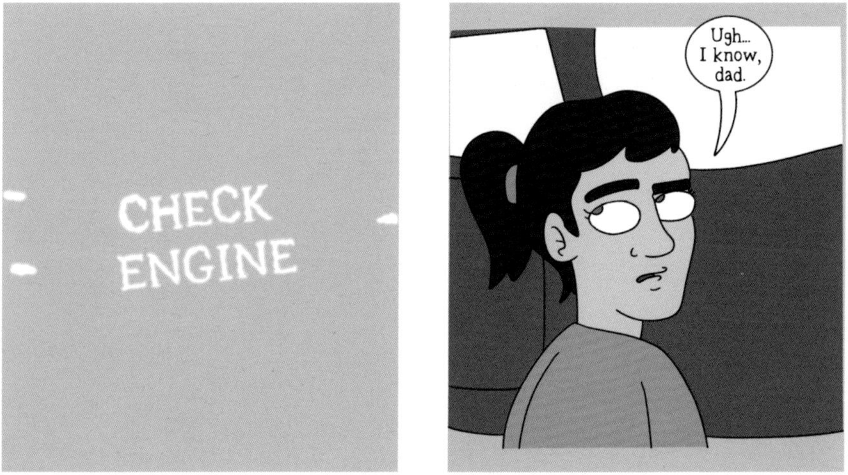
CHECK ENGINE
Ugh... I know, dad.

Life of Ryan

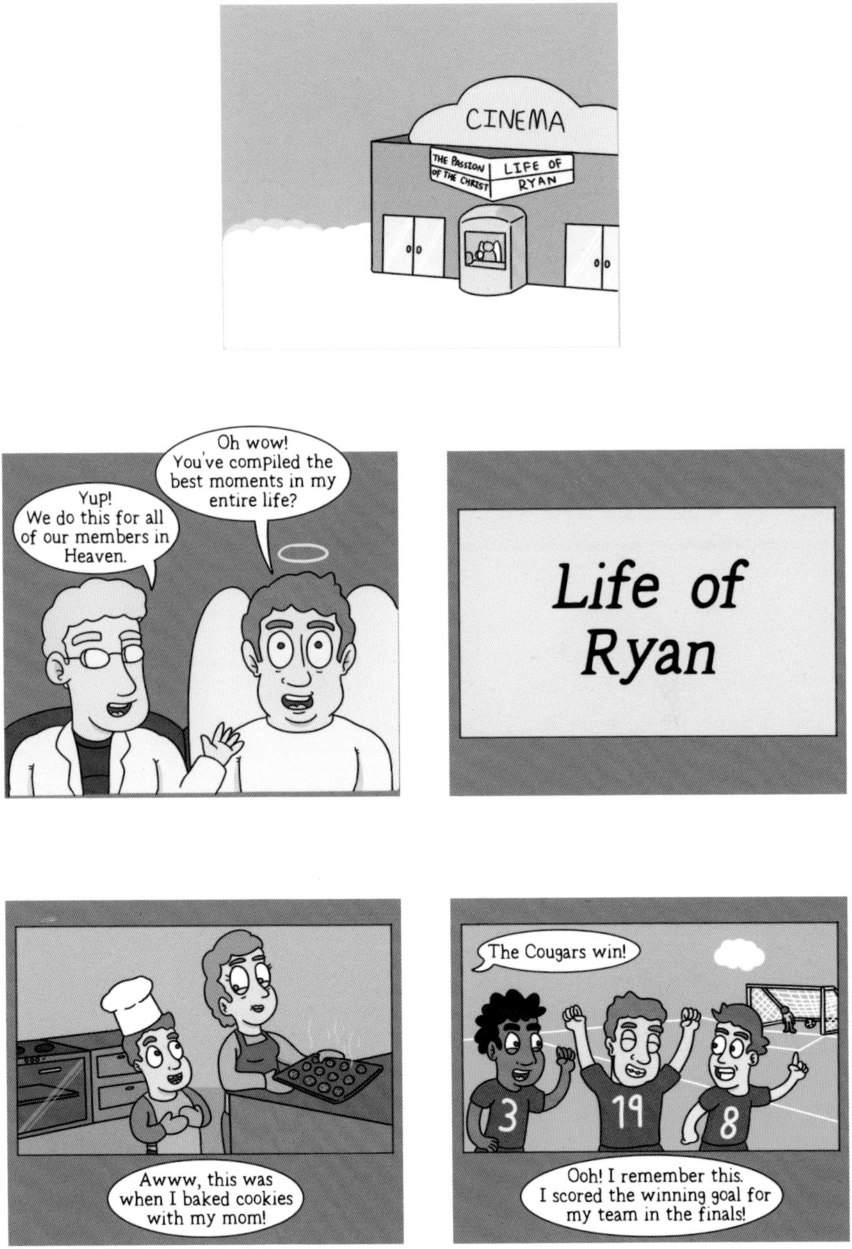
CINEMA
THE PASSION OF THE CHRIST
LIFE OF RYAN
Oh wow! You've compiled the best moments in my entire life?
Yup! We do this for all of our members in Heaven.
Life of Ryan
Awww, this was when I baked cookies with my mom!
The Cougars win!
3
19
8
Ooh! I remember this. I scored the winning goal for my team in the finals!

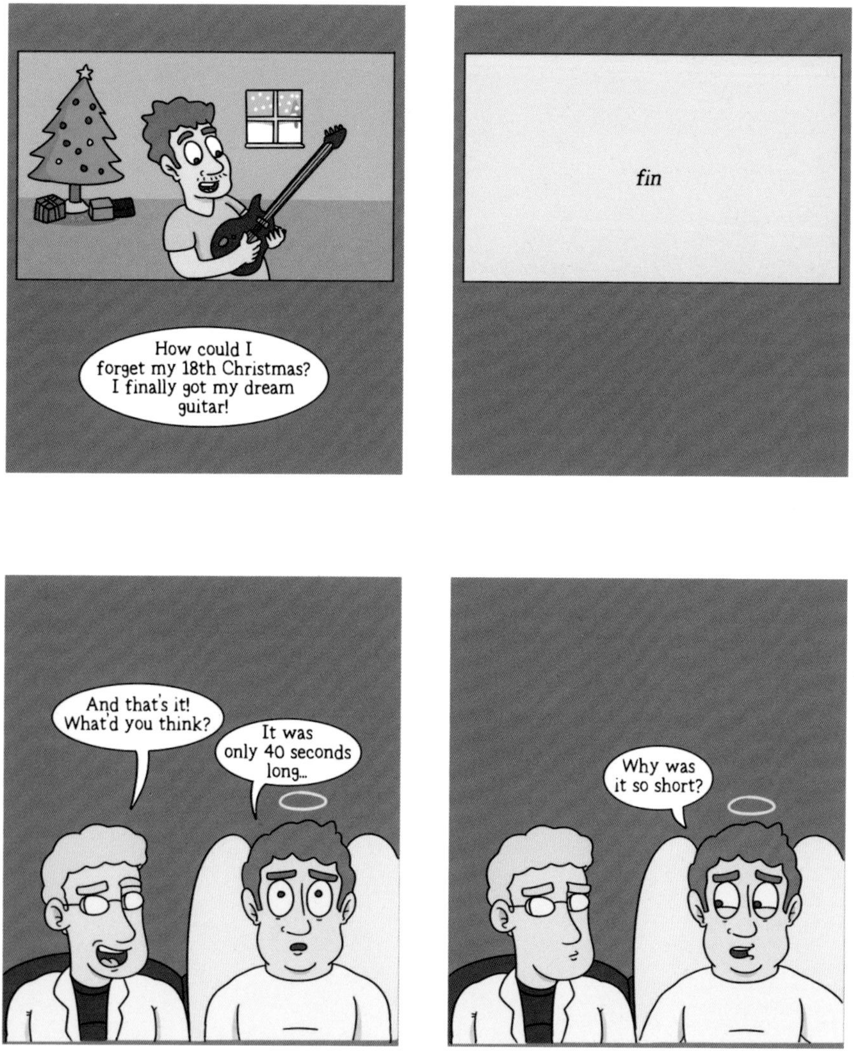
How could I forget my 18th Christmas? I finally got my dream guitar!
fin
And that's it! What'd you think?
It was only 40 seconds long...
Why was it so short?

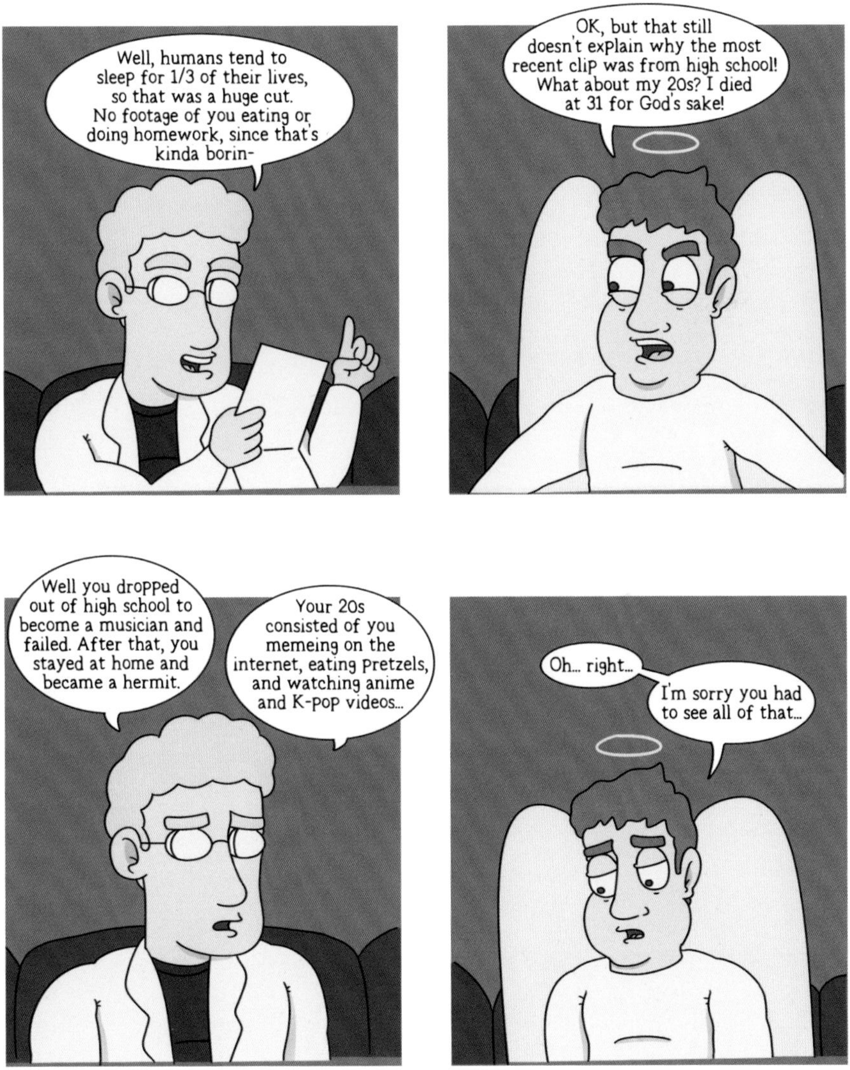
Well, humans tend to sleep for 1/3 of their lives, so that was a huge cut. No footage of you eating or doing homework, since that's kinda borin-
OK, but that still doesn't explain why the most recent clip was from high school! What about my 20s? I died at 31 for God's sake!
Well you dropped out of high school to become a musician and failed. After that, you stayed at home and became a hermit.
Your 20s consisted of you memeing on the internet, eating pretzels, and watching anime and K-pop videos...
Oh... right...
I'm sorry you had to see all of that...

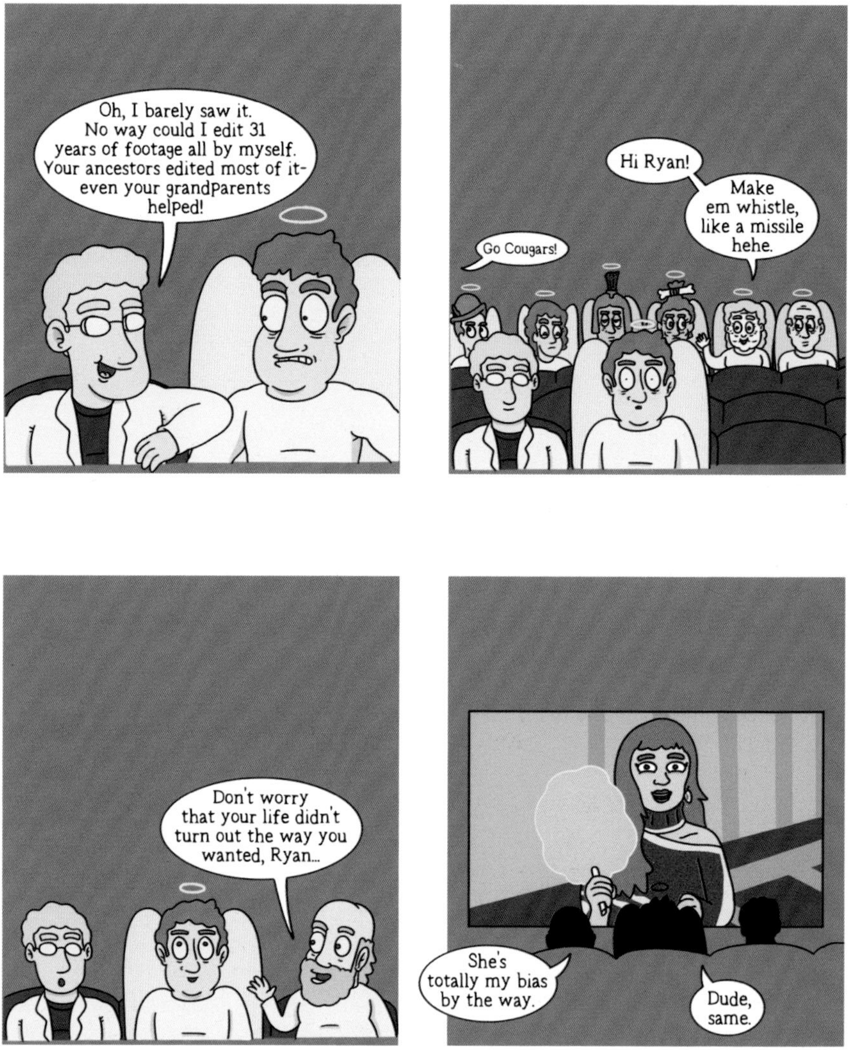
Oh, I barely saw it. No way could I edit 31 years of footage all by myself. Your ancestors edited most of it- even your grandparents helped!
Hi Ryan!
Make em whistle, like a missile hehe.
Go Cougars!
Don't worry that your life didn't turn out the way you wanted, Ryan...
She's totally my bias by the way.
Dude, same.

Noah's Ark: Snakes on a Boat

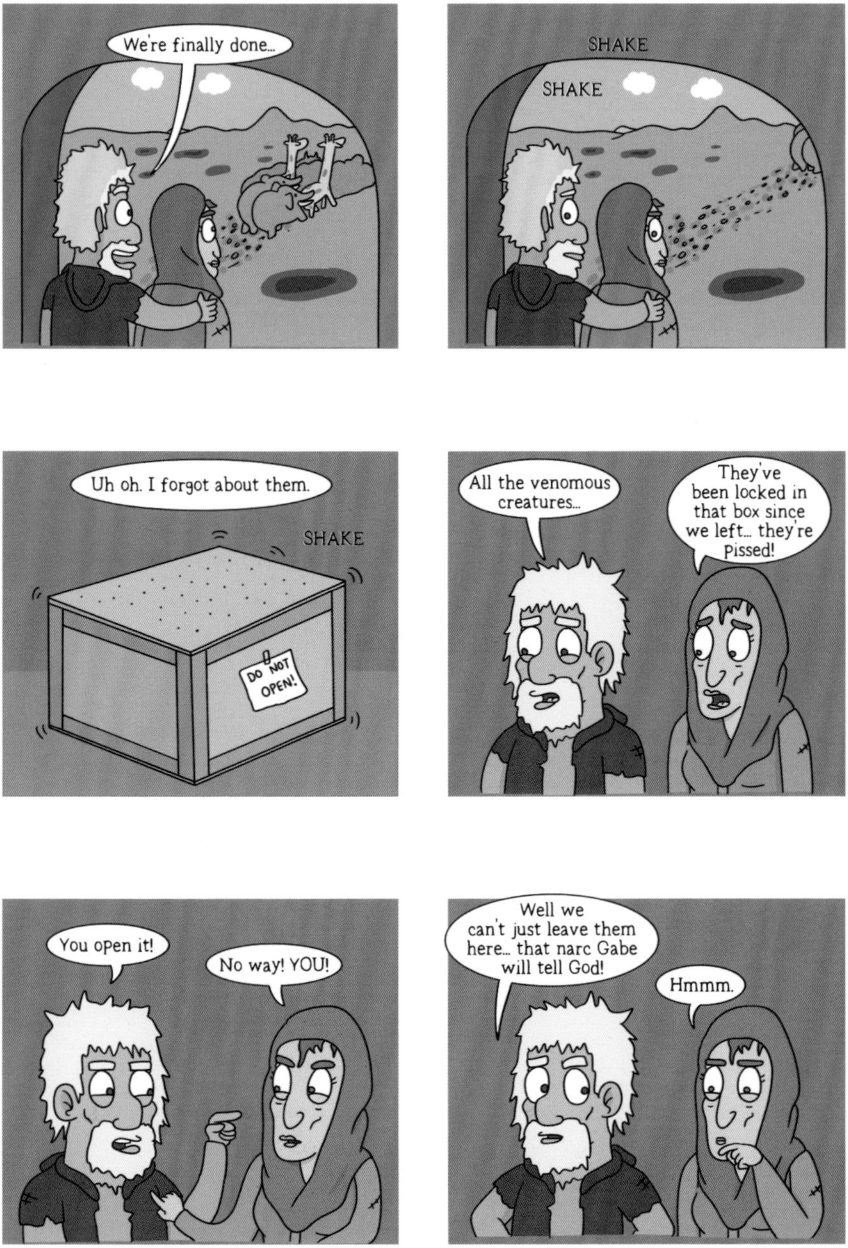

We're finally done...
SHAKE
SHAKE
Uh oh. I forgot about them.
SHAKE
DO NOT OPEN!
All the venomous creatures...
They've been locked in that box since we left... they're pissed!
You open it!
No way! YOU!
Well we can't just leave them here... that narc Gabe will tell God!
Hmmm.

ADIOS!
Oi!

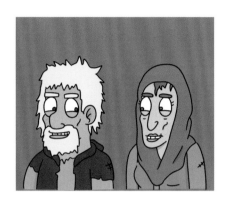

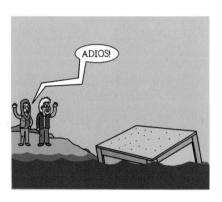

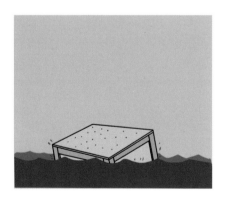

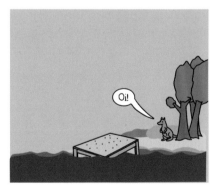

New mates!
HOORAY!

BONUS

Hold on, I'm missing some snakes and spiders like the funnel web, the eastern brown snake, the...
Ehh, screw it.

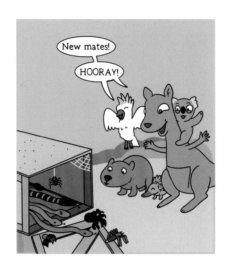

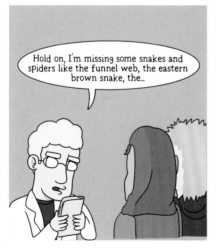

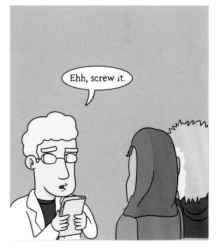

Plan

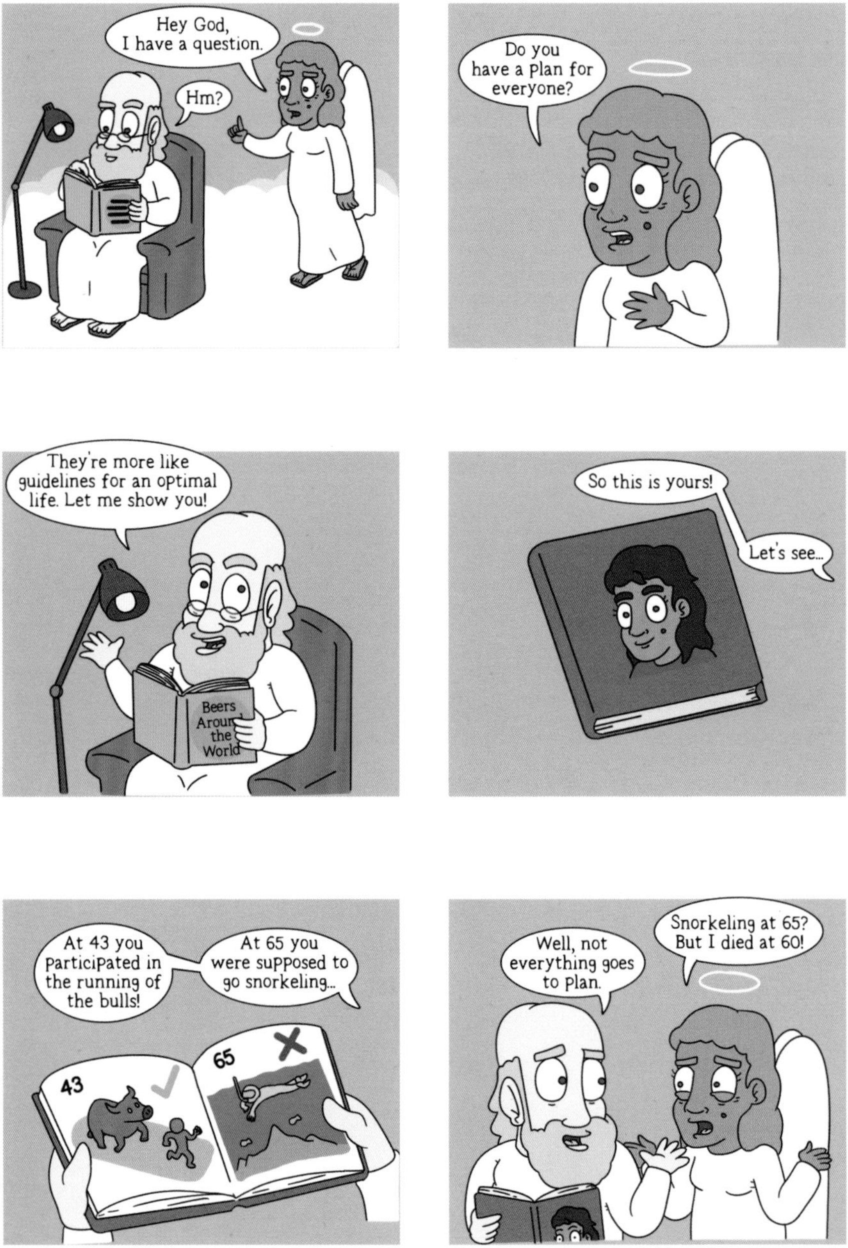
Hey God,
I have a question.
Hm?
Do you have a plan for everyone?
They're more like guidelines for an optimal life. Let me show you!
Beers Around the World
So this is yours!
Let's see...
At 43 you participated in the running of the bulls!
At 65 you were supposed to go snorkeling...
43
65
Snorkeling at 65? But I died at 60!
Well, not everything goes to plan.

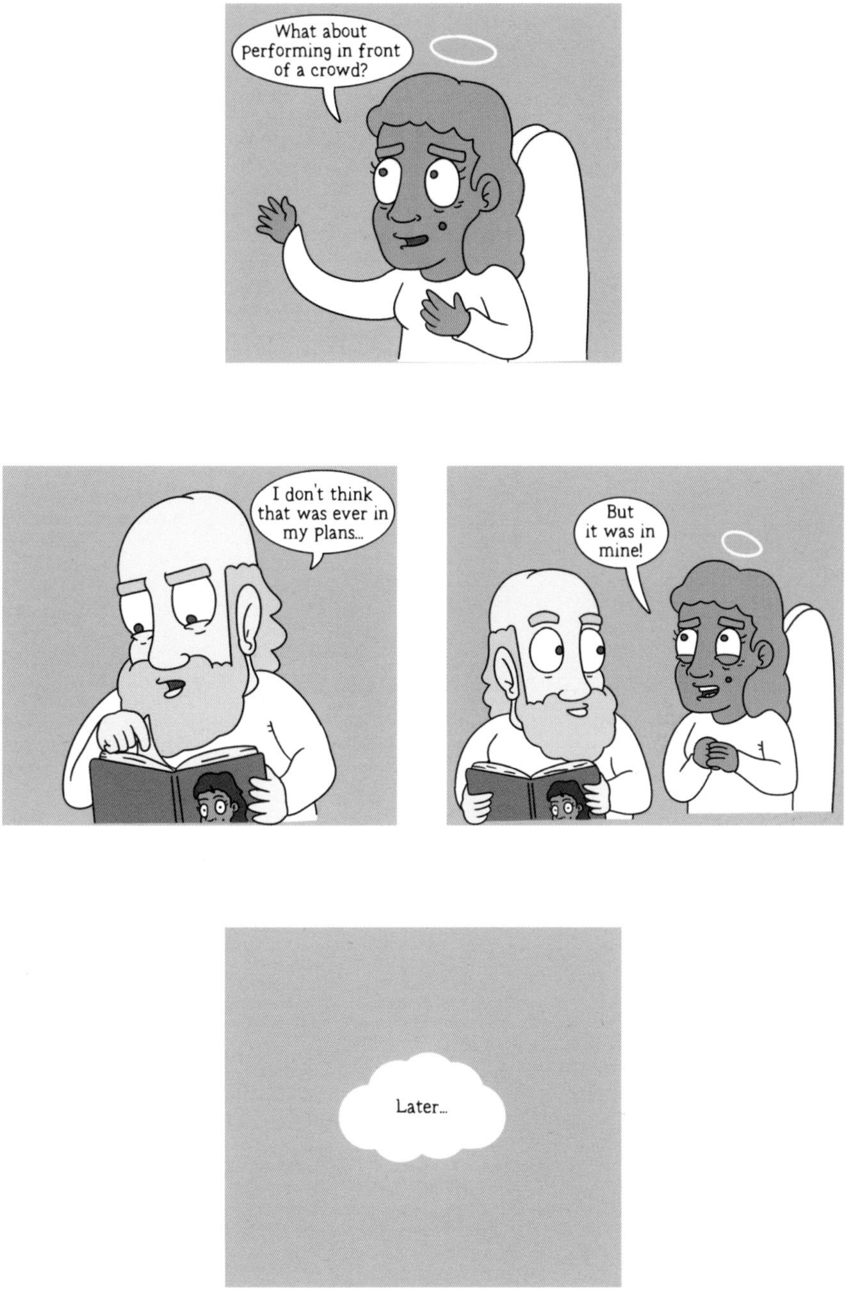
What about performing in front of a crowd?
I don't think that was ever in my plans...
But it was in mine!
Later...

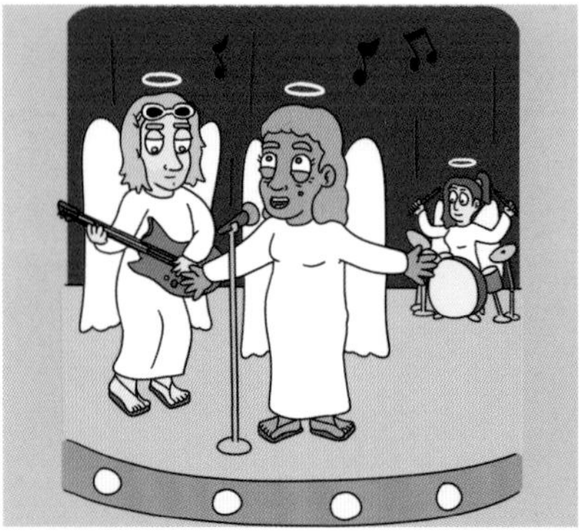

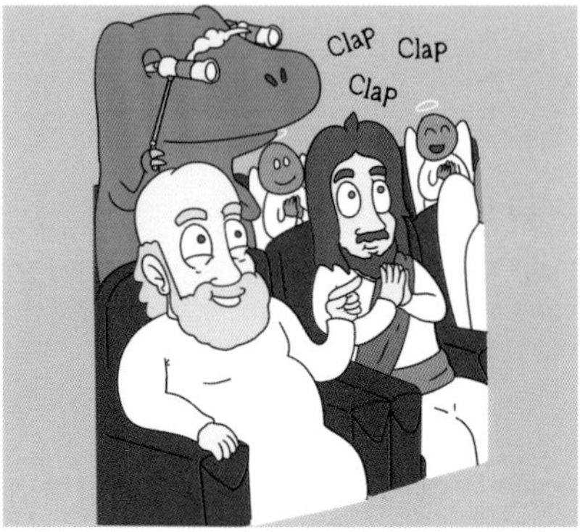
Clap
Clap
Clap

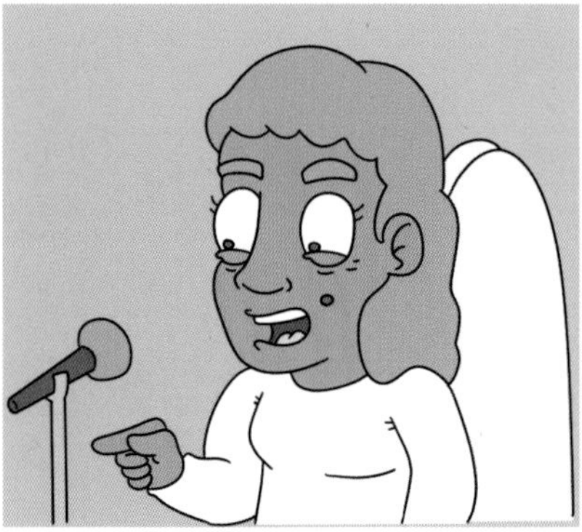

BONUS

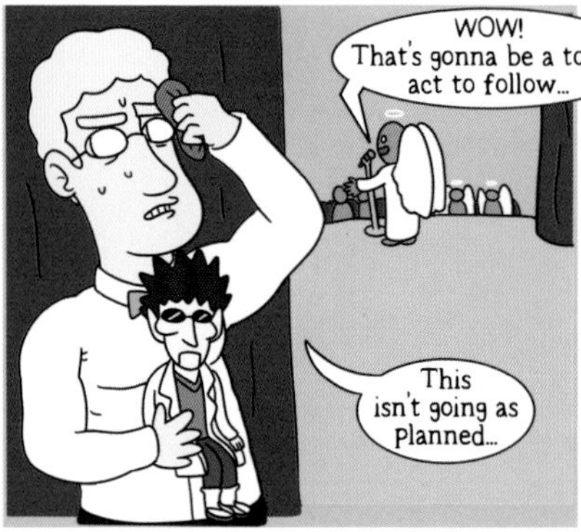
WOW! That's gonna be a tough act to follow...
This isn't going as planned...

Y'all Need Jesus

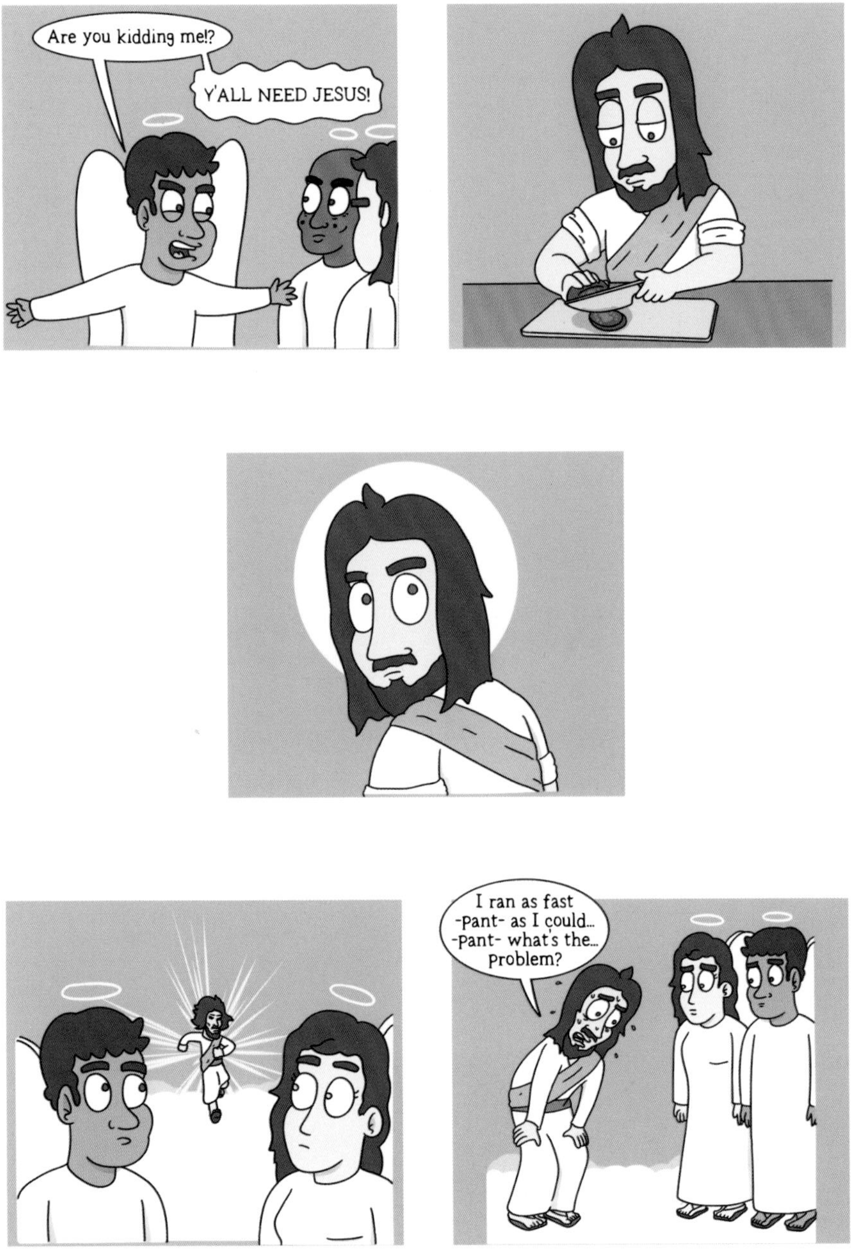

Are you kidding me!?
Y'ALL NEED JESUS!
I ran as fast -pant- as I could... -pant- what's the... problem?

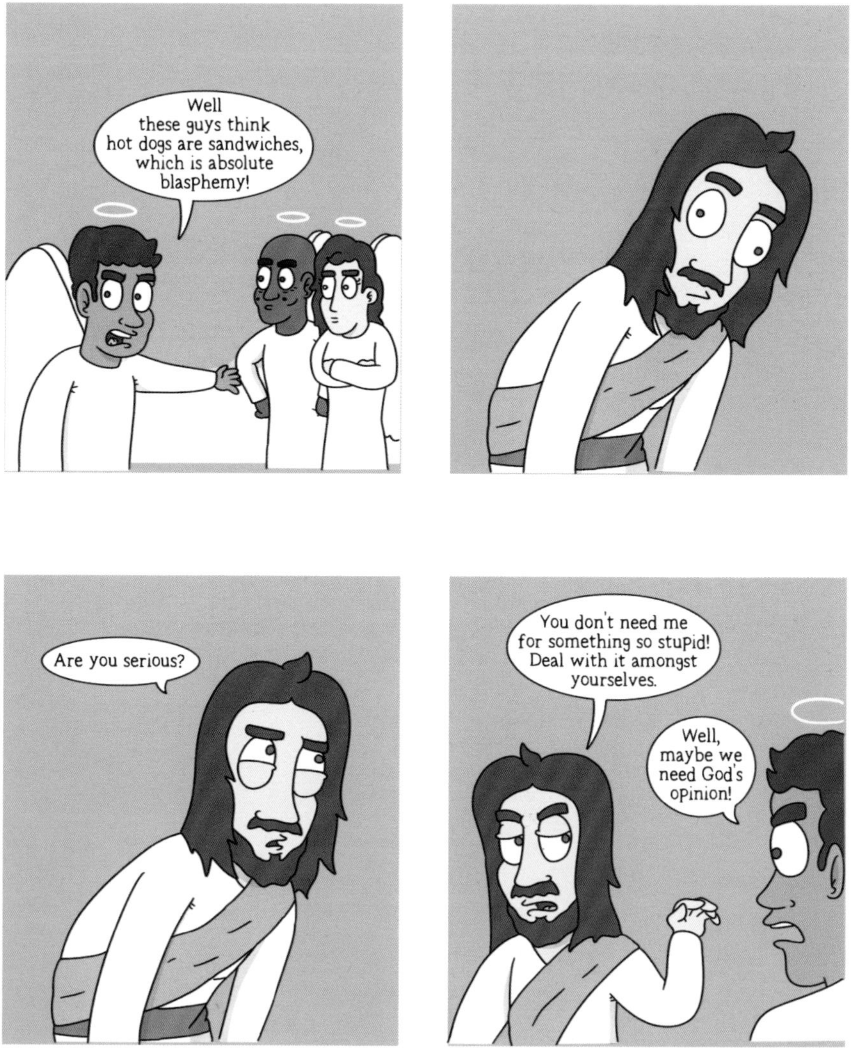
Well these guys think hot dogs are sandwiches, which is absolute blasphemy!
Are you serious?
You don't need me for something so stupid! Deal with it amongst yourselves.
Well, maybe we need God's opinion!

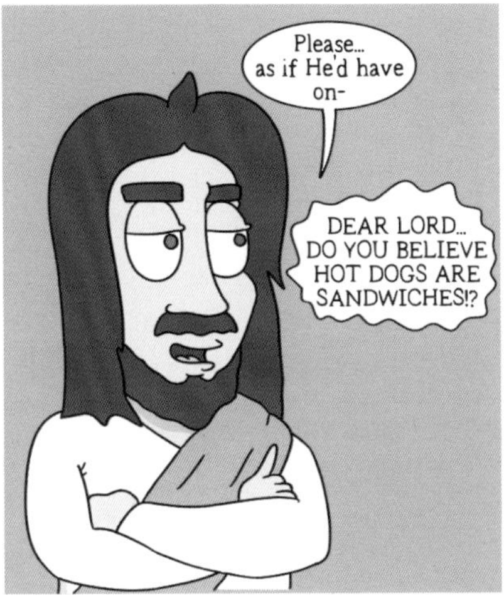
Please... as if He'd have on-
DEAR LORD... DO YOU BELIEVE HOT DOGS ARE SANDWICHES!?

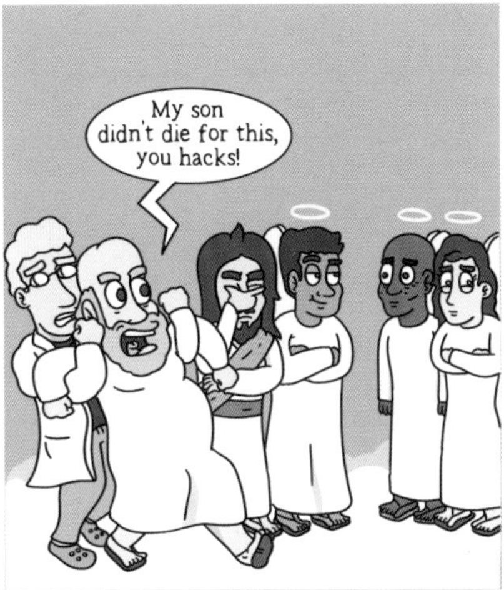
My son didn't die for this, you hacks!

BONUS

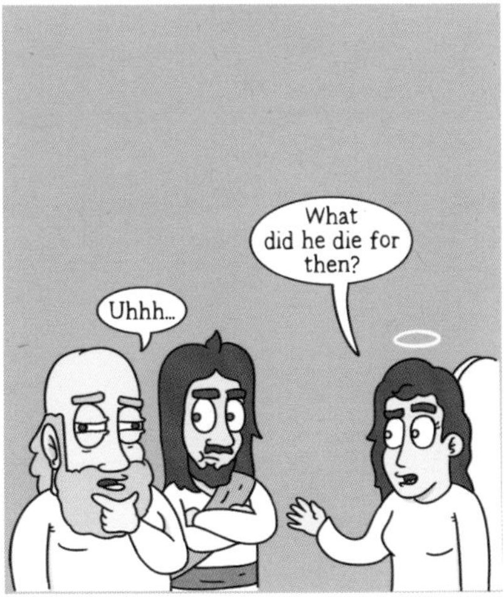
What did he die for then?
Uhhh...

Letter to Satan

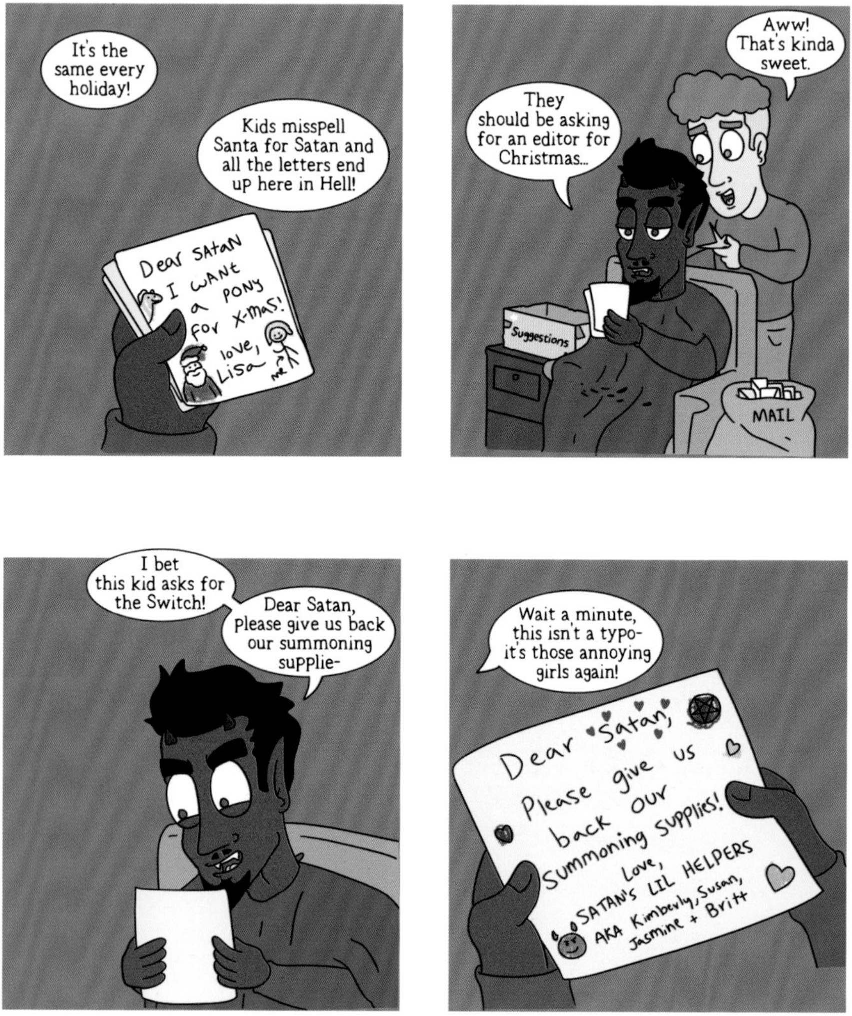
It's the same every holiday!
Kids misspell Santa for Satan and all the letters end up here in Hell!
Dear SAtaN I WANT a PONY for X-mas! love, Lisa
They should be asking for an editor for Christmas...
Aww! That's kinda sweet.
Suggestions
MAIL
I bet this kid asks for the Switch!
Dear Satan, Please give us back our summoning supplie-
Wait a minute, this isn't a typo-it's those annoying girls again!
Dear Satan, Please give us back our summoning supplies! Love, SATAN'S LIL HELPERS AKA Kimberly, Susan, Jasmine + Britt

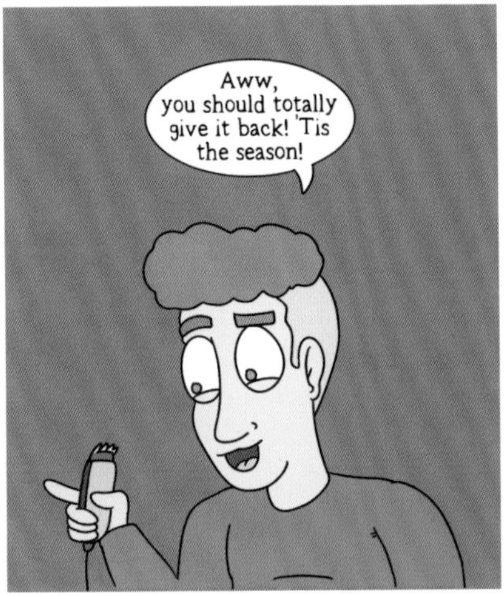
Aww, you should totally give it back! 'Tis the season!

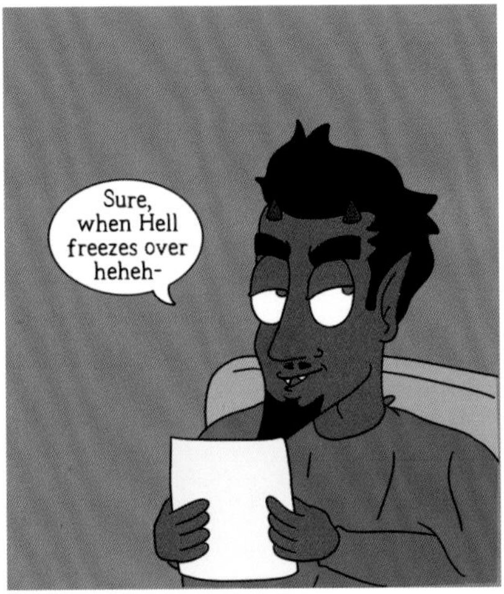
Sure, when Hell freezes over heheh-

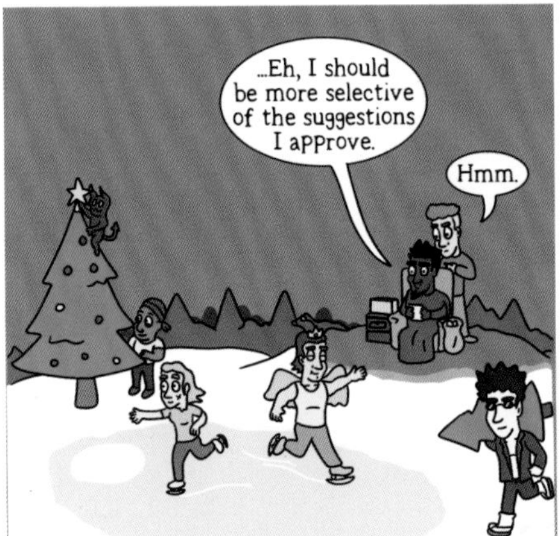
...Eh, I should be more selective of the suggestions I approve.
Hmm.

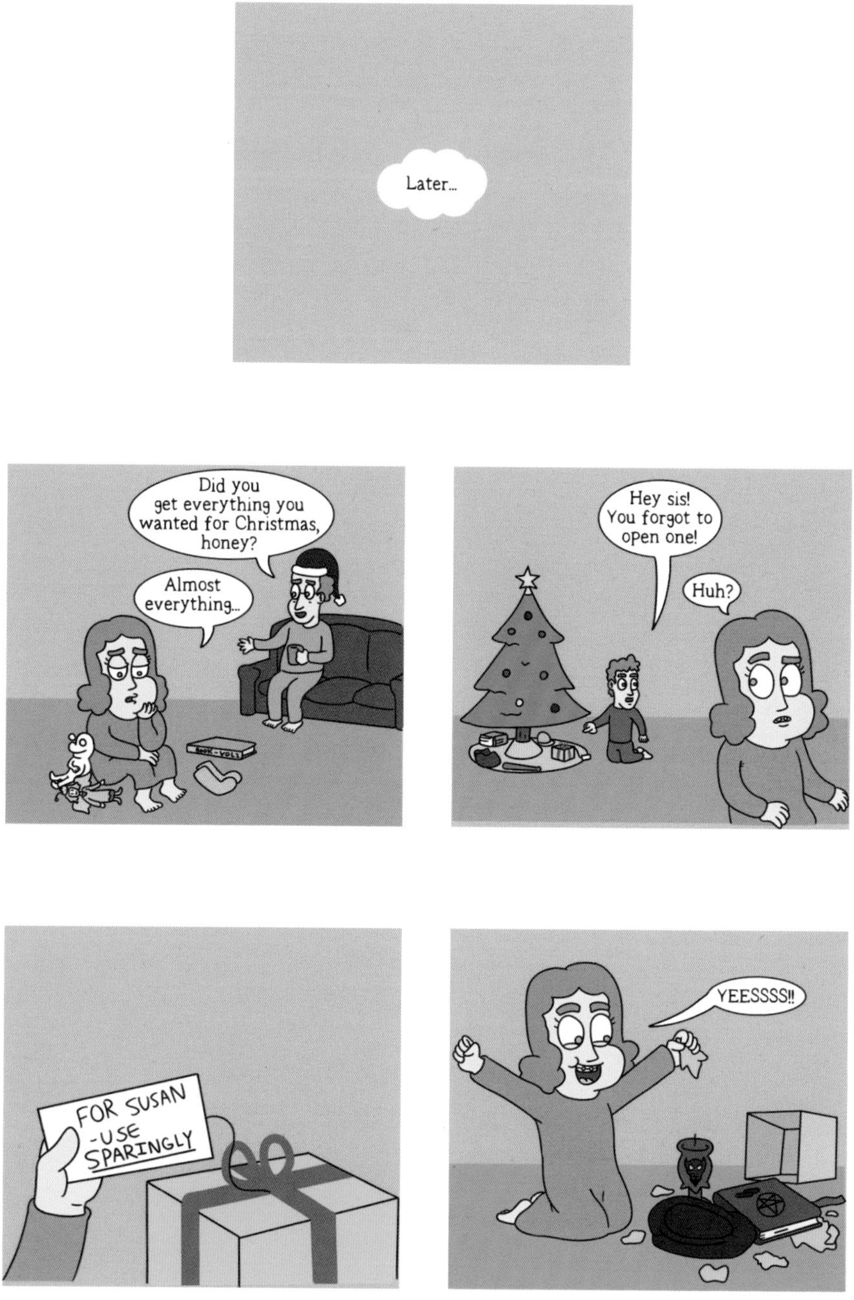
Later...
Did you get everything you wanted for Christmas, honey?
Almost everything...
Hey sis! You forgot to open one!
Huh?
FOR SUSAN -USE SPARINGLY
YEESSSS!!

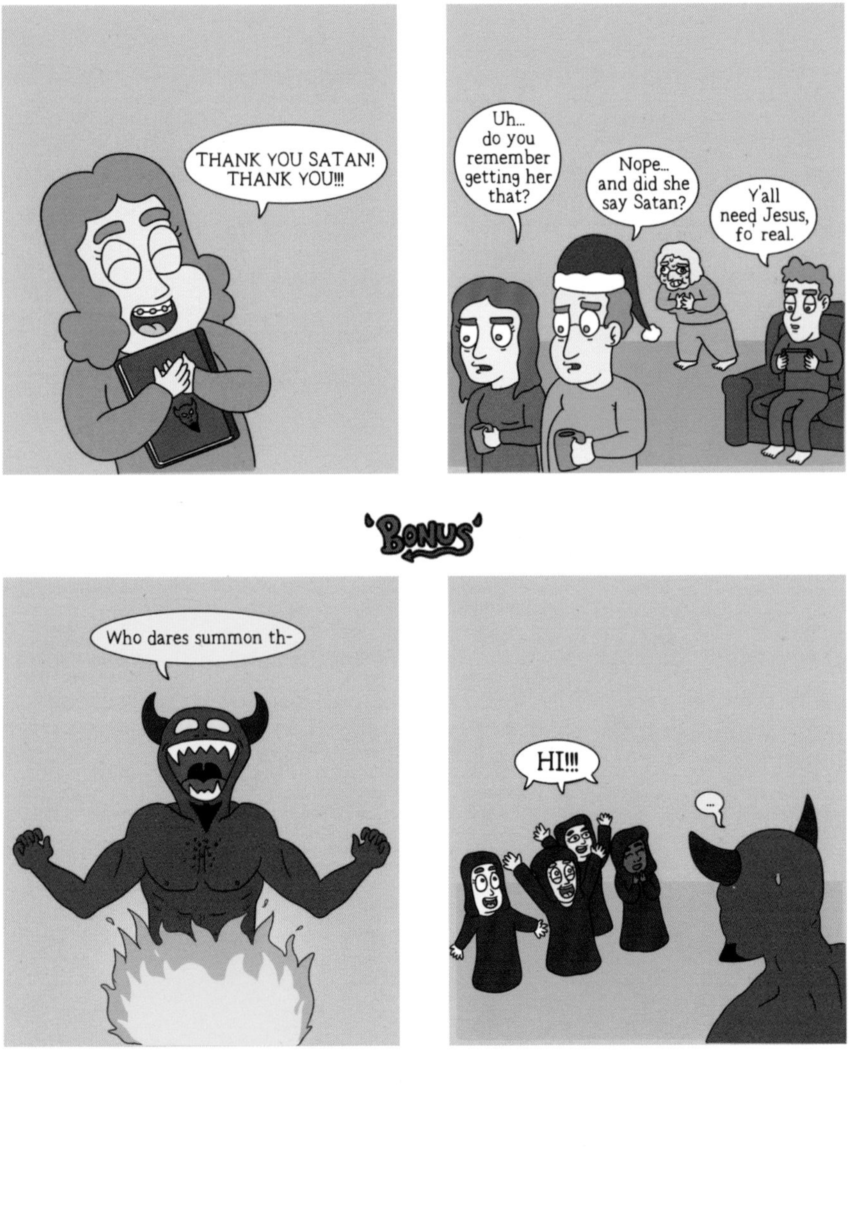
THANK YOU SATAN! THANK YOU!!!
Uh... do you remember getting her that?
Nope... and did she say Satan?
Y'all need Jesus, fo' real.
BONUS
Who dares summon th-
HI!!!
...

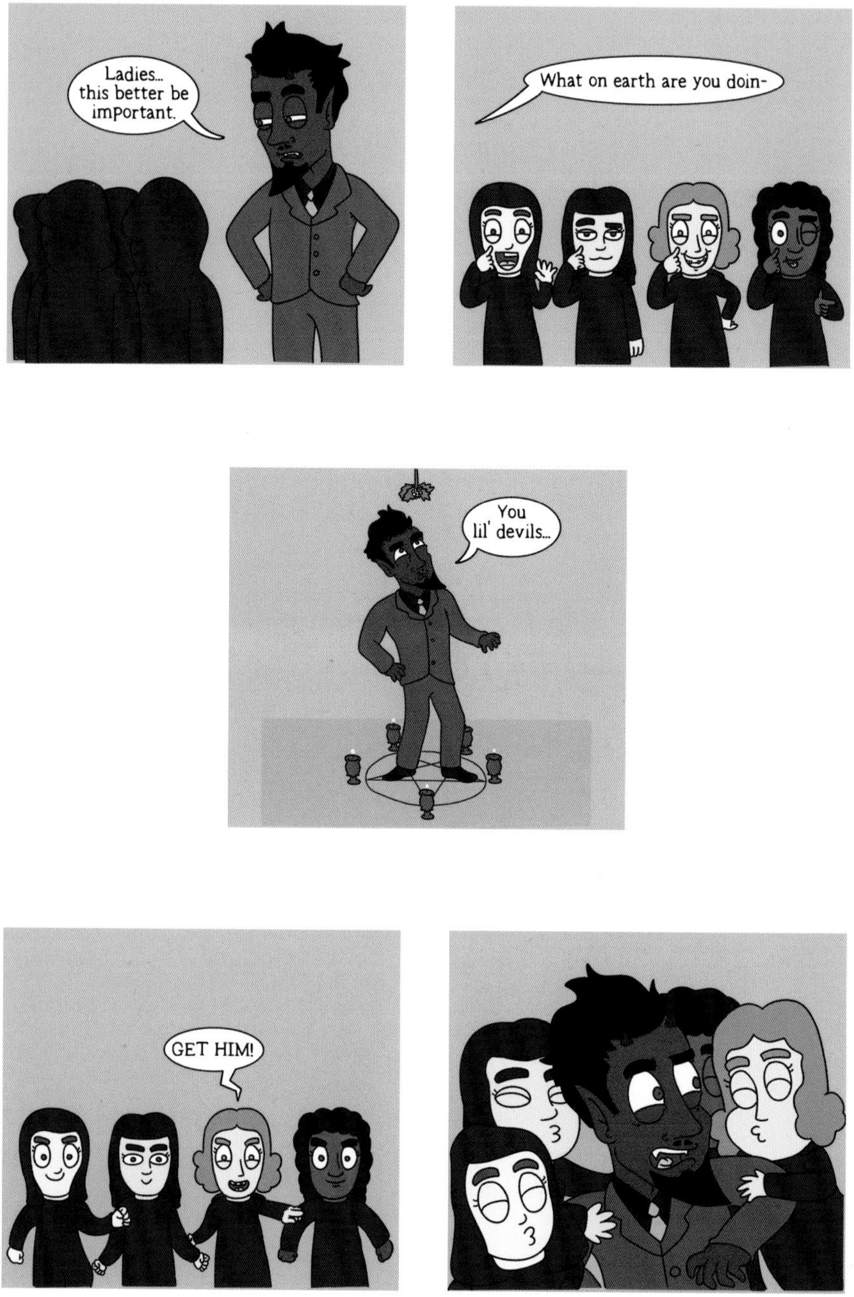
Ladies... this better be important.
What on earth are you doin-
You lil' devils...
GET HIM!

Faith Healing

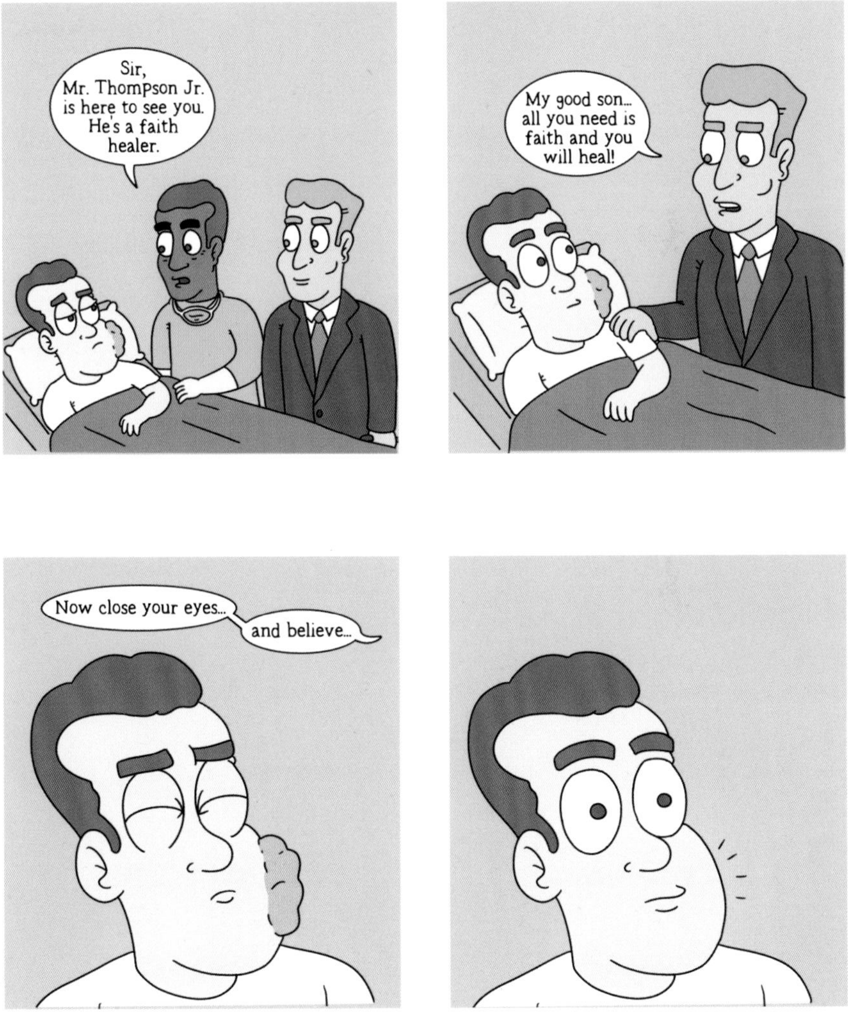
Sir, Mr. Thompson Jr. is here to see you. He's a faith healer.
My good son... all you need is faith and you will heal!
Now close your eyes...
and believe...

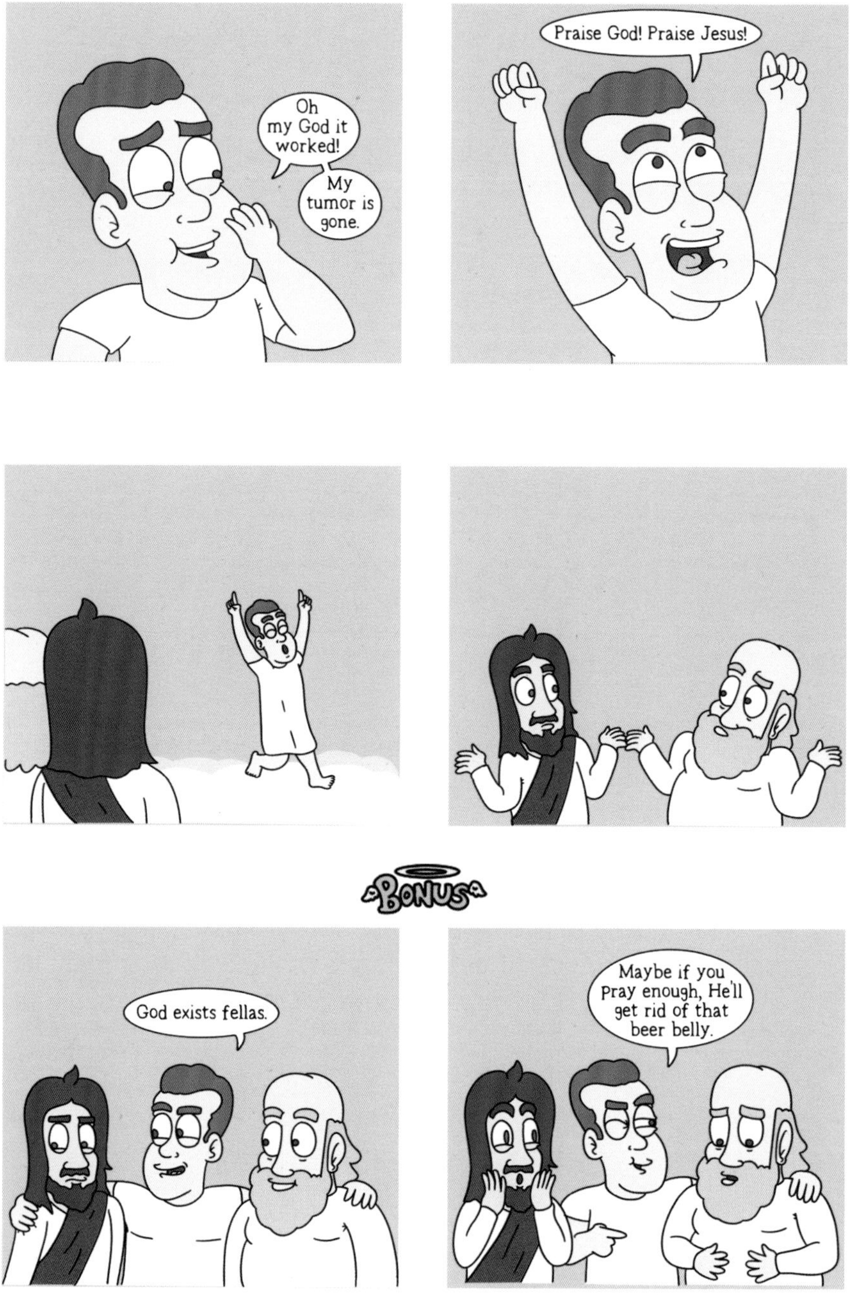
Oh my God it worked!
My tumor is gone.
Praise God! Praise Jesus!
BONUS
God exists fellas.
Maybe if you pray enough, He'll get rid of that beer belly.

2018

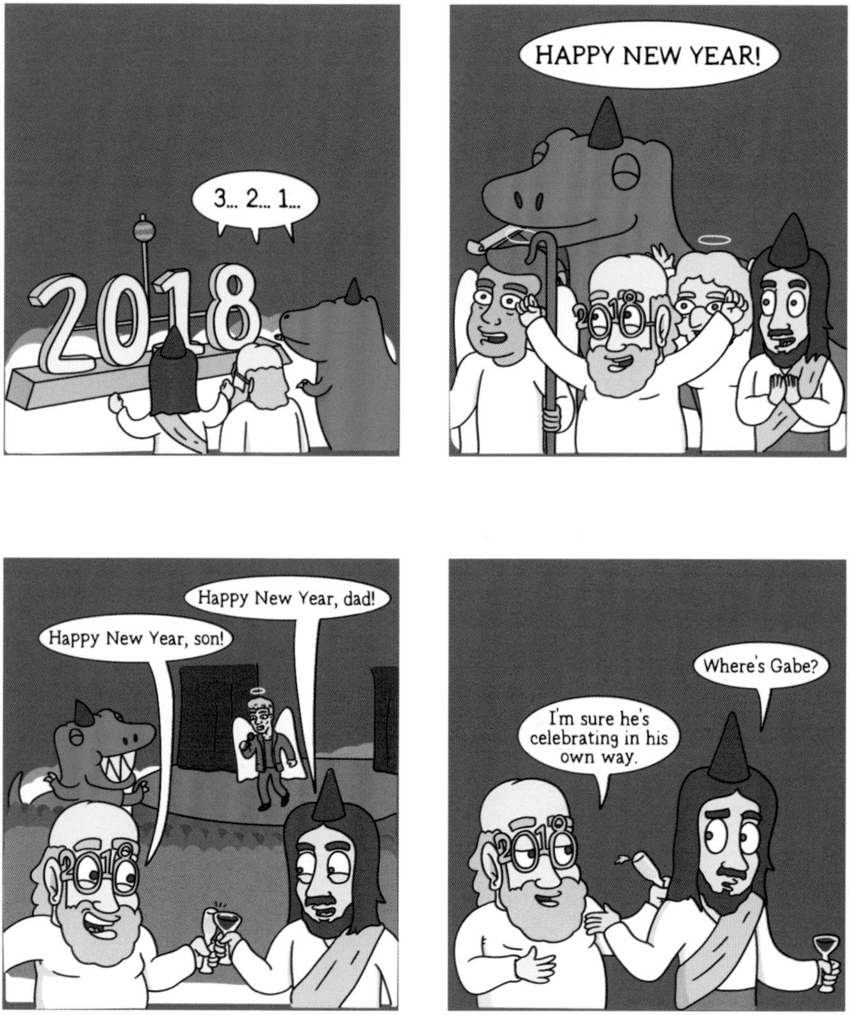
3... 2... 1...
HAPPY NEW YEAR!
Happy New Year, son!
Happy New Year, dad!
Where's Gabe?
I'm sure he's celebrating in his own way.

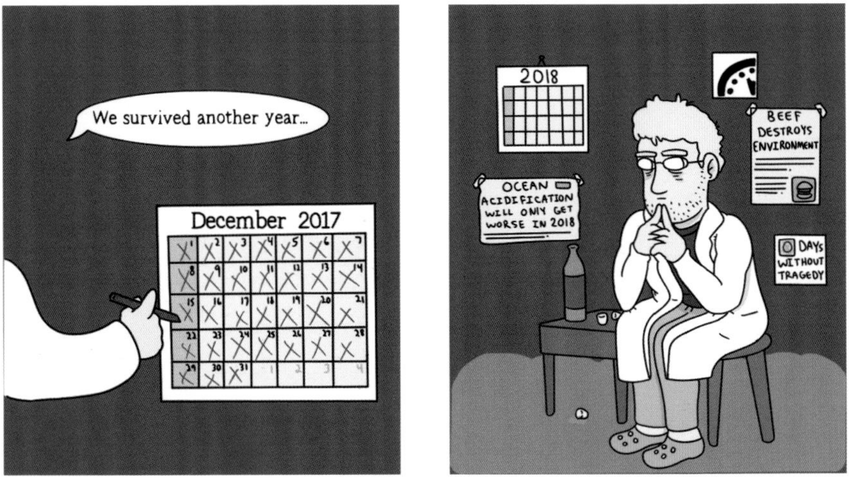
We survived another year...
December 2017
2018
OCEAN ACIDIFICATION WILL ONLY GET WORSE IN 2018
BEEF DESTROYS ENVIRONMENT
DAYS WITHOUT TRAGEDY

BONUS

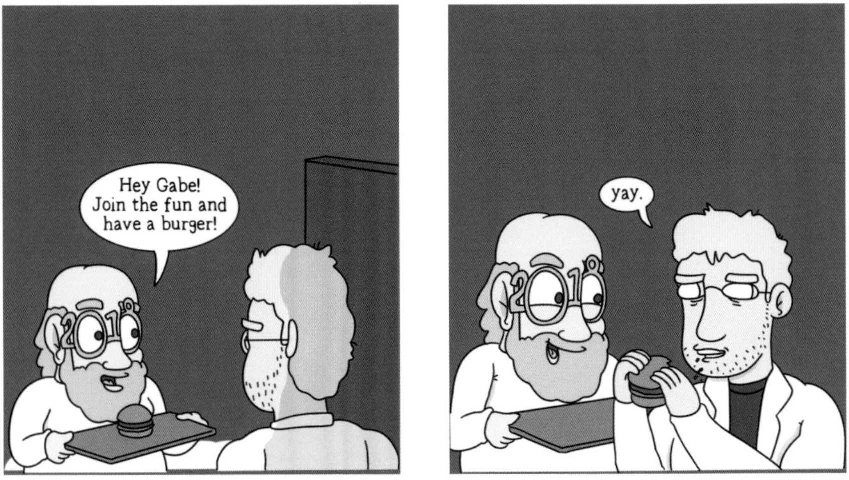
Hey Gabe! Join the fun and have a burger!
yay.

The 9 + 1 Commandments

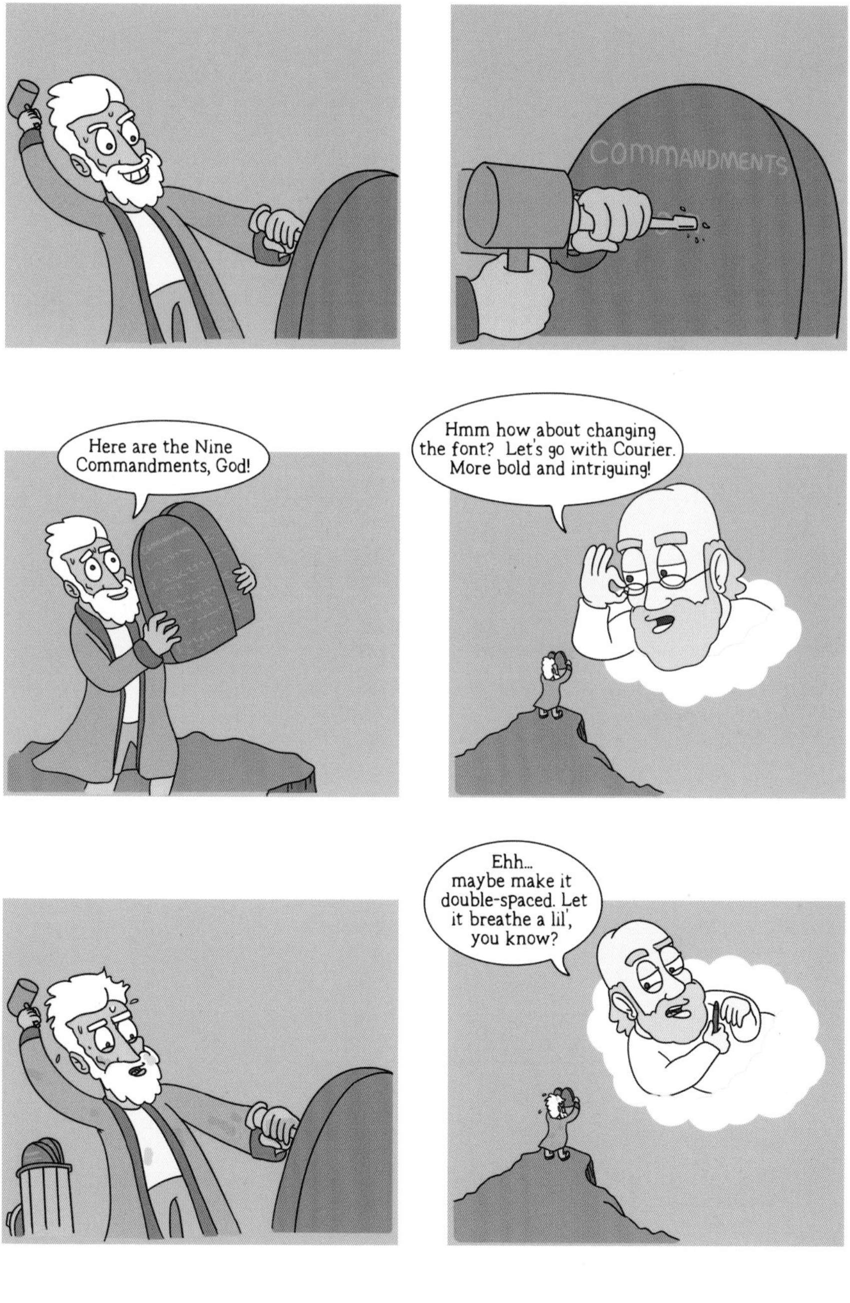
COMMANDMENTS
Here are the Nine Commandments, God!
Hmm how about changing the font? Let's go with Courier. More bold and intriguing!
Ehh... maybe make it double-spaced. Let it breathe a lil', you know?

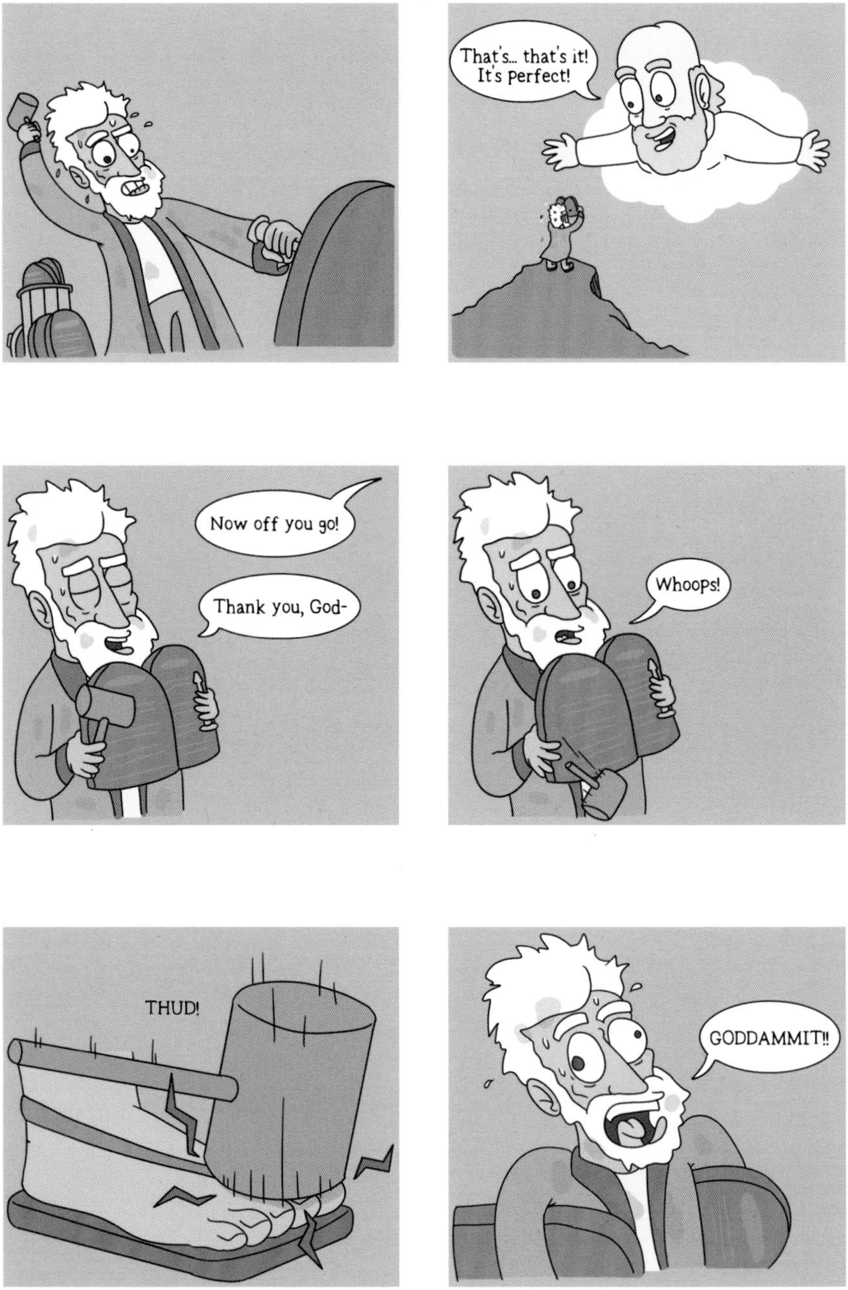
That's... that's it!
It's perfect!
Now off you go!
Thank you, God-
Whoops!
THUD!
GODDAMMIT!!

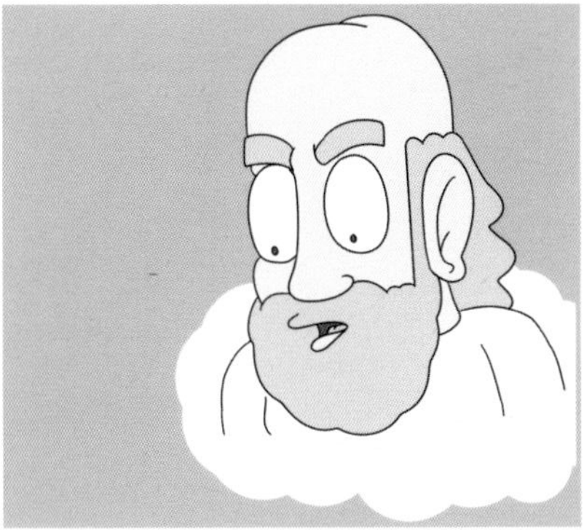

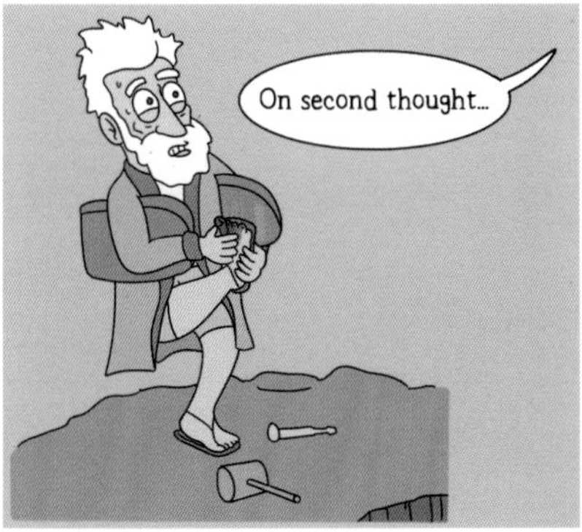
On second thought...

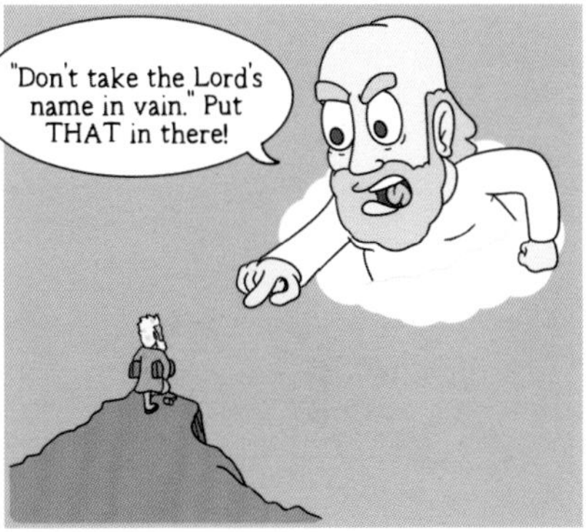
"Don't take the Lord's name in vain." Put THAT in there!

BONUS

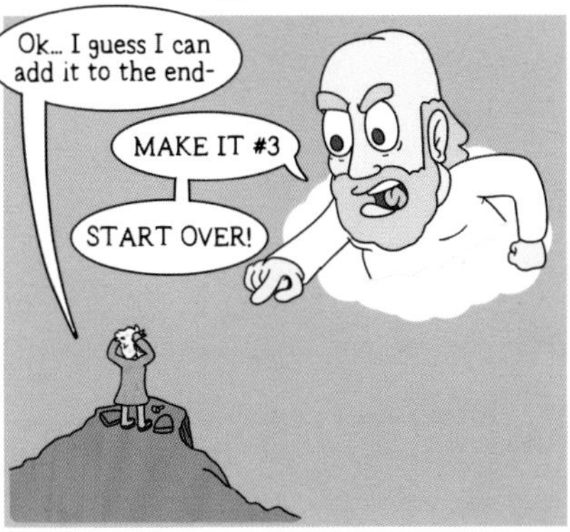
Ok... I guess I can add it to the end-
MAKE IT #3
START OVER!

Mistake

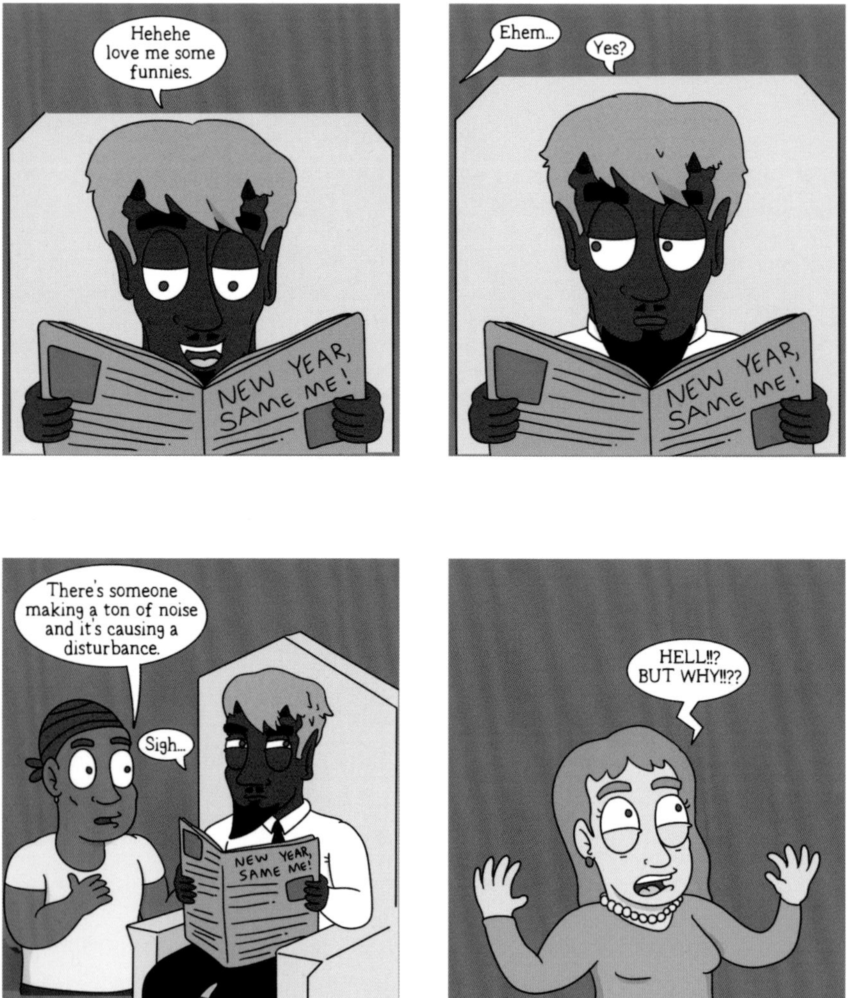
Hehehe love me some funnies.
NEW YEAR, SAME ME!
Ehem...
Yes?
NEW YEAR, SAME ME!
There's someone making a ton of noise and it's causing a disturbance.
Sigh...
NEW YEAR, SAME ME!
HELL!!? BUT WHY!!??

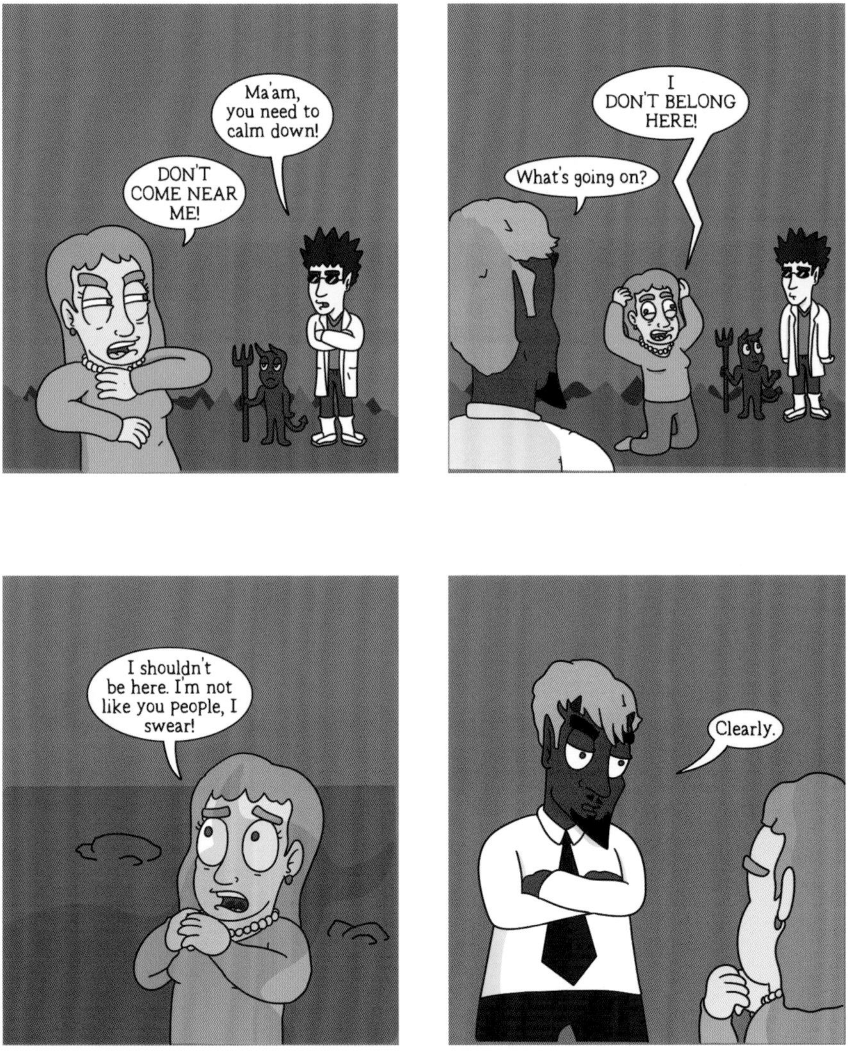
Ma'am, you need to calm down!
DON'T COME NEAR ME!
I DON'T BELONG HERE!
What's going on?
I shouldn't be here. I'm not like you people, I swear!
Clearly.

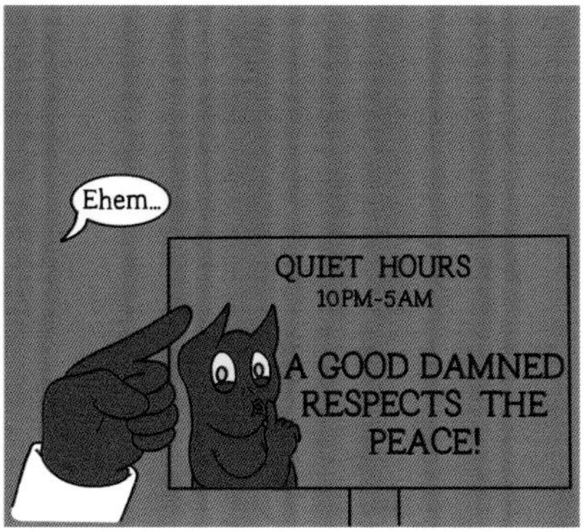
Ehem...
QUIET HOURS
10PM-5AM
A GOOD DAMNED RESPECTS THE PEACE!

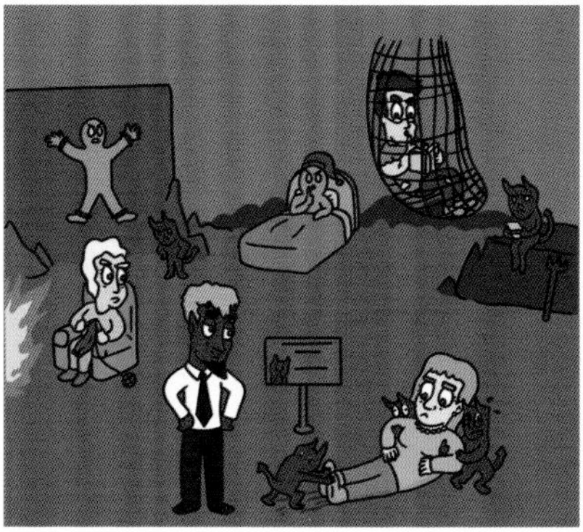

BONUS

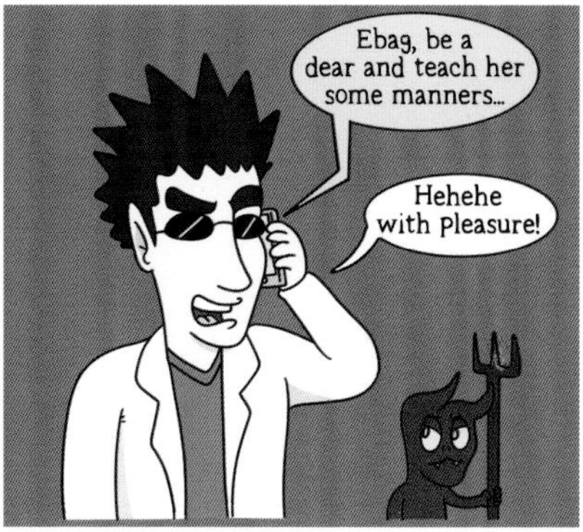
Ebag, be a dear and teach her some manners...
Hehehe with Pleasure!

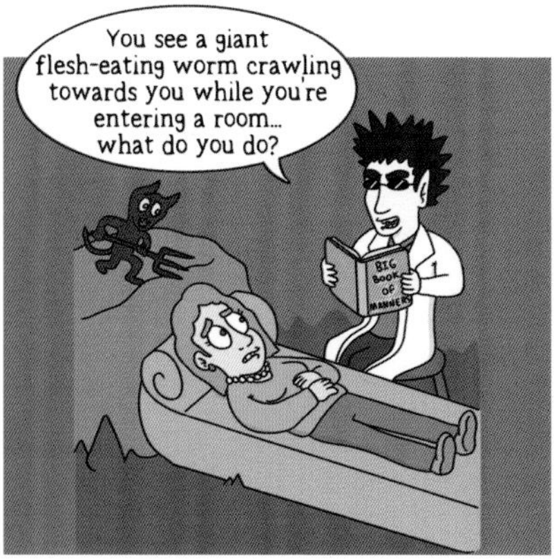
You see a giant flesh-eating worm crawling towards you while you're entering a room... what do you do?
BIG BOOK OF MANNERS

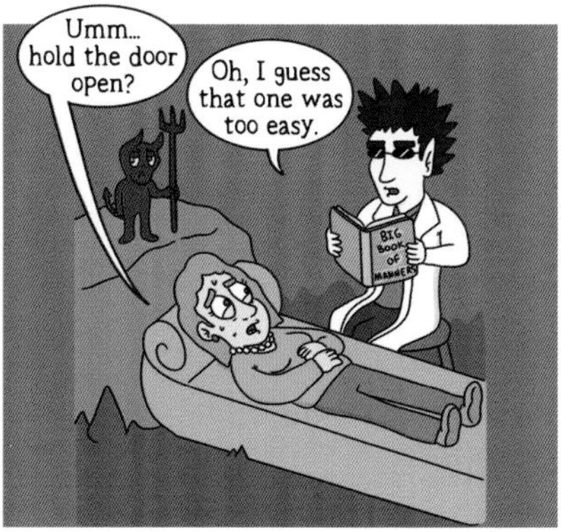
Umm... hold the door open?
Oh, I guess that one was too easy.
BIG BOOK OF MANNERS

Visitors

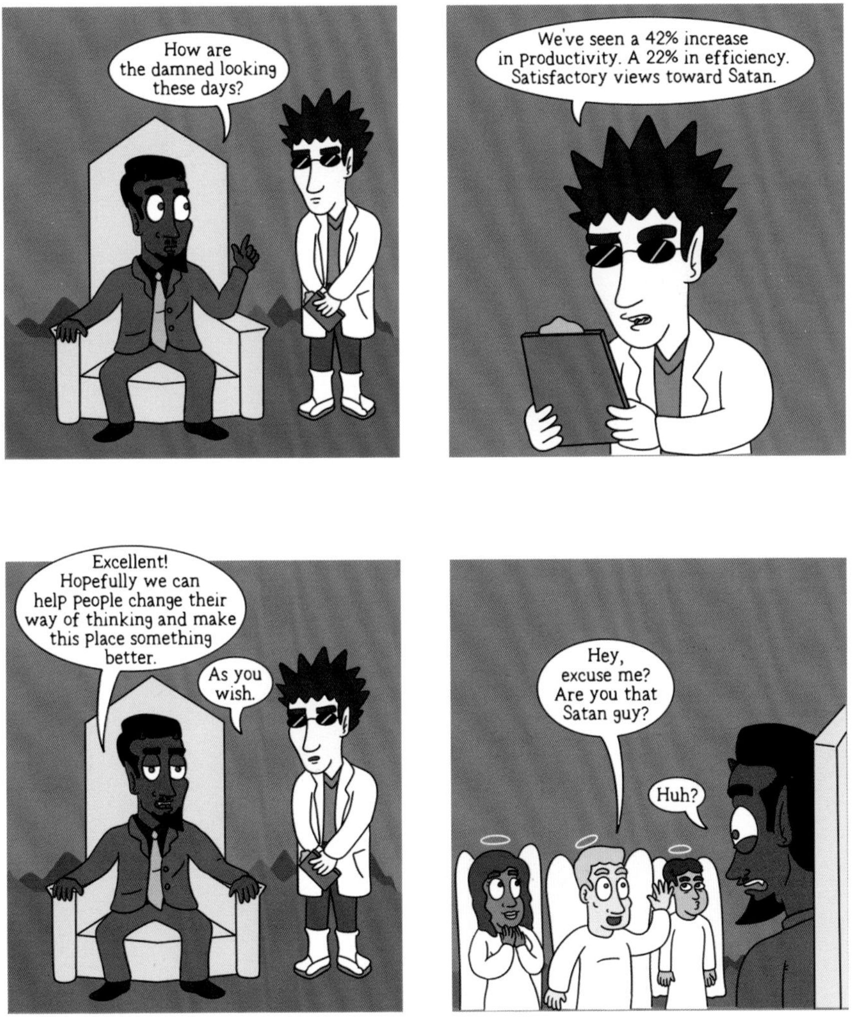
How are the damned looking these days?
We've seen a 42% increase in productivity. A 22% in efficiency. Satisfactory views toward Satan.
Excellent! Hopefully we can help people change their way of thinking and make this place something better.
As you wish.
Hey, excuse me? Are you that Satan guy?
Huh?

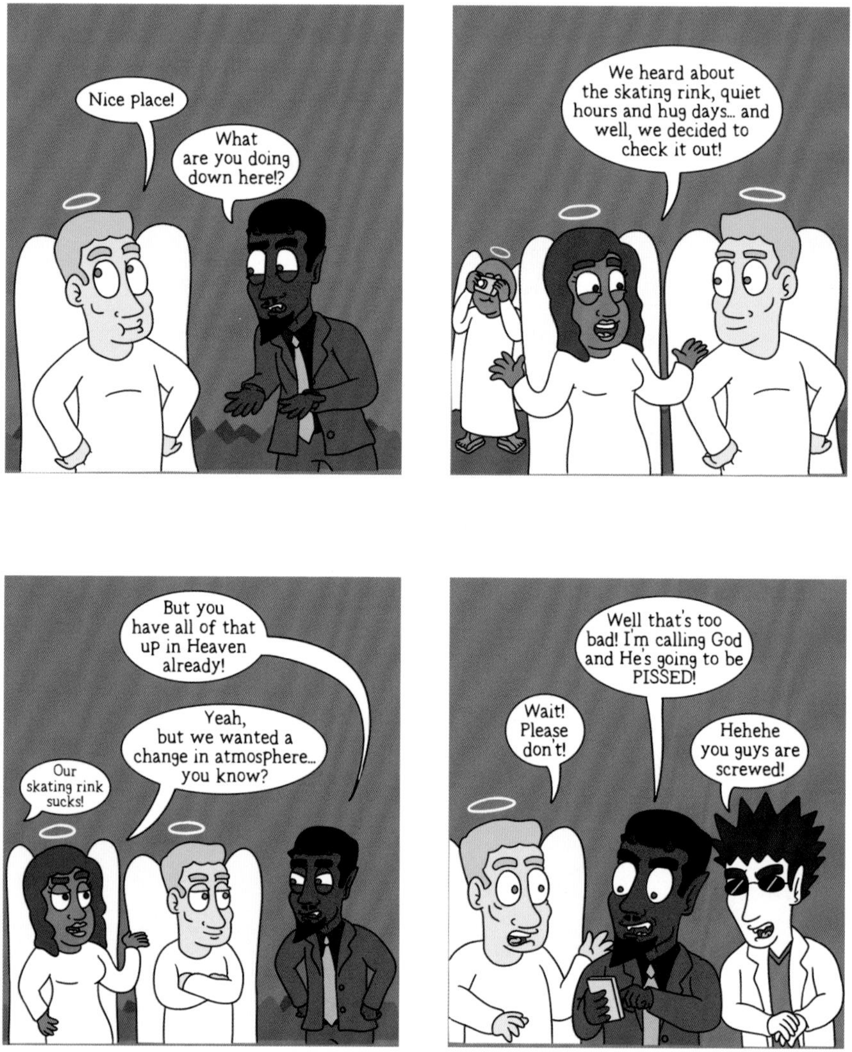
Nice place!
What are you doing down here!?
We heard about the skating rink, quiet hours and hug days... and well, we decided to check it out!
But you have all of that up in Heaven already!
Yeah, but we wanted a change in atmosphere... you know?
Our skating rink sucks!
Well that's too bad! I'm calling God and He's going to be PISSED!
Wait! Please don't!
Hehehe you guys are screwed!

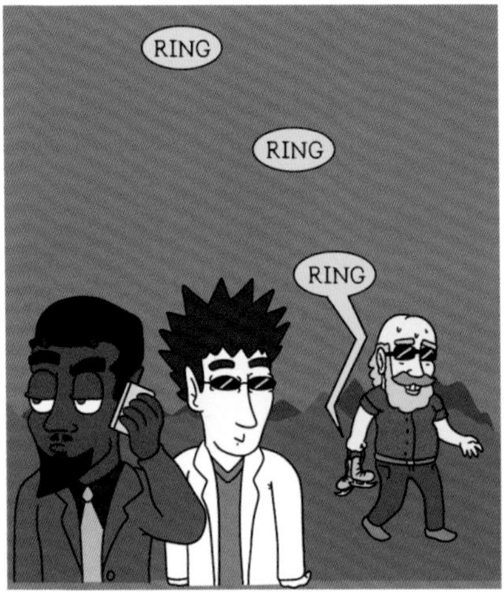
RING
RING
RING

BONUS

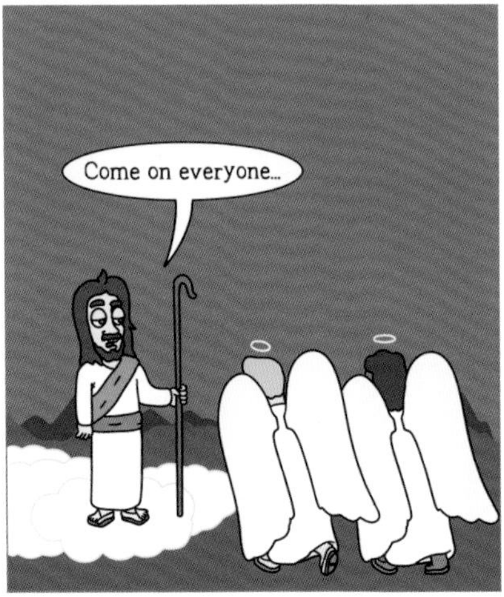
Come on everyone...

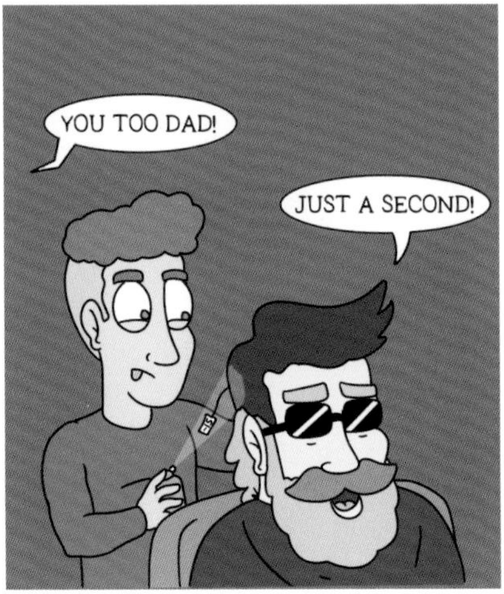
YOU TOO DAD!
JUST A SECOND!

Snow

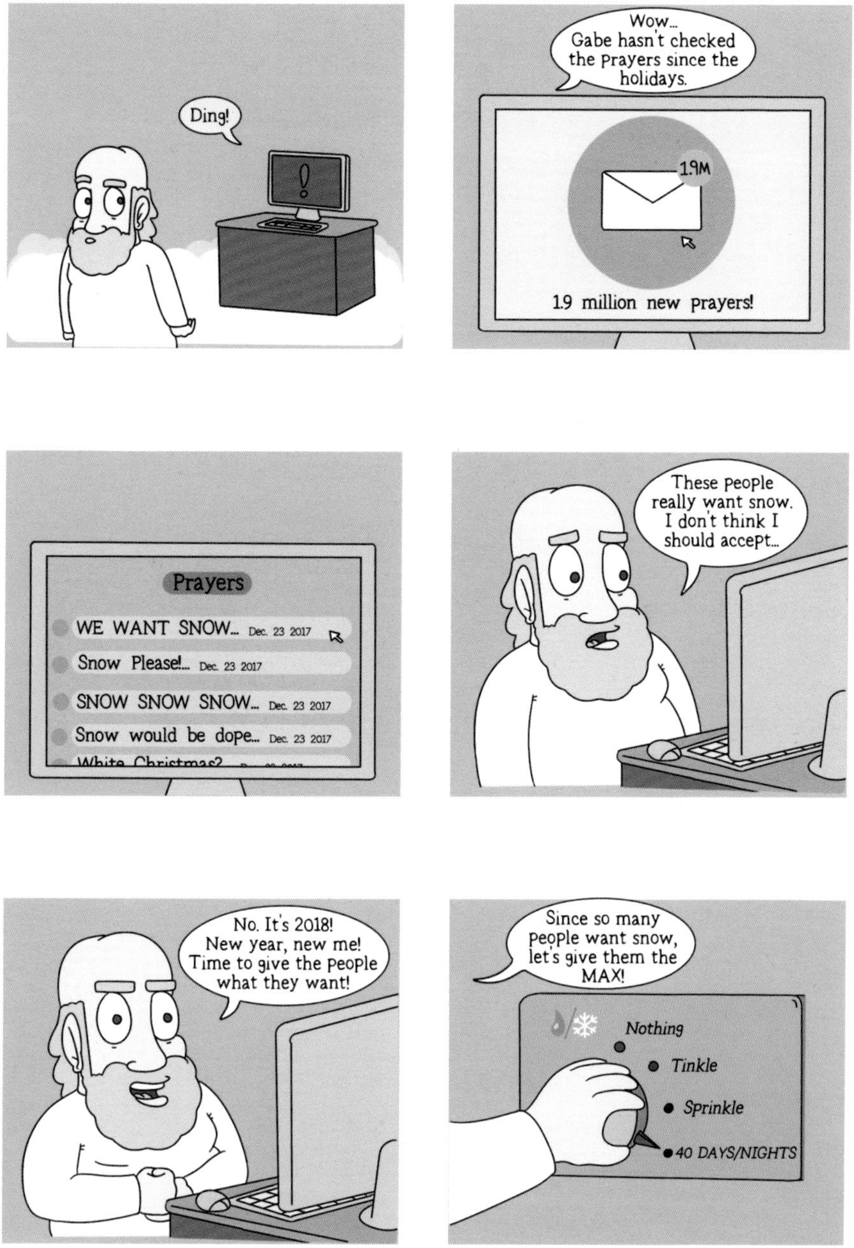
Ding!
Wow... Gabe hasn't checked the prayers since the holidays.
1.9M
1.9 million new prayers!
Prayers
WE WANT SNOW... Dec. 23 2017
Snow Please!... Dec. 23 2017
SNOW SNOW SNOW... Dec. 23 2017
Snow would be dope... Dec. 23 2017
These people really want snow. I don't think I should accept...
No. It's 2018! New year, new me! Time to give the people what they want!
Since so many people want snow, let's give them the MAX!
Nothing
Tinkle
Sprinkle
40 DAYS/NIGHTS

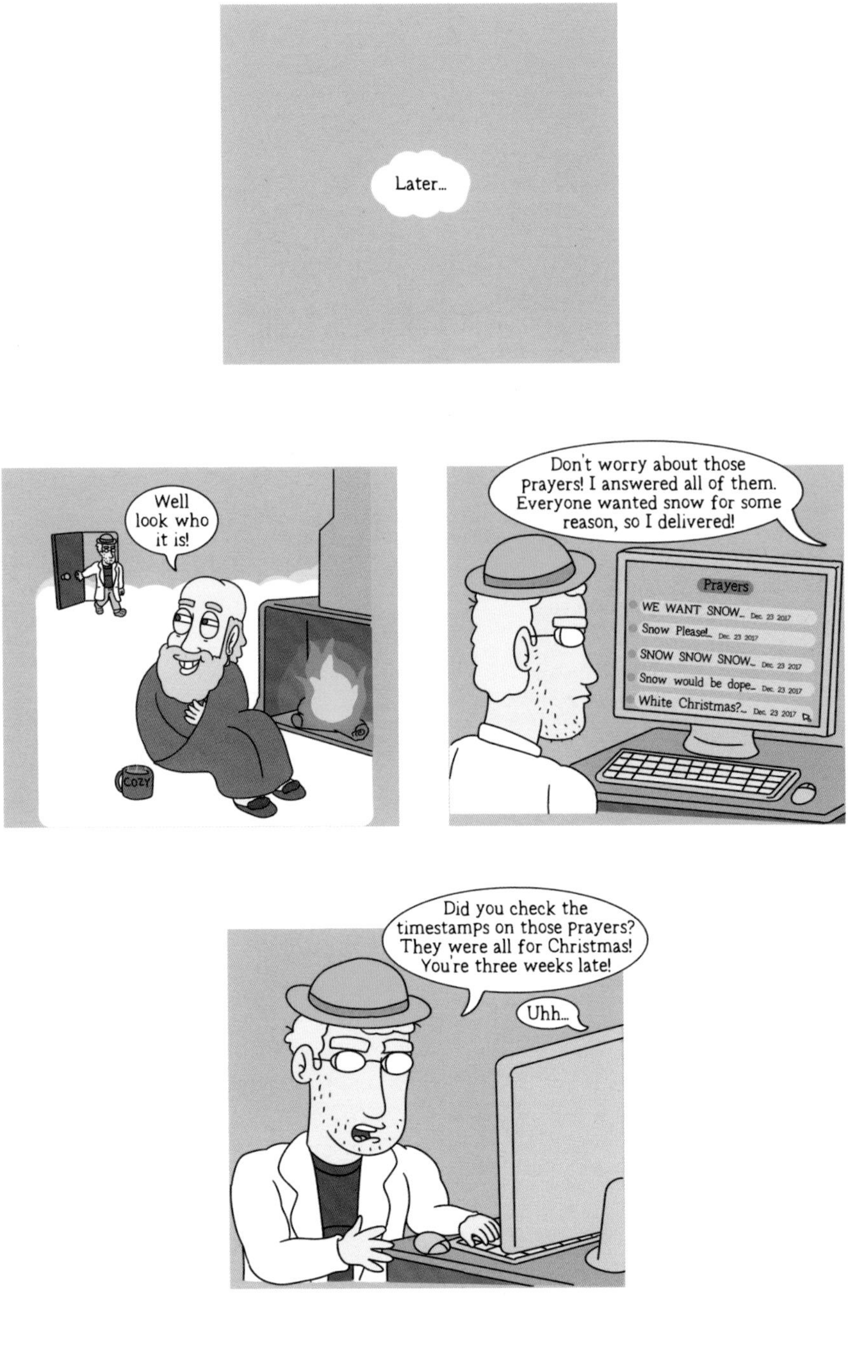
Later...
Well look who it is!
Don't worry about those prayers! I answered all of them. Everyone wanted snow for some reason, so I delivered!
Prayers
WE WANT SNOW... Dec. 23 2017
Snow Please!... Dec. 23 2017
SNOW SNOW SNOW... Dec. 23 2017
Snow would be dope... Dec. 23 2017
White Christmas?... Dec. 23 2017
COZY
Did you check the timestamps on those prayers? They were all for Christmas! You're three weeks late!
Uhh...

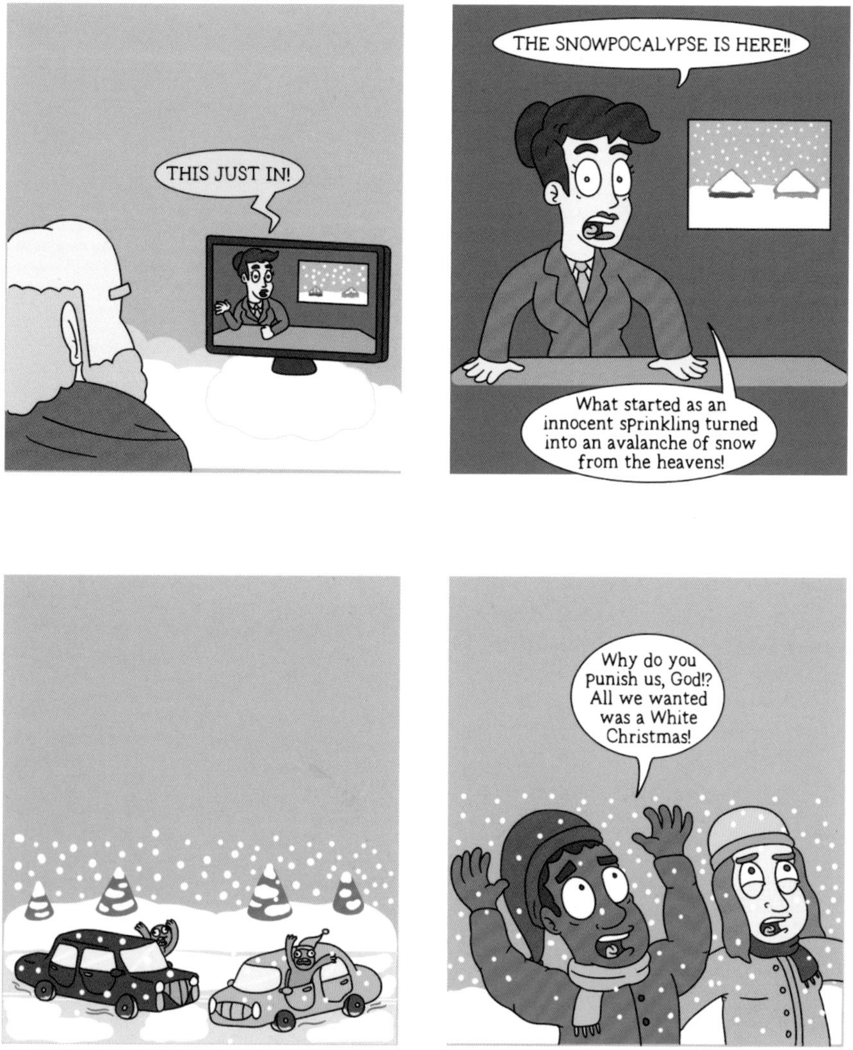
THIS JUST IN!
THE SNOWPOCALYPSE IS HERE!!
What started as an innocent sprinkling turned into an avalanche of snow from the heavens!
Why do you punish us, God!? All we wanted was a White Christmas!

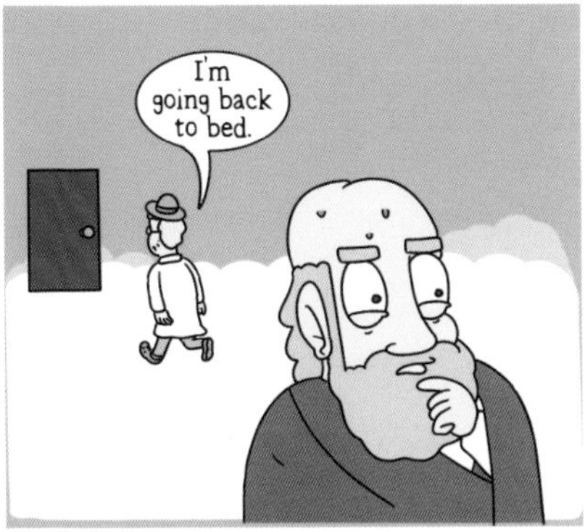
I'm going back to bed.

BONUS

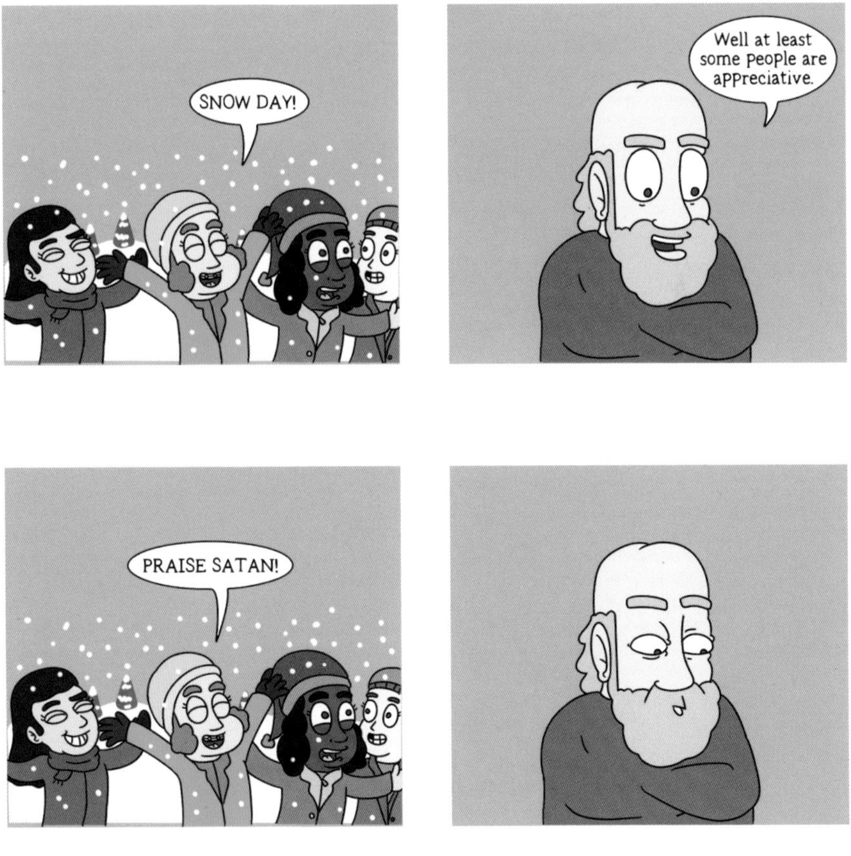
SNOW DAY!
Well at least some people are appreciative.
PRAISE SATAN!

Sad Gabe

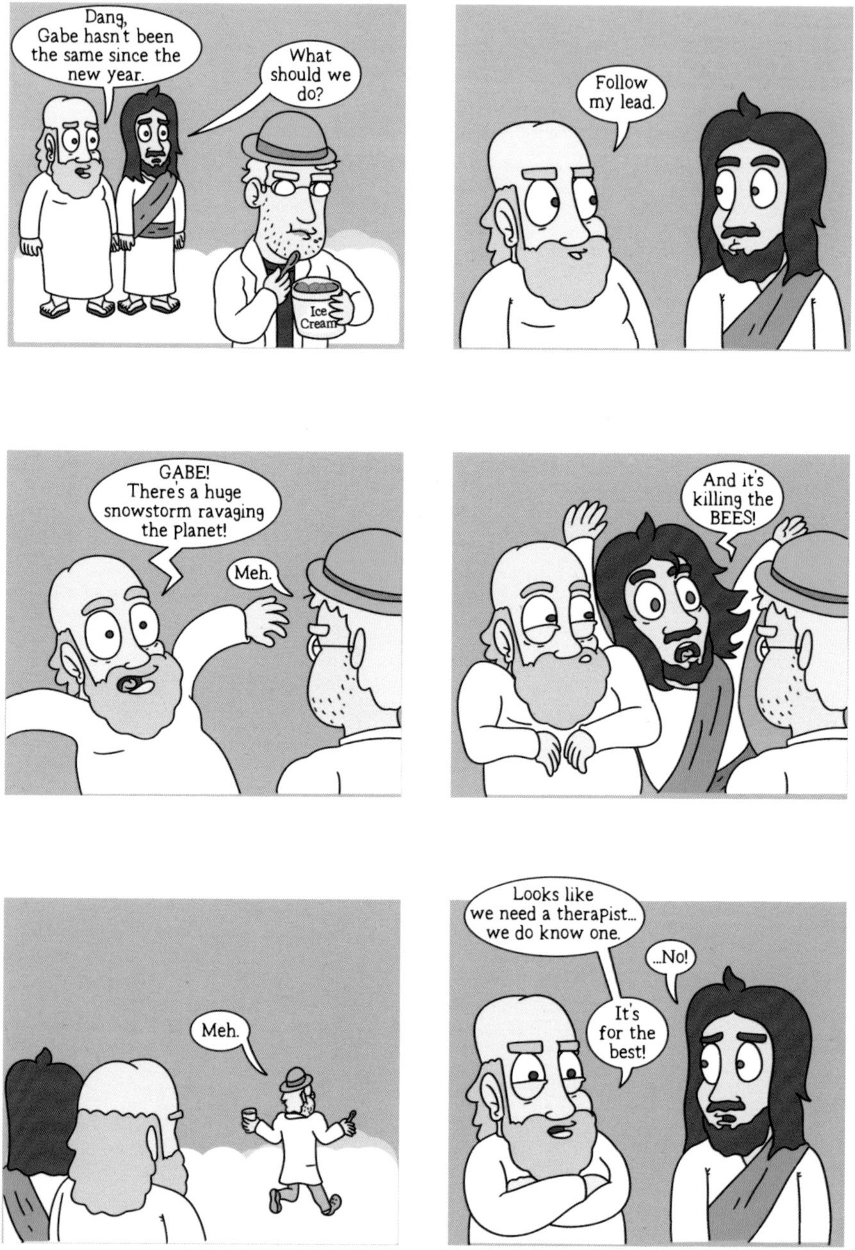

Dang, Gabe hasn't been the same since the new year.
What should we do?
Ice Cream
Follow my lead.
GABE! There's a huge snowstorm ravaging the planet!
Meh.
And it's killing the BEES!
Meh.
Looks like we need a therapist... we do know one.
...No!
It's for the best!

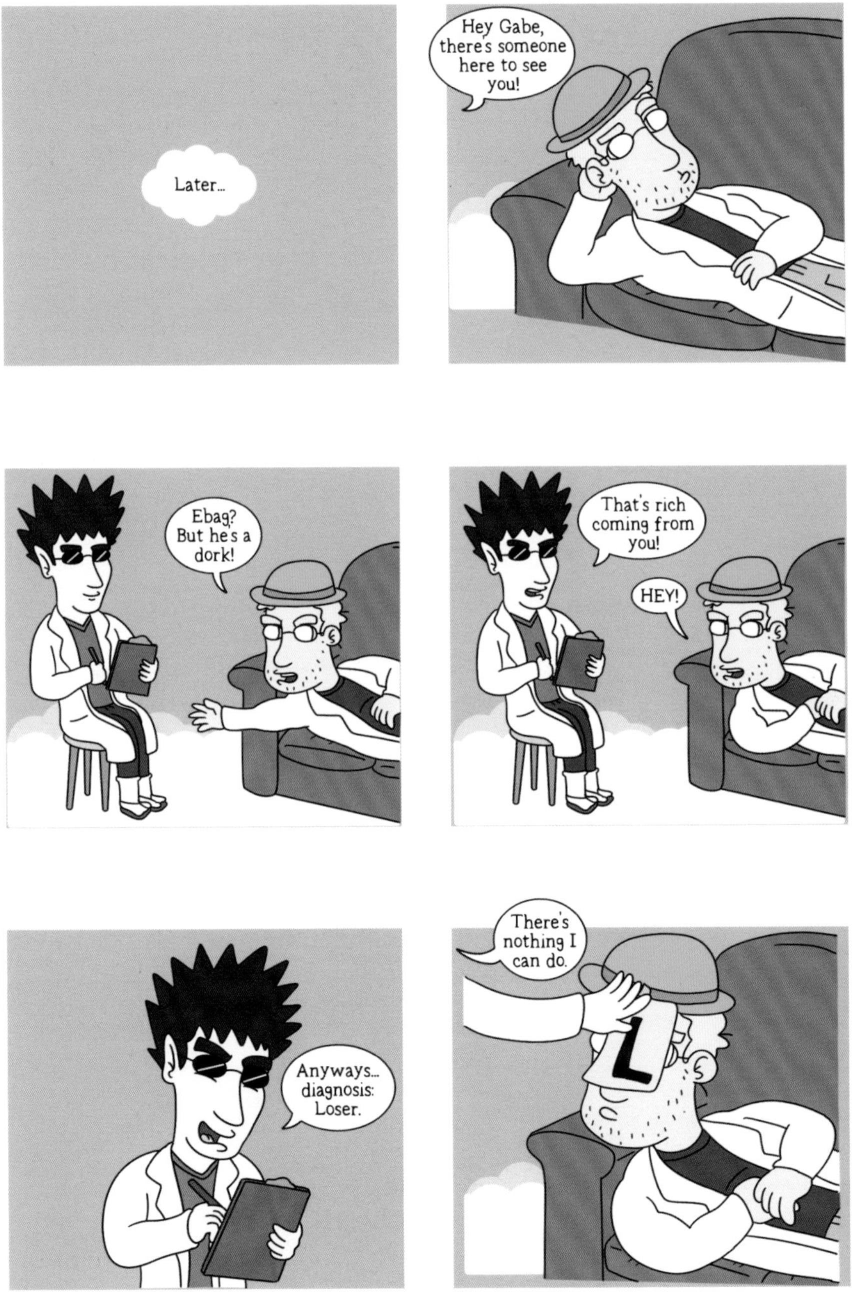
Later...
Hey Gabe, there's someone here to see you!
Ebag? But he's a dork!
That's rich coming from you!
HEY!
Anyways... diagnosis: Loser.
There's nothing I can do.
L

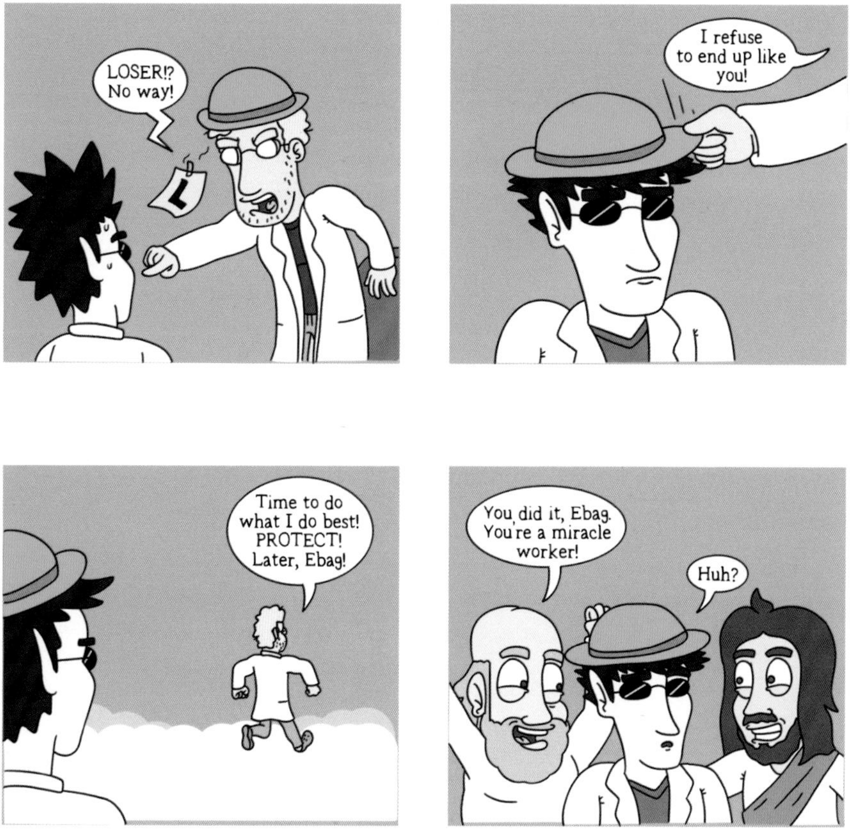
LOSER!? No way!
L
I refuse to end up like you!
Time to do what I do best! PROTECT! Later, Ebag!
You did it, Ebag. You're a miracle worker!
Huh?

BONUS

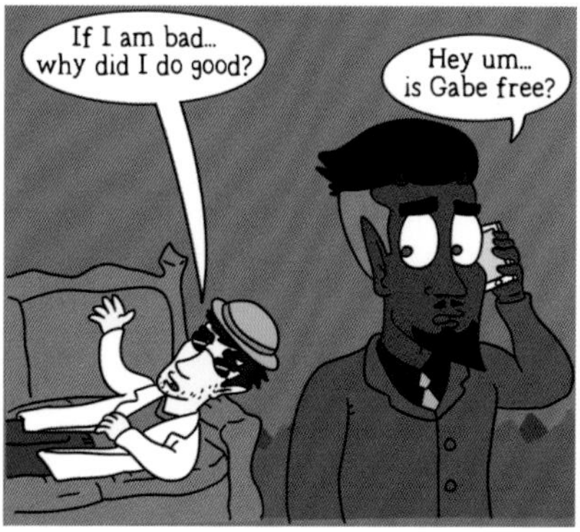
If I am bad... why did I do good?
Hey um... is Gabe free?

Reward

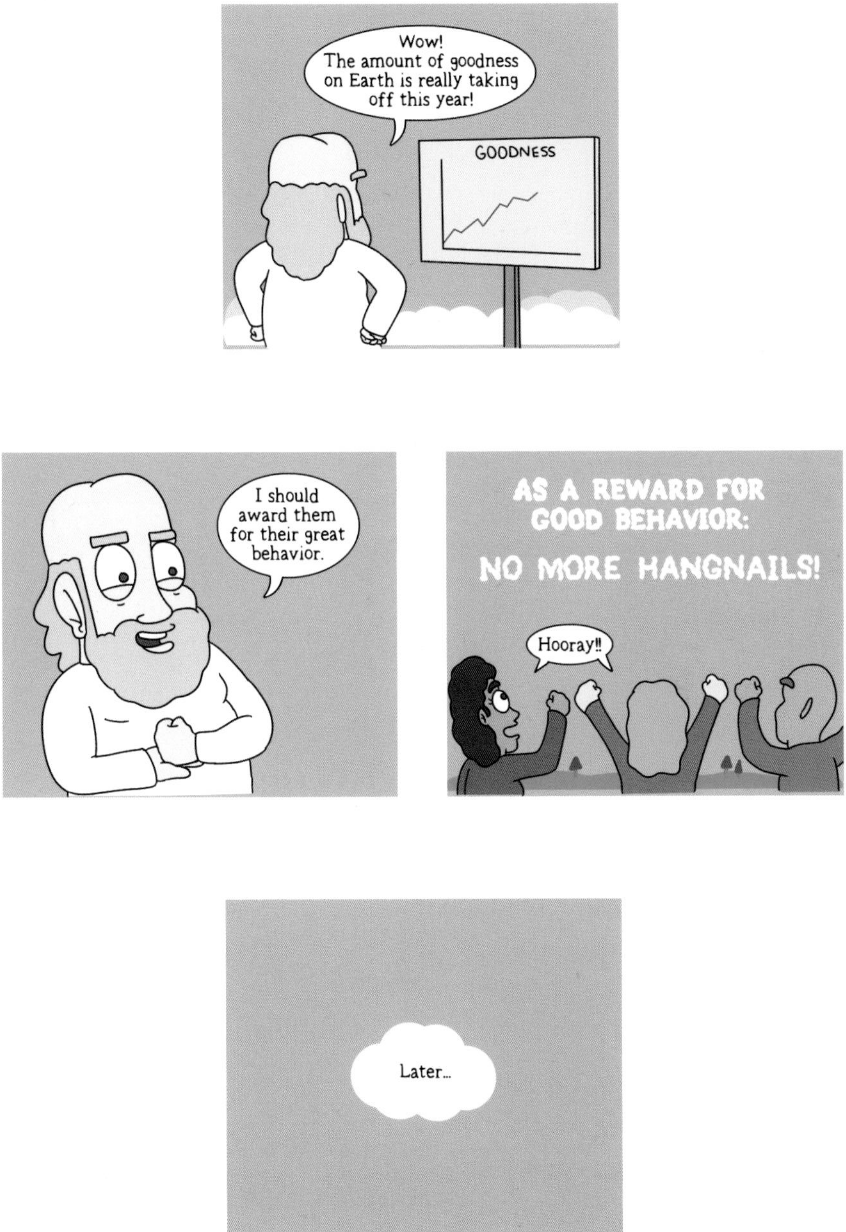
Wow!
The amount of goodness on Earth is really taking off this year!
GOODNESS
I should award them for their great behavior.
AS A REWARD FOR GOOD BEHAVIOR:
NO MORE HANGNAILS!
Hooray!!
Later...

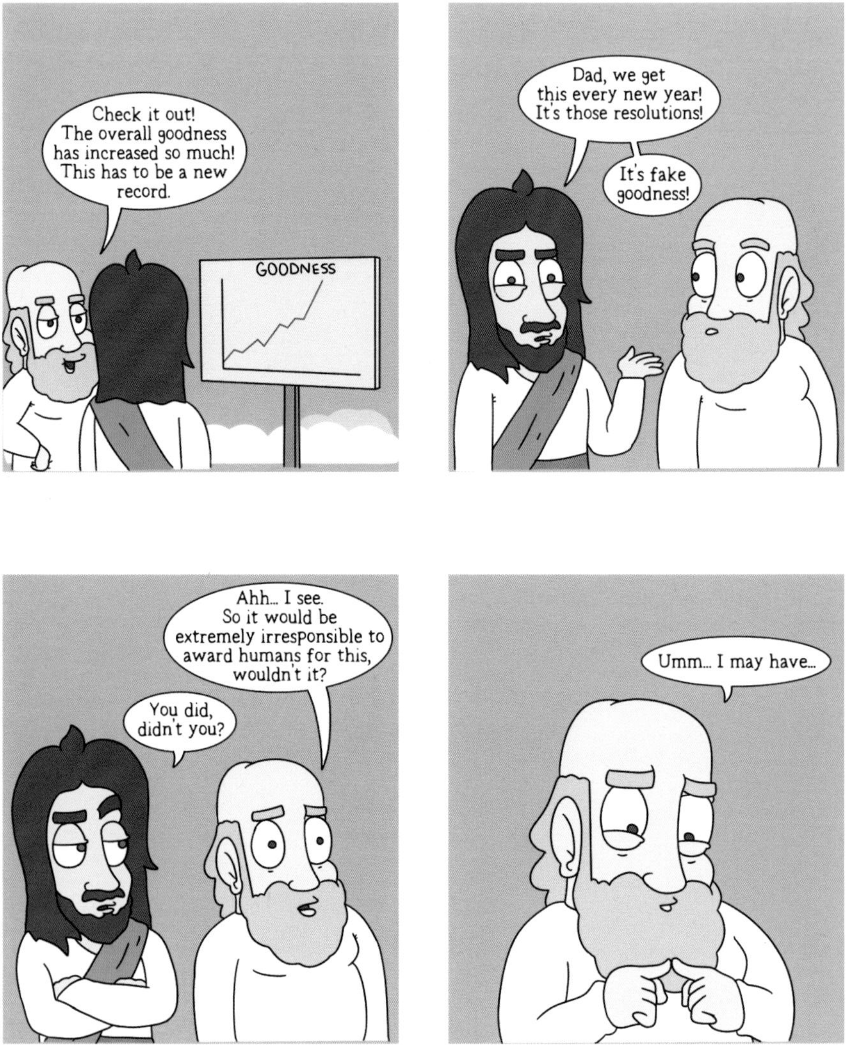
Check it out! The overall goodness has increased so much! This has to be a new record.
GOODNESS
Dad, we get this every new year! It's those resolutions!
It's fake goodness!
Ahh... I see. So it would be extremely irresponsible to award humans for this, wouldn't it?
You did, didn't you?
Umm... I may have...

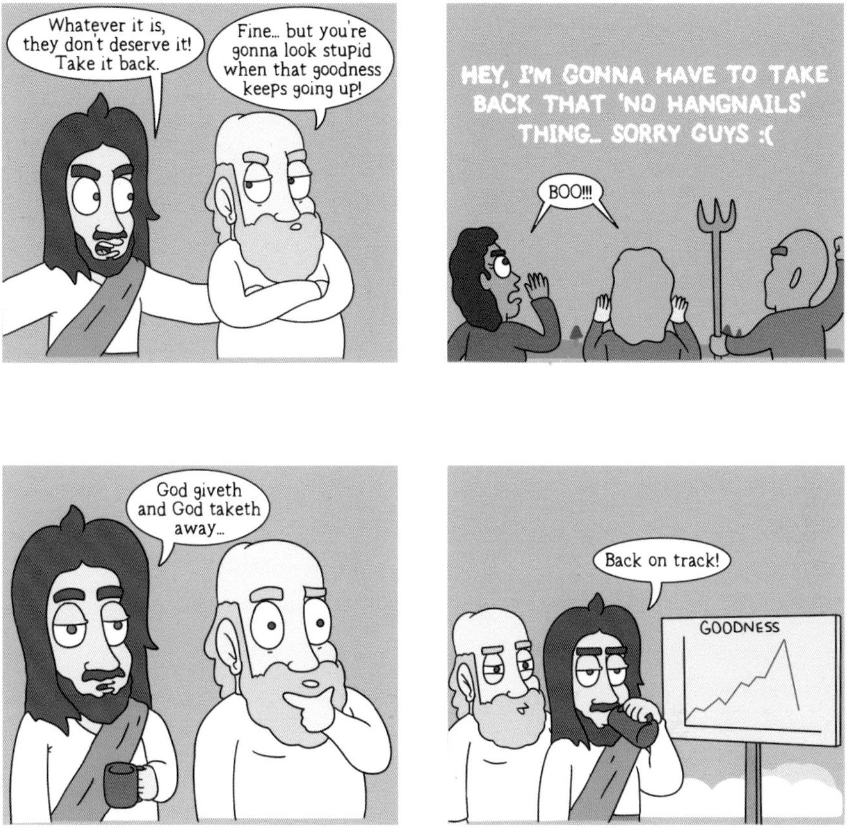
Whatever it is, they don't deserve it! Take it back.
Fine... but you're gonna look stupid when that goodness keeps going up!
HEY, I'M GONNA HAVE TO TAKE BACK THAT 'NO HANGNAILS' THING... SORRY GUYS :(
BOO!!!
God giveth and God taketh away...
Back on track!
GOODNESS

BONUS

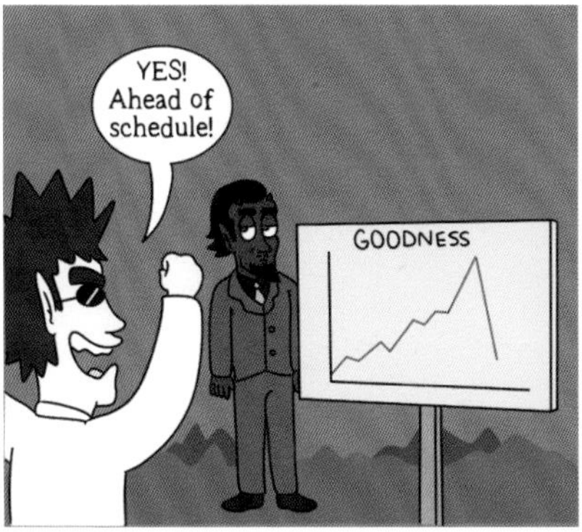
YES! Ahead of schedule!
GOODNESS

Lure

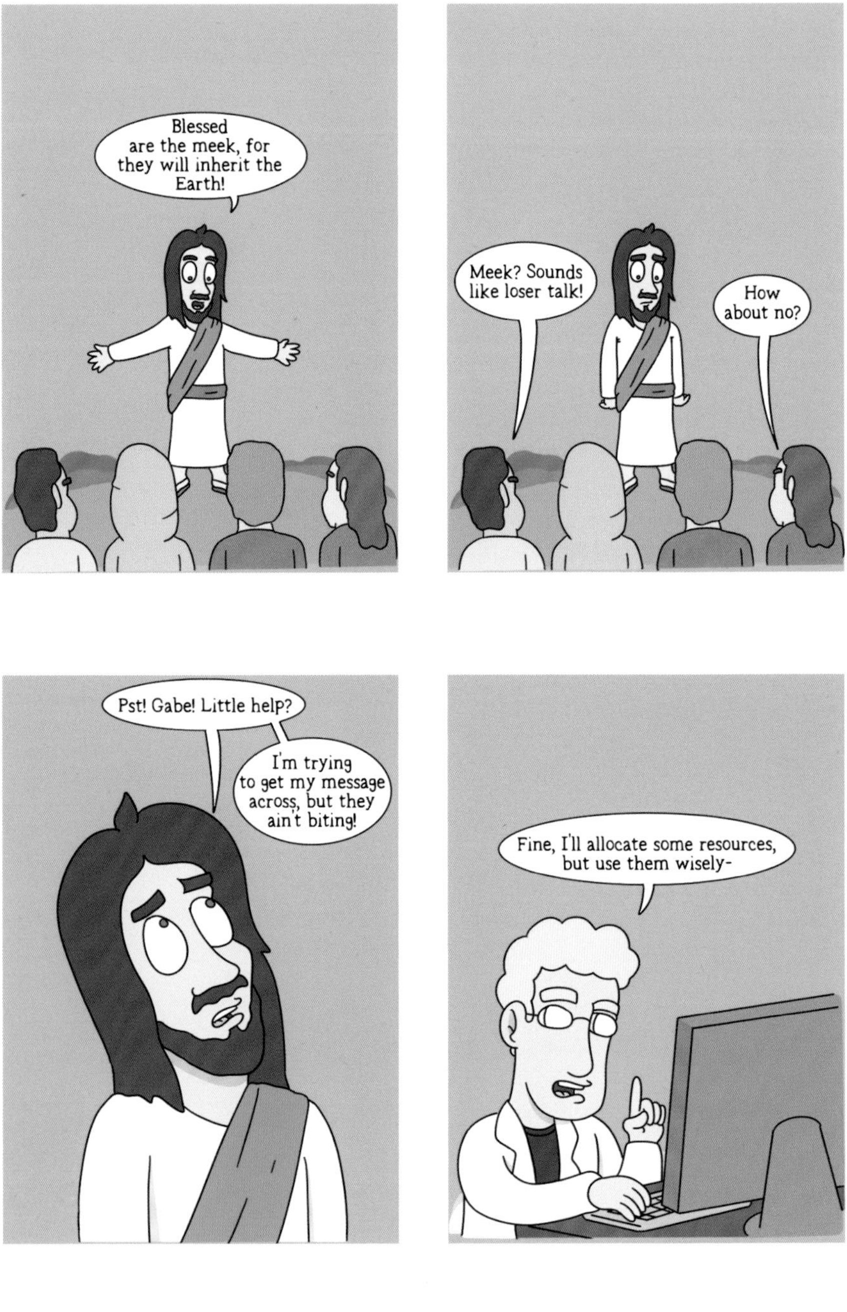

Blessed are the meek, for they will inherit the Earth!
Meek? Sounds like loser talk!
How about no?
Pst! Gabe! Little help?
I'm trying to get my message across, but they ain't biting!
Fine, I'll allocate some resources, but use them wisely-

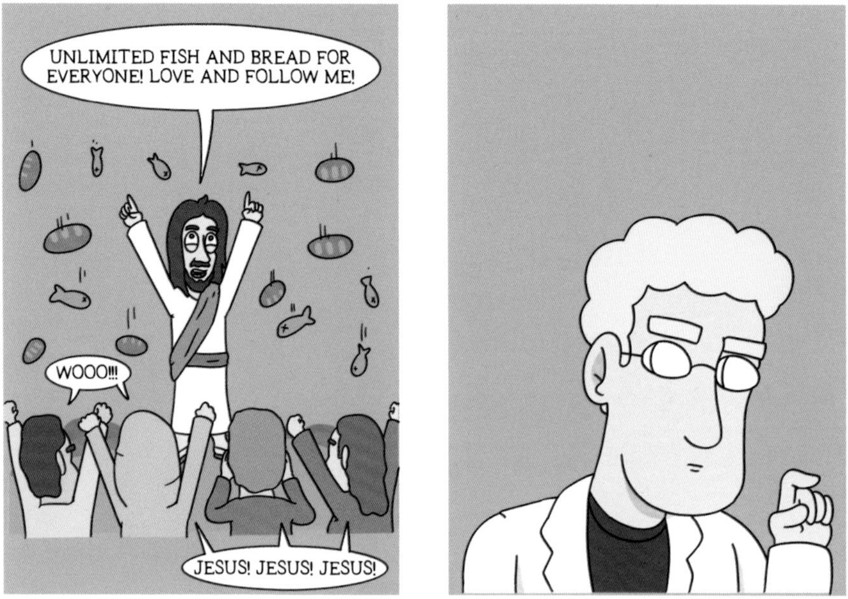
UNLIMITED FISH AND BREAD FOR EVERYONE! LOVE AND FOLLOW ME!
WOOO!!!
JESUS! JESUS! JESUS!

BONUS

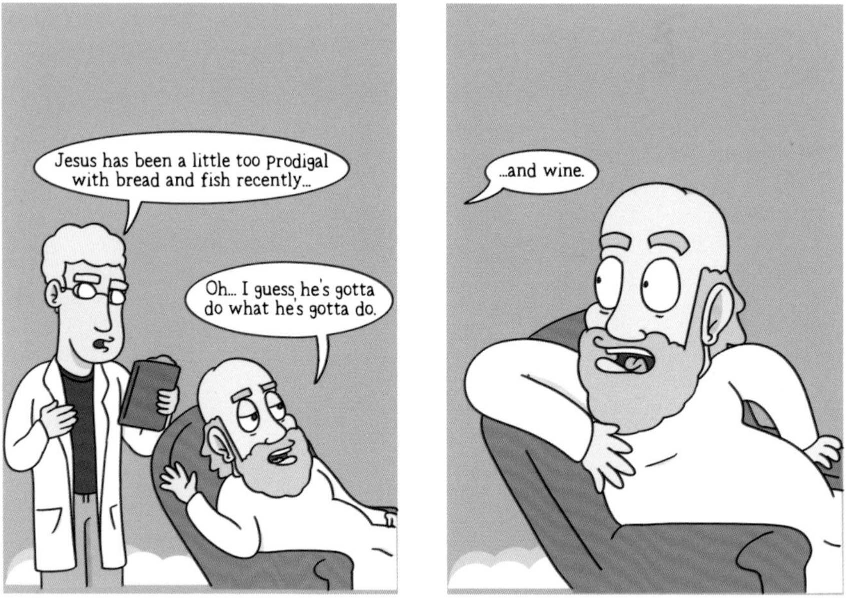
Jesus has been a little too prodigal with bread and fish recently...
Oh... I guess he's gotta do what he's gotta do.
...and wine.

Questions

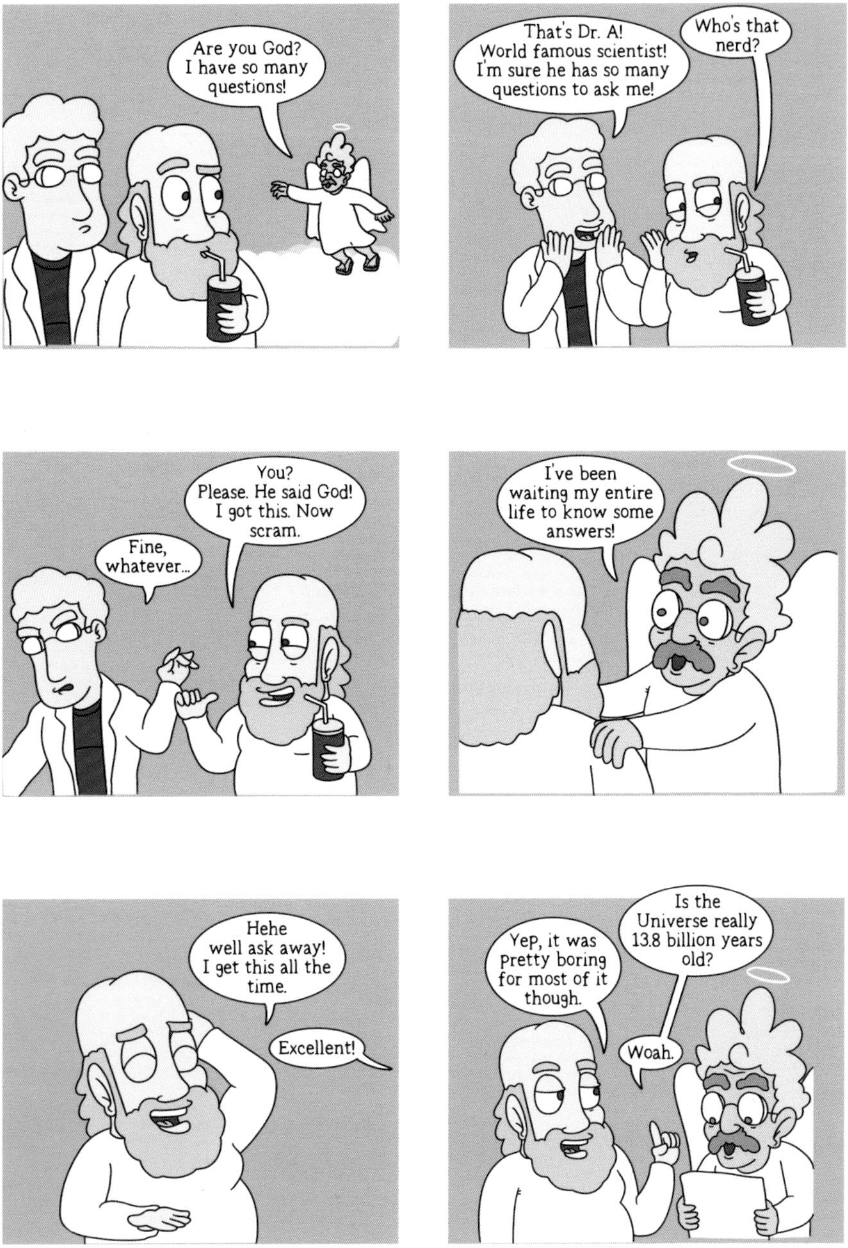
Are you God? I have so many questions!
That's Dr. A! World famous scientist! I'm sure he has so many questions to ask me!
Who's that nerd?
Fine, whatever...
You? Please. He said God! I got this. Now scram.
I've been waiting my entire life to know some answers!
Hehe well ask away! I get this all the time.
Excellent!
Is the Universe really 13.8 billion years old?
Yep, it was pretty boring for most of it though.
Woah.

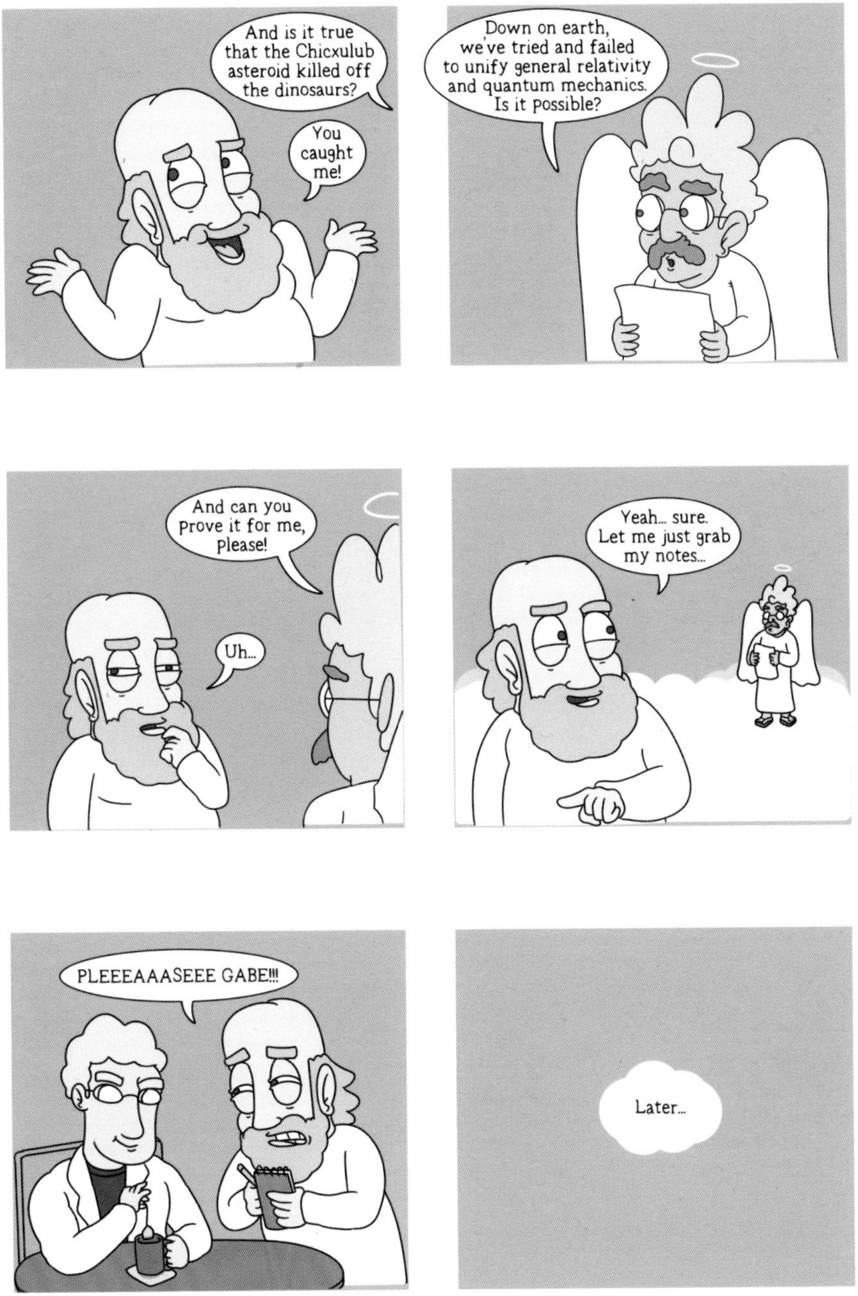
And is it true that the Chicxulub asteroid killed off the dinosaurs?
You caught me!
Down on earth, we've tried and failed to unify general relativity and quantum mechanics. Is it possible?
And can you prove it for me, please!
Uh...
Yeah... sure. Let me just grab my notes...
PLEEEAAASEEE GABE!!!
Later...

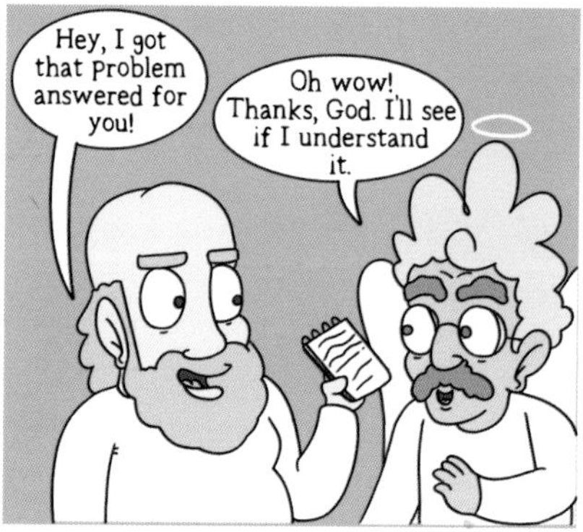
Hey, I got that problem answered for you!
Oh wow! Thanks, God. I'll see if I understand it.

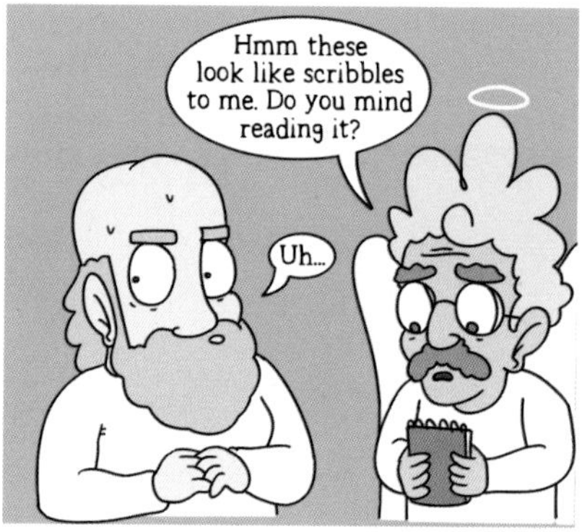
Hmm these look like scribbles to me. Do you mind reading it?
Uh...

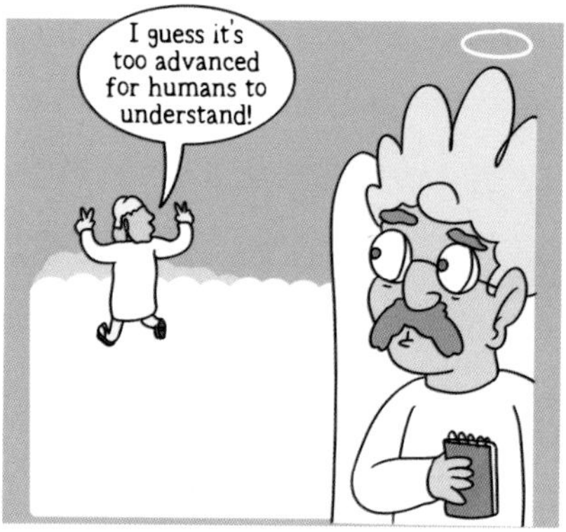
I guess it's too advanced for humans to understand!

BONUS

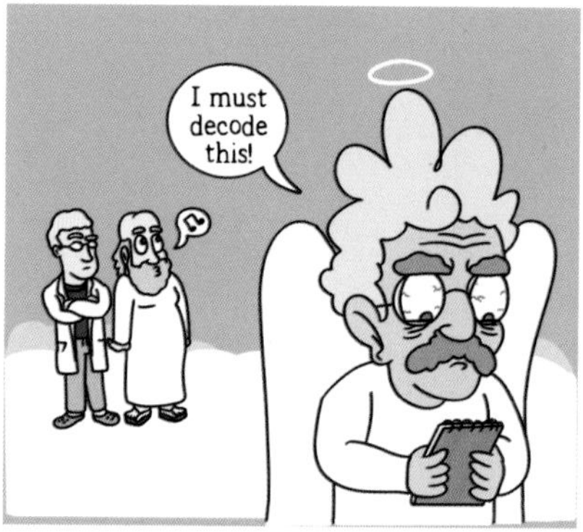
I must decode this!

Promised

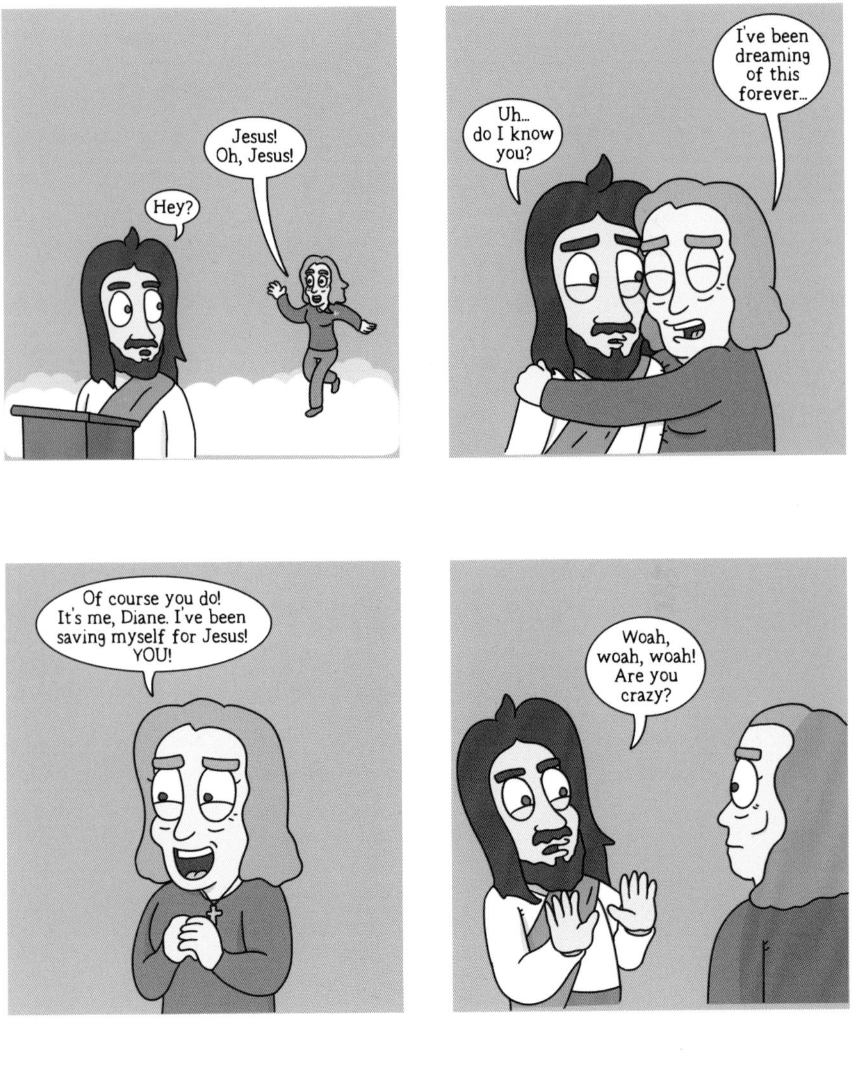
Jesus! Oh, Jesus!
Hey?
Uh... do I know you?
I've been dreaming of this forever...
Of course you do! It's me, Diane. I've been saving myself for Jesus! YOU!
Woah, woah, woah! Are you crazy?

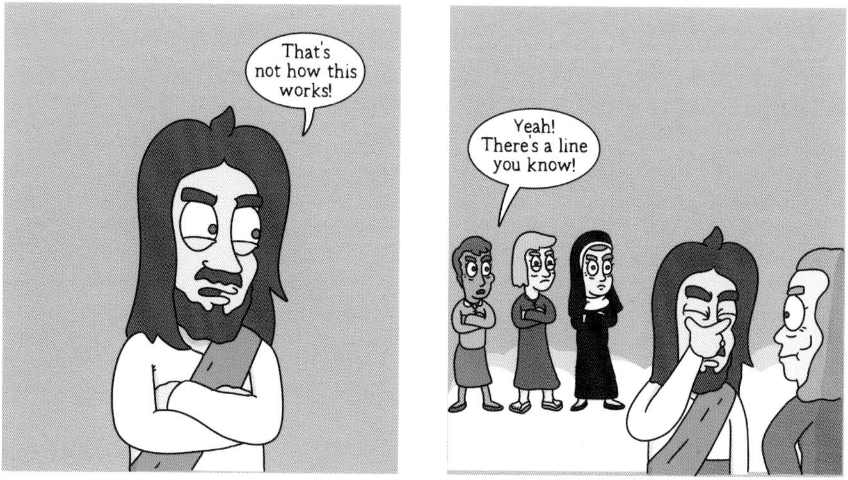
That's not how this works!
Yeah! There's a line you know!

BONUS

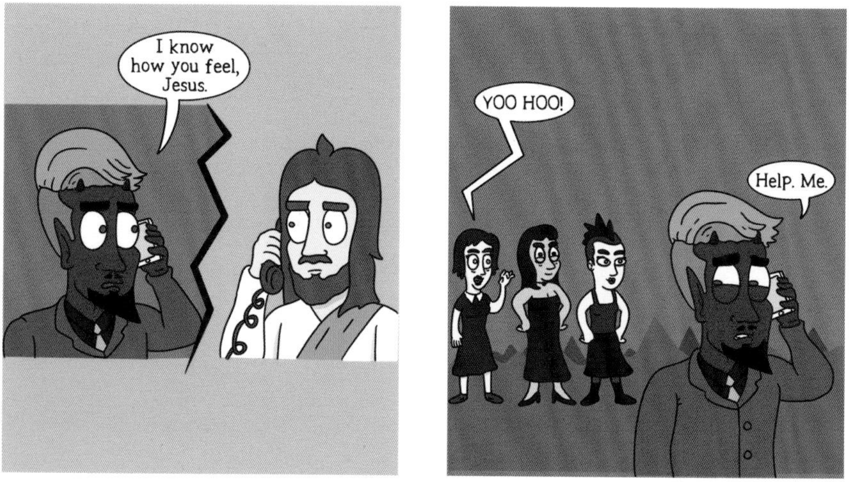
I know how you feel, Jesus.
YOO HOO!
Help. Me.

Cat Duty

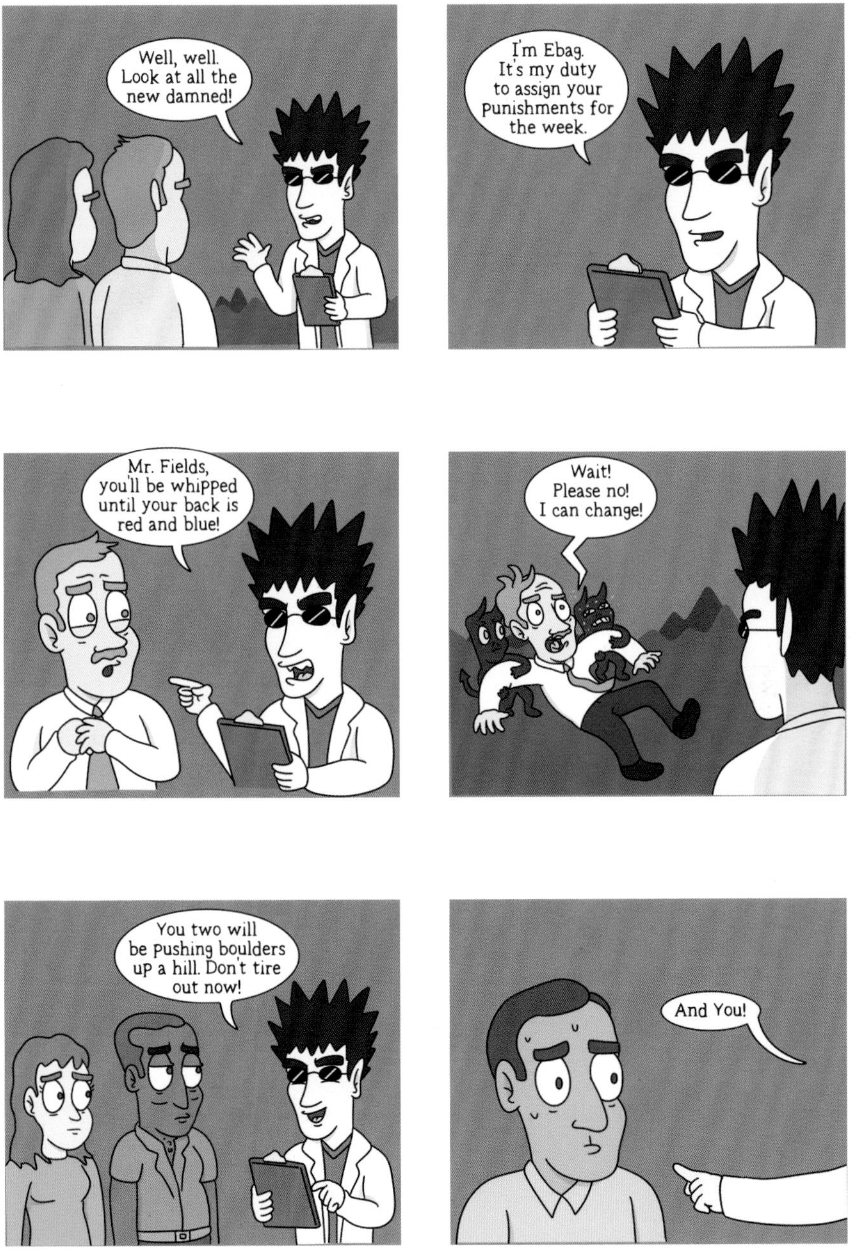
Well, well. Look at all the new damned!
I'm Ebag. It's my duty to assign your punishments for the week.
Mr. Fields, you'll be whipped until your back is red and blue!
Wait! Please no! I can change!
You two will be pushing boulders up a hill. Don't tire out now!
And You!

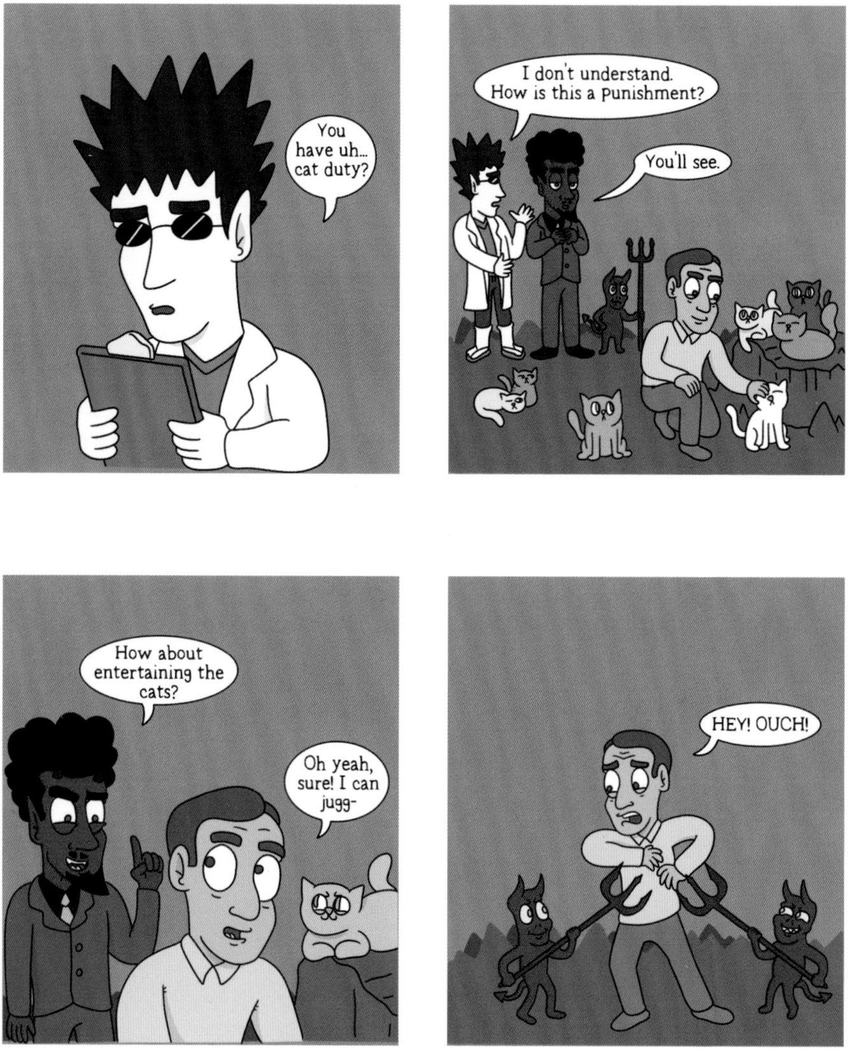
You have uh... cat duty?
I don't understand. How is this a punishment?
You'll see.
How about entertaining the cats?
Oh yeah, sure! I can jugg-
HEY! OUCH!

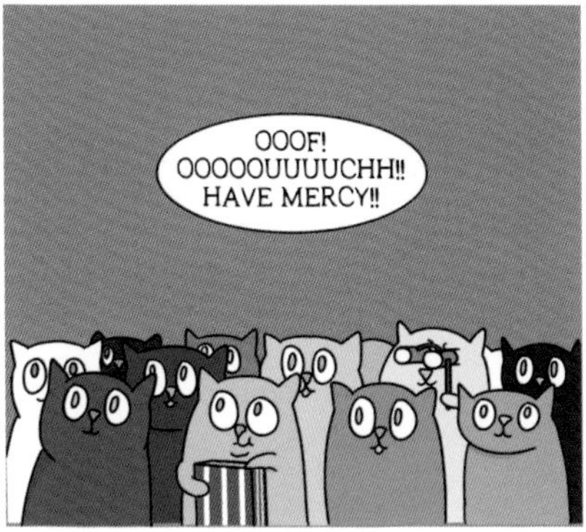
OOOF!
OOOOOUUUUCHH!!
HAVE MERCY!!

BONUS

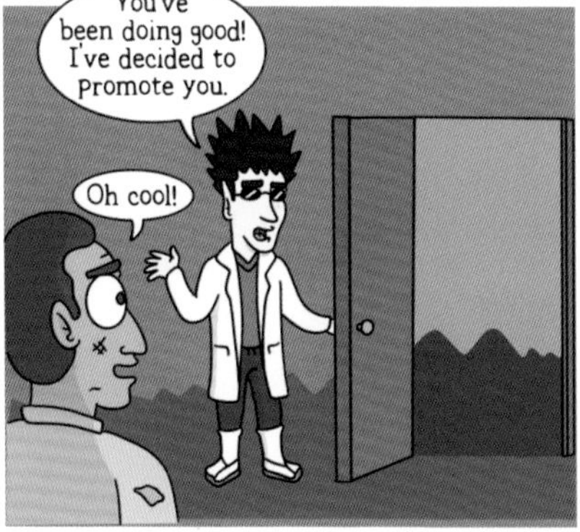
You've been doing good! I've decided to promote you.
Oh cool!

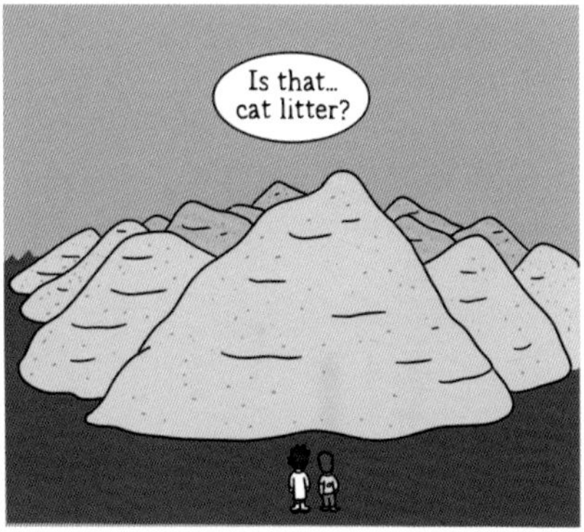
Is that... cat litter?

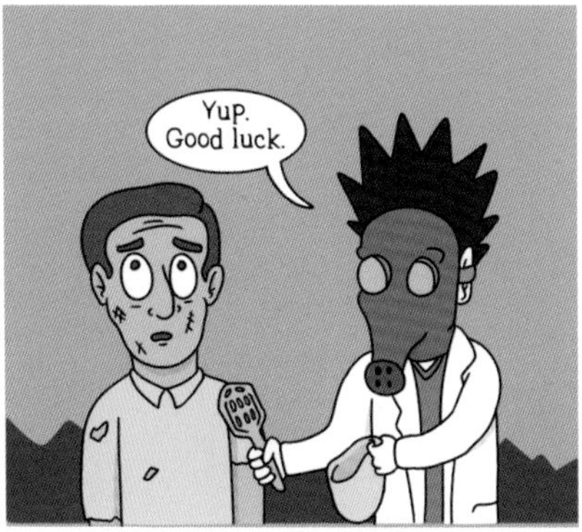
Yup. Good luck.

Bad Gabe

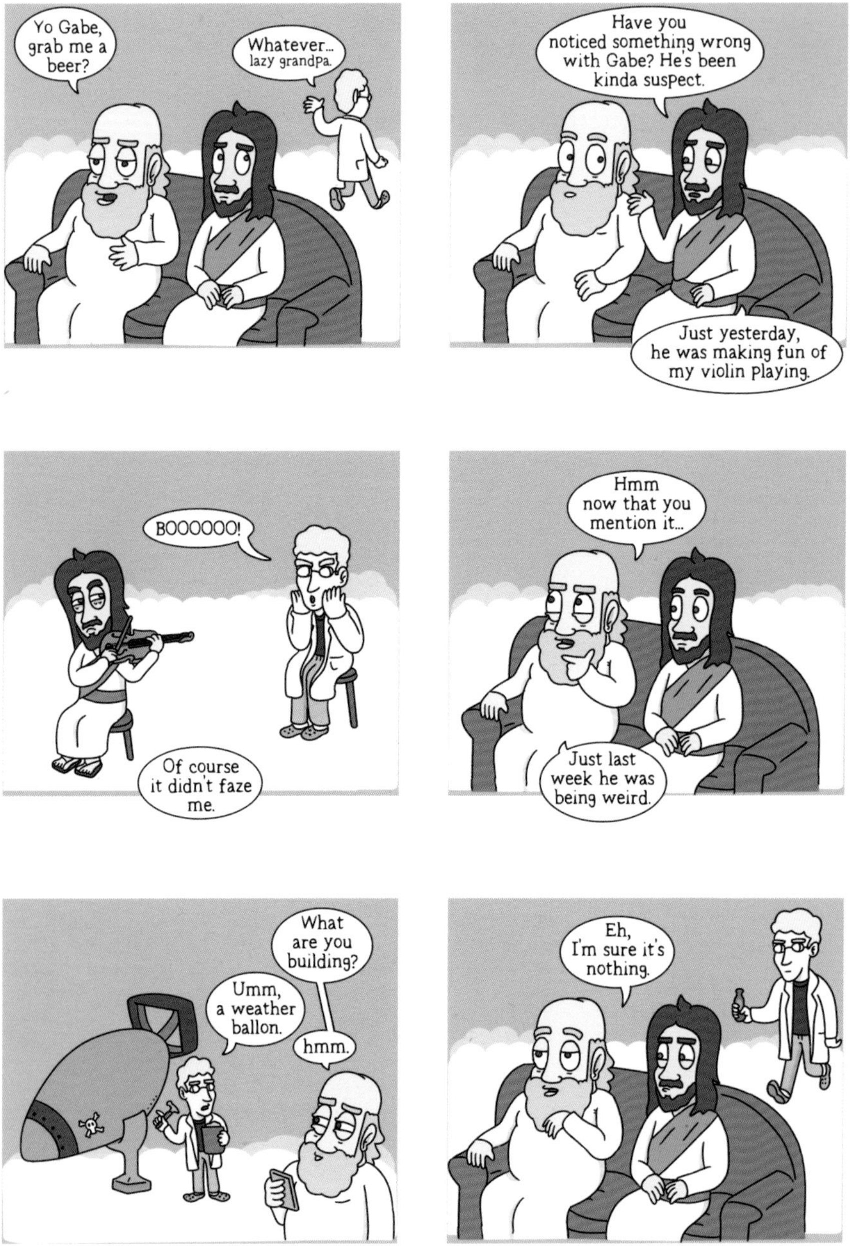
Yo Gabe, grab me a beer?
Whatever... lazy grandpa.
Have you noticed something wrong with Gabe? He's been kinda suspect.
Just yesterday, he was making fun of my violin playing.
BOOOOOO!
Of course it didn't faze me.
Hmm now that you mention it...
Just last week he was being weird.
What are you building?
Umm, a weather ballon.
hmm.
Eh, I'm sure it's nothing.

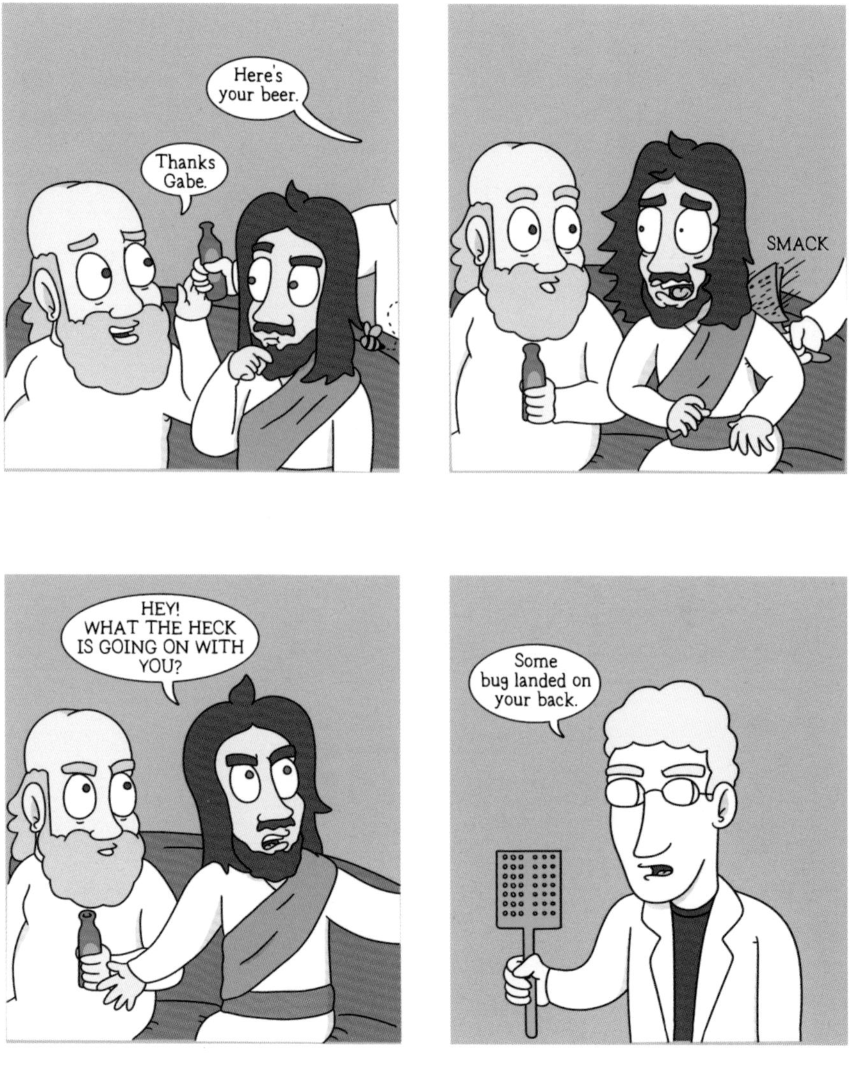
Here's your beer.
Thanks Gabe.
SMACK
HEY! WHAT THE HECK IS GOING ON WITH YOU?
Some bug landed on your back.

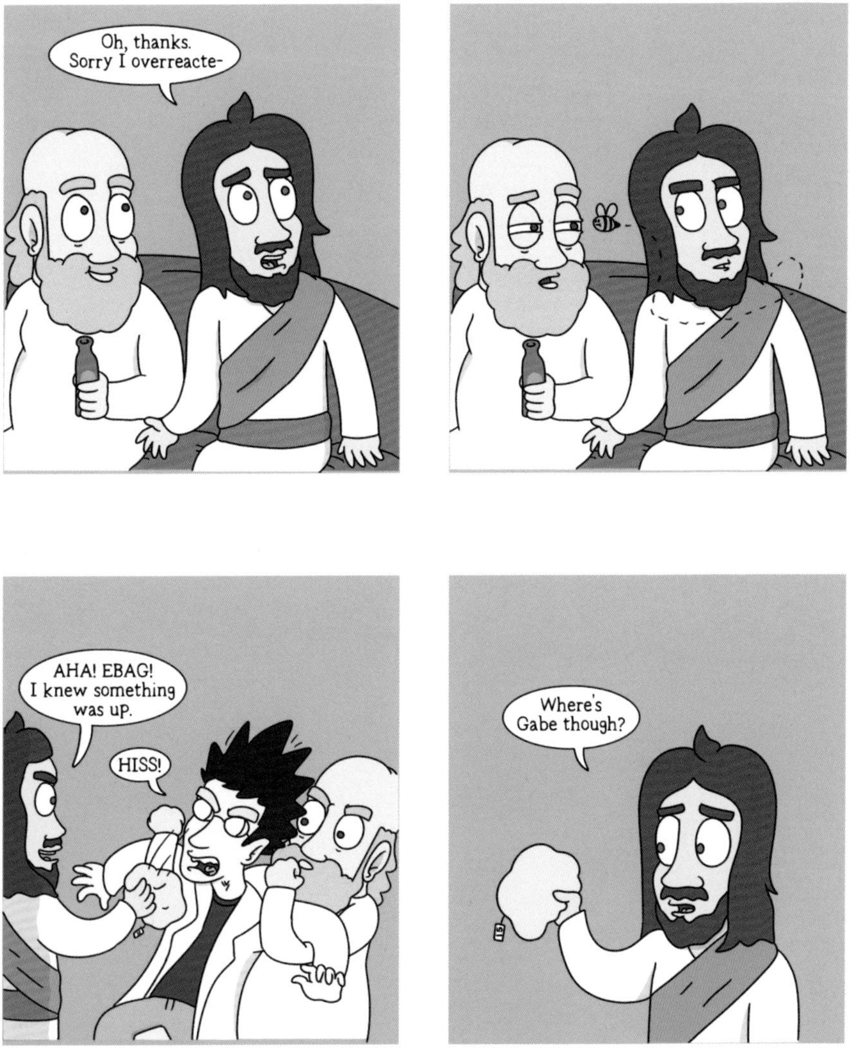
Oh, thanks.
Sorry I overreacte-
AHA! EBAG!
I knew something
was up.
HISS!
Where's
Gabe though?

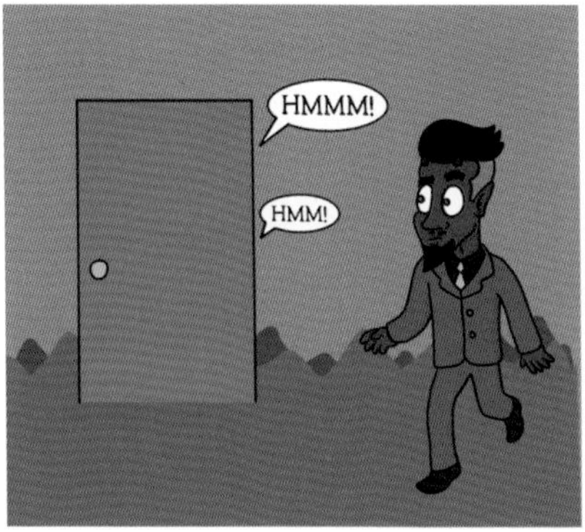
HMMM!
HMM!

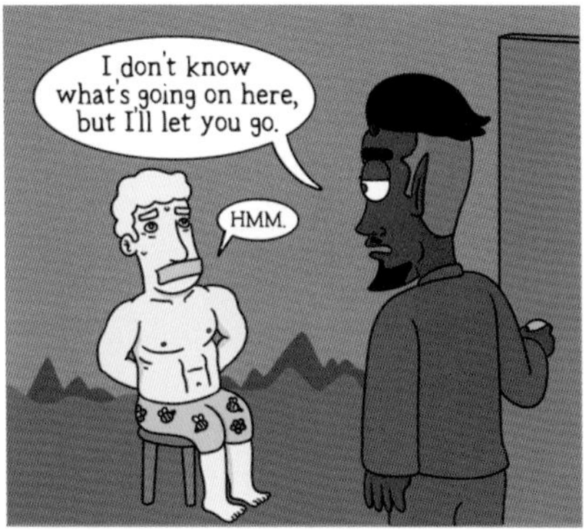
I don't know what's going on here, but I'll let you go.
HMM.

BONUS

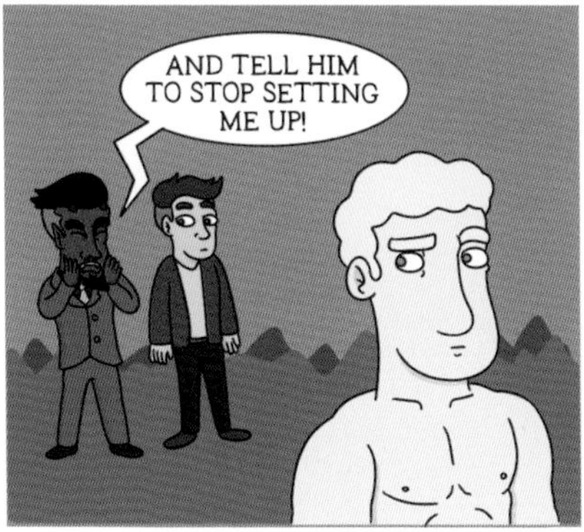
AND TELL HIM TO STOP SETTING ME UP!

Apocryphal

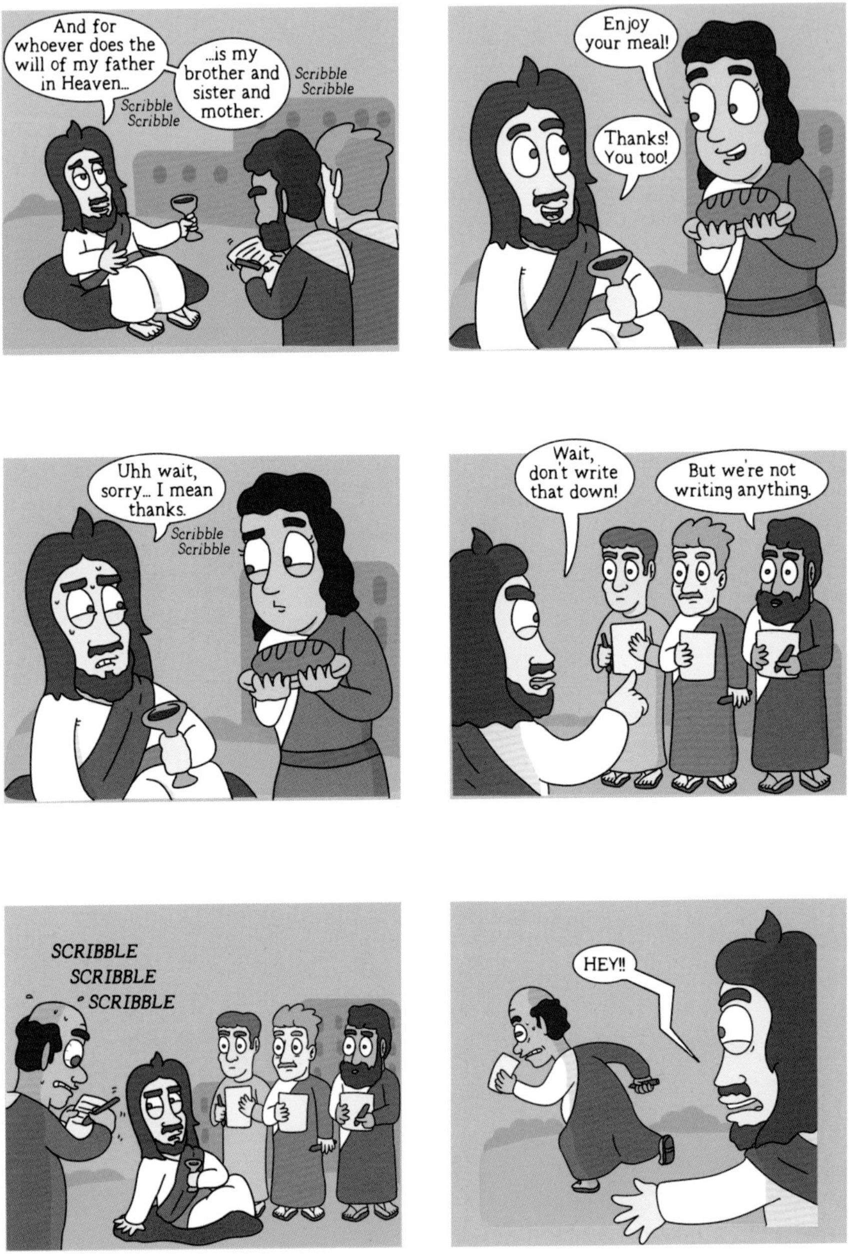
And for whoever does the will of my father in Heaven...
...is my brother and sister and mother.
Scribble Scribble
Scribble Scribble
Enjoy your meal!
Thanks! You too!
Uhh wait, sorry... I mean thanks.
Scribble Scribble
Wait, don't write that down!
But we're not writing anything.
SCRIBBLE
SCRIBBLE
SCRIBBLE
HEY!!

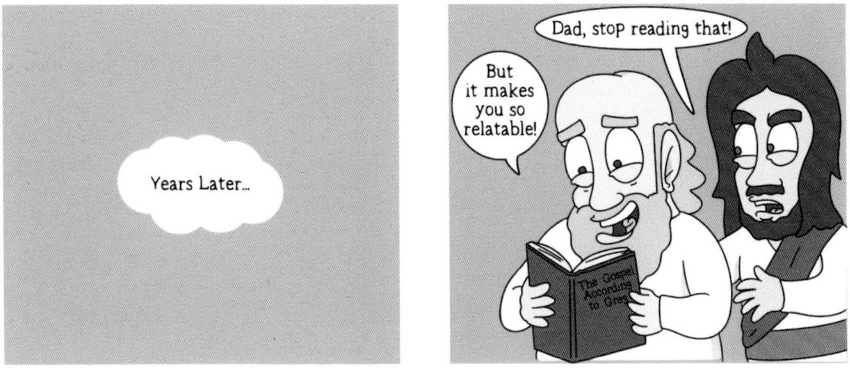
Years Later...
Dad, stop reading that!
But it makes you so relatable!

BONUS

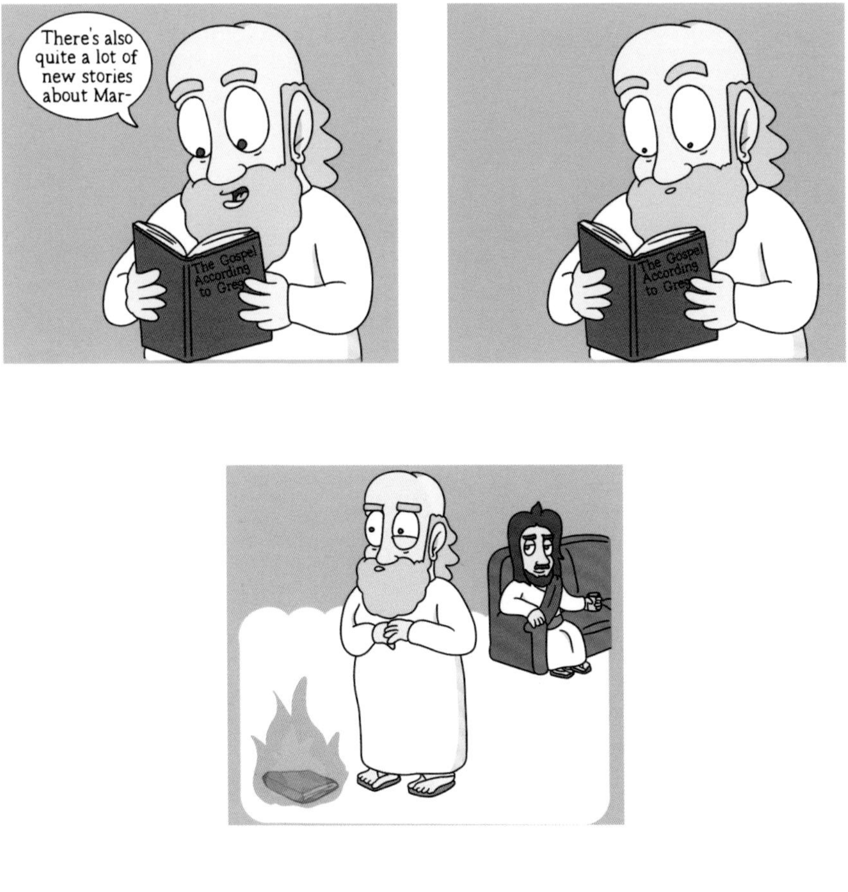
There's also quite a lot of new stories about Mar-

Pope?

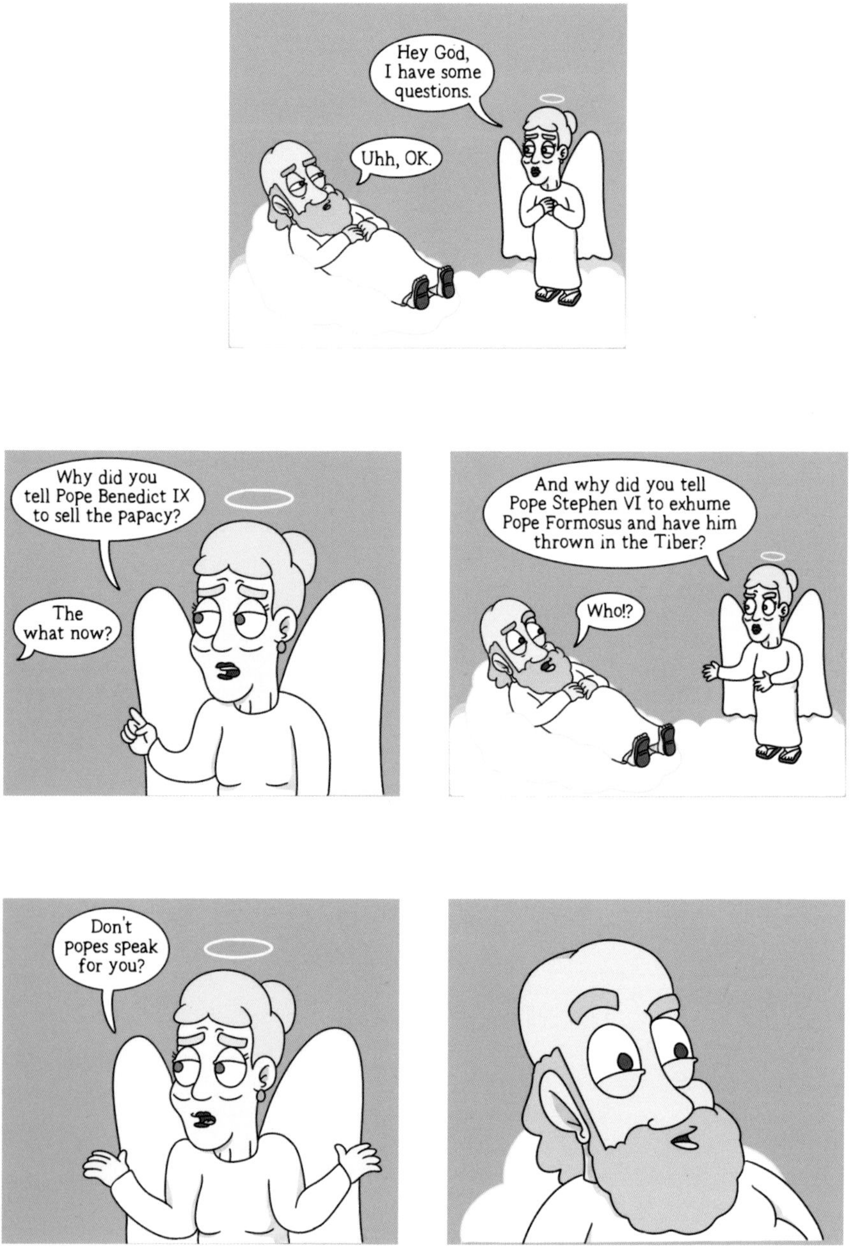

Hey God, I have some questions.
Uhh, OK.
Why did you tell Pope Benedict IX to sell the papacy?
The what now?
And why did you tell Pope Stephen VI to exhume Pope Formosus and have him thrown in the Tiber?
Who!?
Don't popes speak for you?

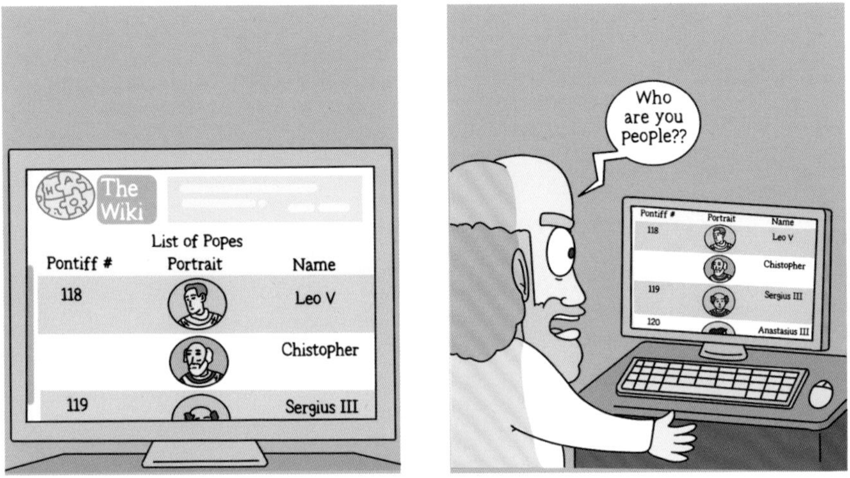

The Wiki
List of Popes
Pontiff #
Portrait
Name
118
Leo V
Chistopher
119
Sergius III
Who are you people??
Pontiff #
Portrait
Name
118
Leo V
Chistopher
119
Sergius III
120
Anastasius III

BONUS

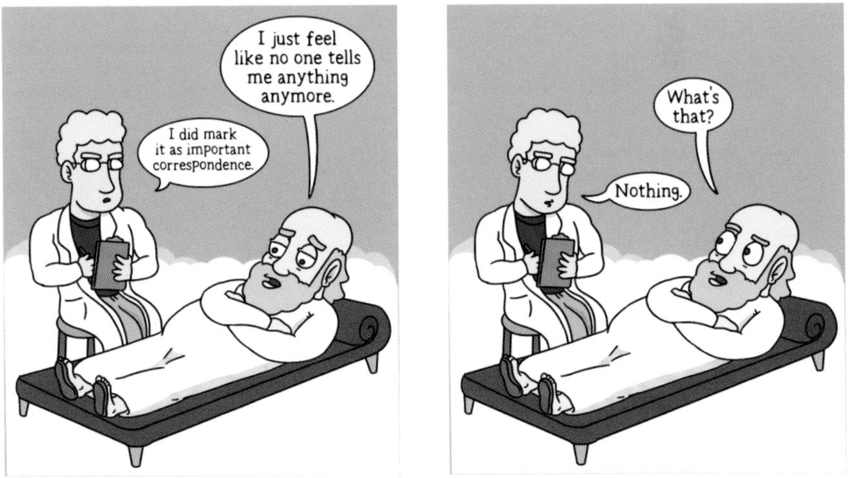

I just feel like no one tells me anything anymore.
I did mark it as important correspondence.
What's that?
Nothing.

Junk

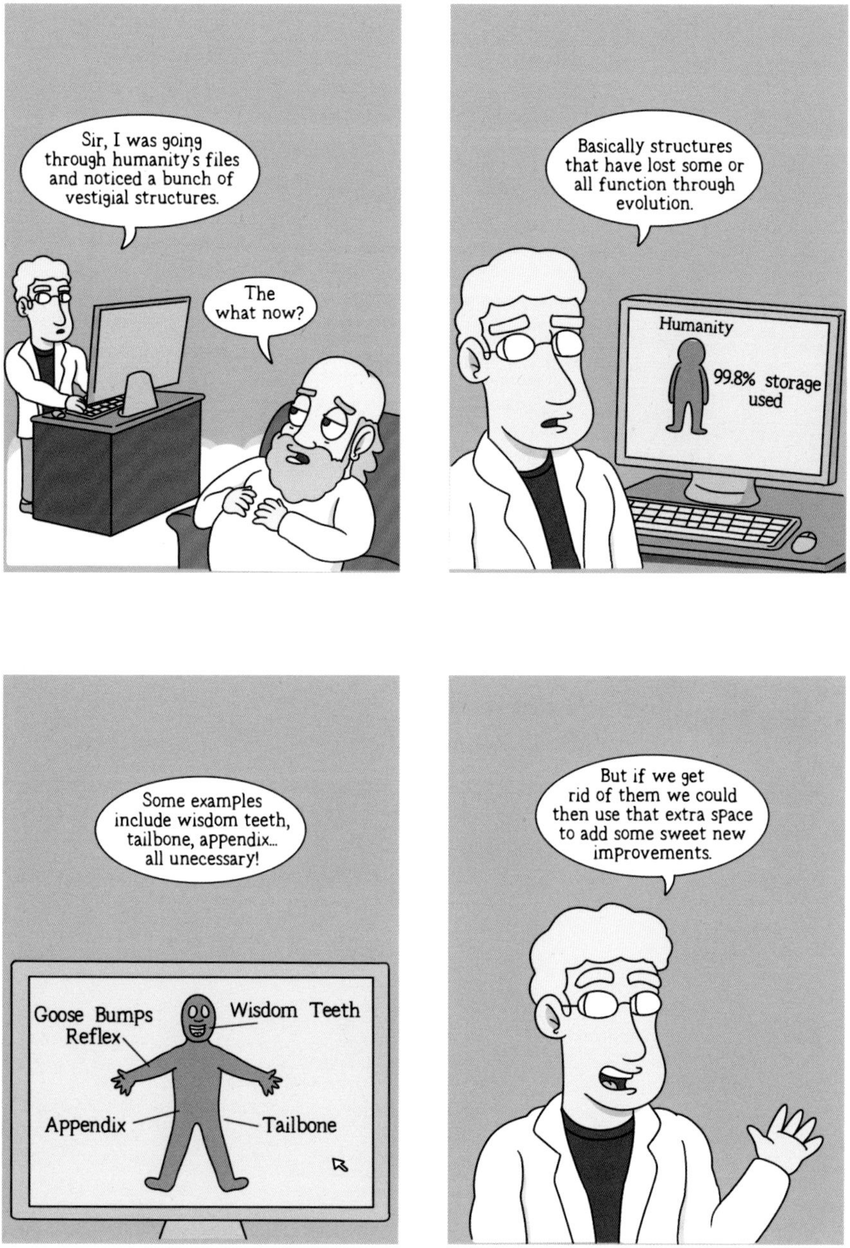

Sir, I was going through humanity's files and noticed a bunch of vestigial structures.
The what now?
Basically structures that have lost some or all function through evolution.
Humanity
99.8% storage used
Some examples include wisdom teeth, tailbone, appendix... all unecessary!
Goose Bumps Reflex
Wisdom Teeth
Appendix
Tailbone
But if we get rid of them we could then use that extra space to add some sweet new improvements.

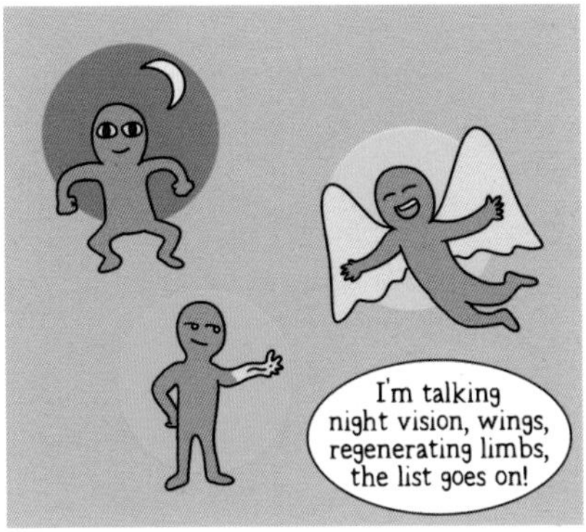
I'm talking night vision, wings, regenerating limbs, the list goes on!

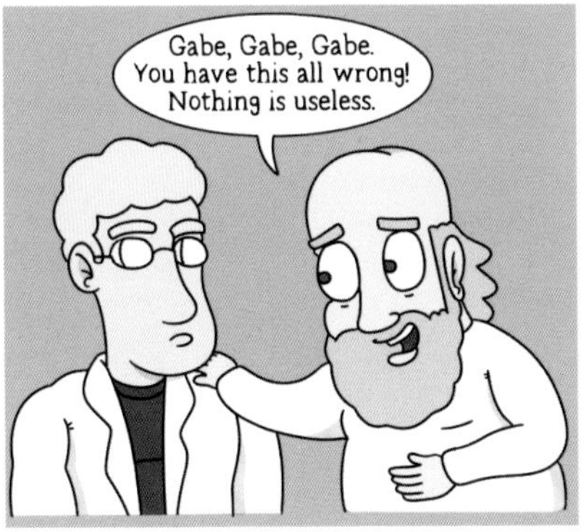
Gabe, Gabe, Gabe. You have this all wrong! Nothing is useless.

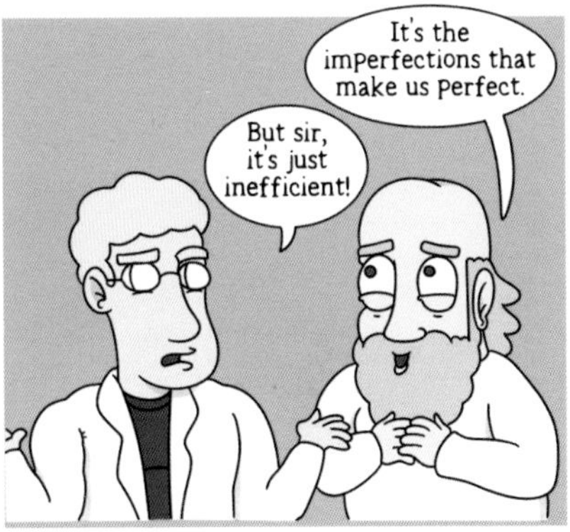
But sir, it's just inefficient!
It's the imperfections that make us perfect.

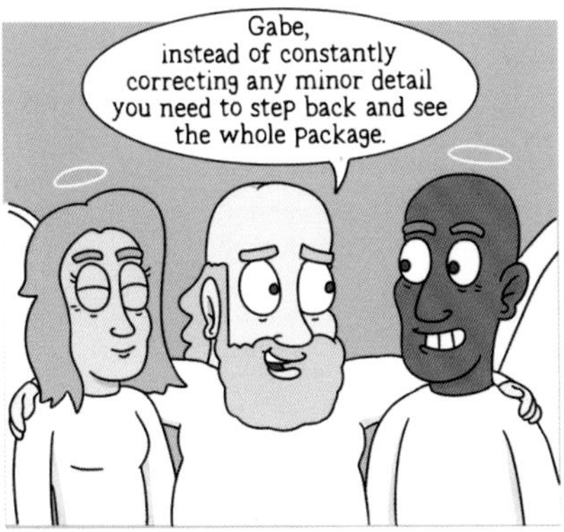
Gabe, instead of constantly correcting any minor detail you need to step back and see the whole package.

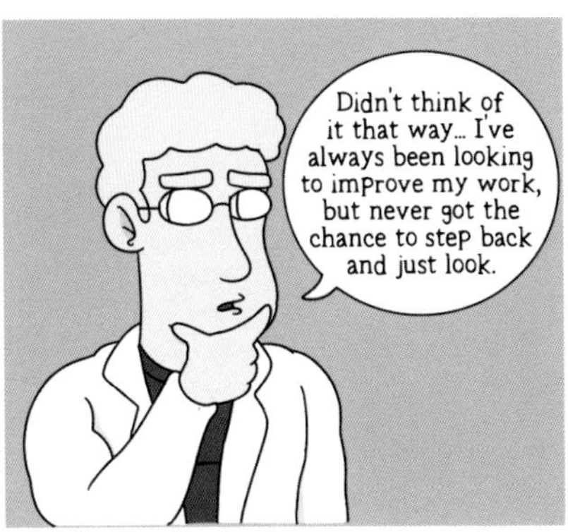
Didn't think of it that way... I've always been looking to improve my work, but never got the chance to step back and just look.

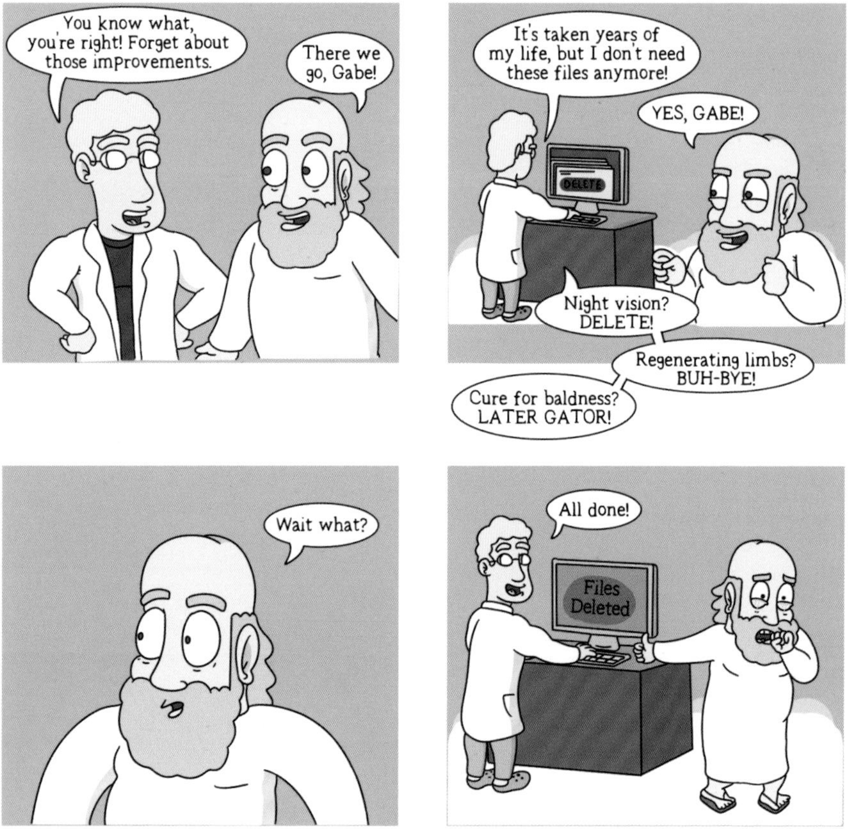
You know what, you're right! Forget about those improvements.
There we go, Gabe!
It's taken years of my life, but I don't need these files anymore!
YES, GABE!
DELETE
Night vision? DELETE!
Regenerating limbs? BUH-BYE!
Cure for baldness? LATER GATOR!
Wait what?
All done!
Files Deleted

BONUS

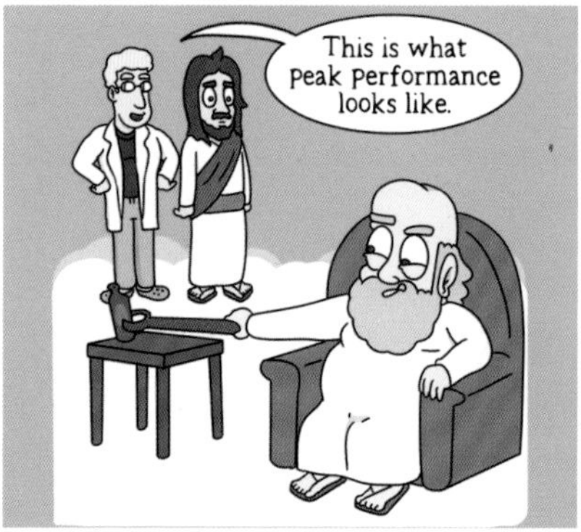
This is what peak performance looks like.

Belong

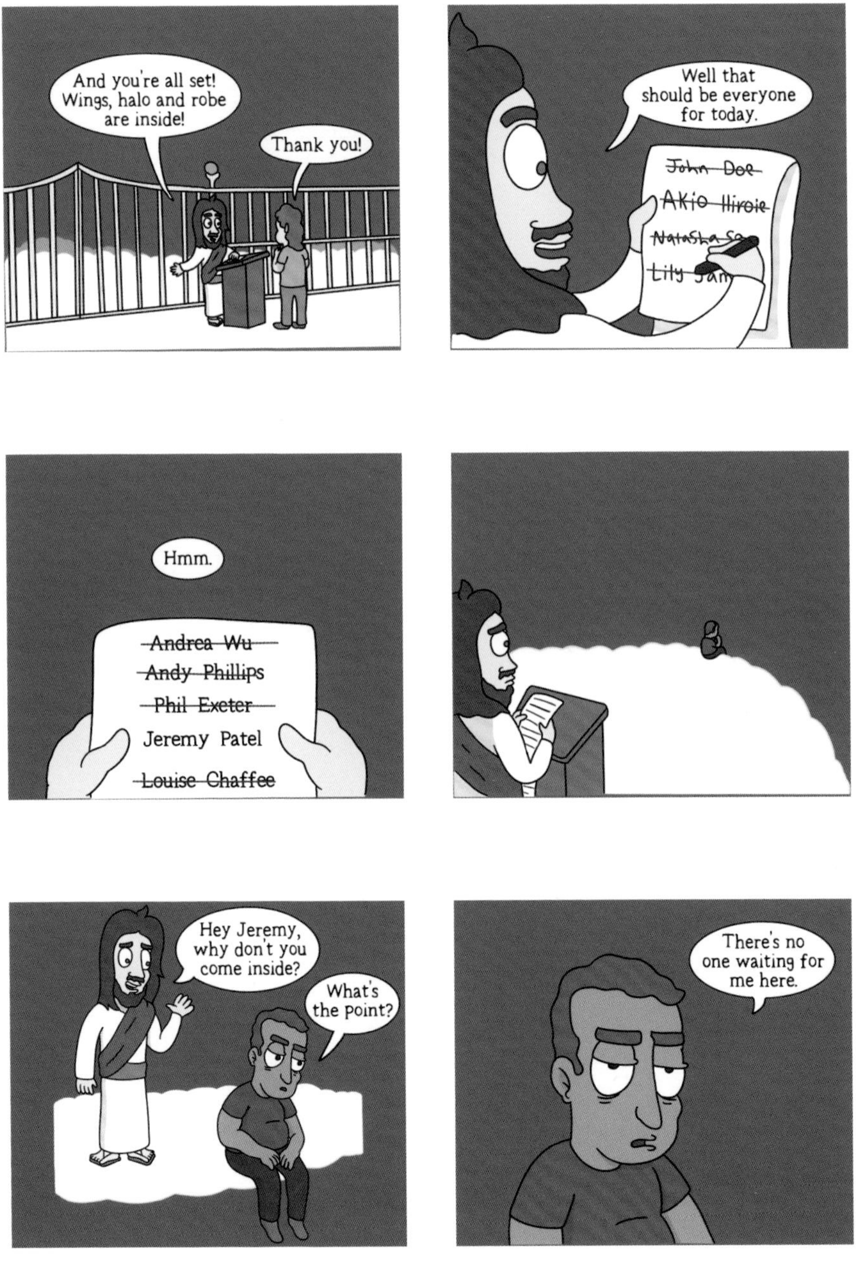
And you're all set! Wings, halo and robe are inside!
Thank you!
Well that should be everyone for today.
John Doe
Akio Hiroie
Natasha
Lily
Hmm.
Andrea Wu
Andy Phillips
Phil Exeter
Jeremy Patel
Louise Chaffee
Hey Jeremy, why don't you come inside?
What's the point?
There's no one waiting for me here.

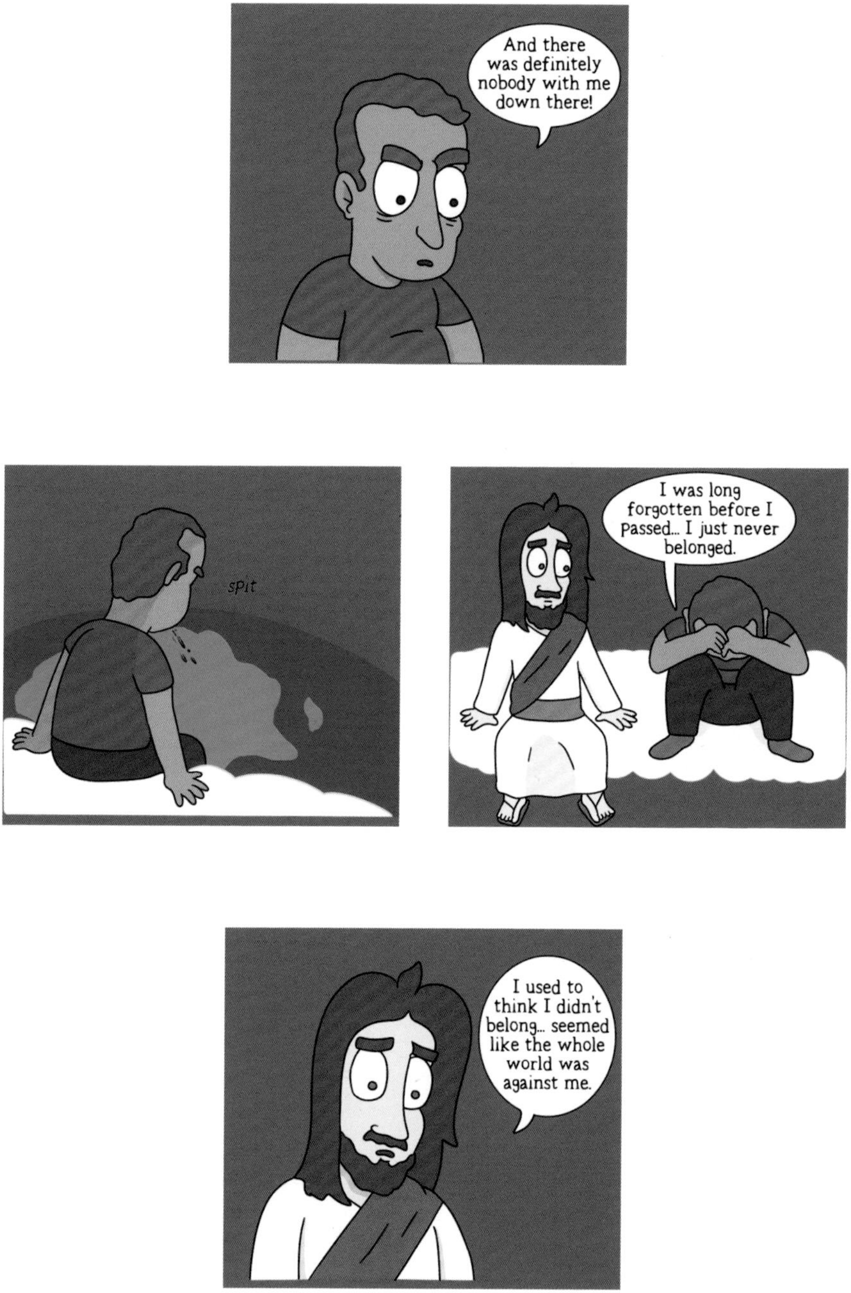
And there was definitely nobody with me down there!
spit
I was long forgotten before I passed... I just never belonged.
I used to think I didn't belong... seemed like the whole world was against me.

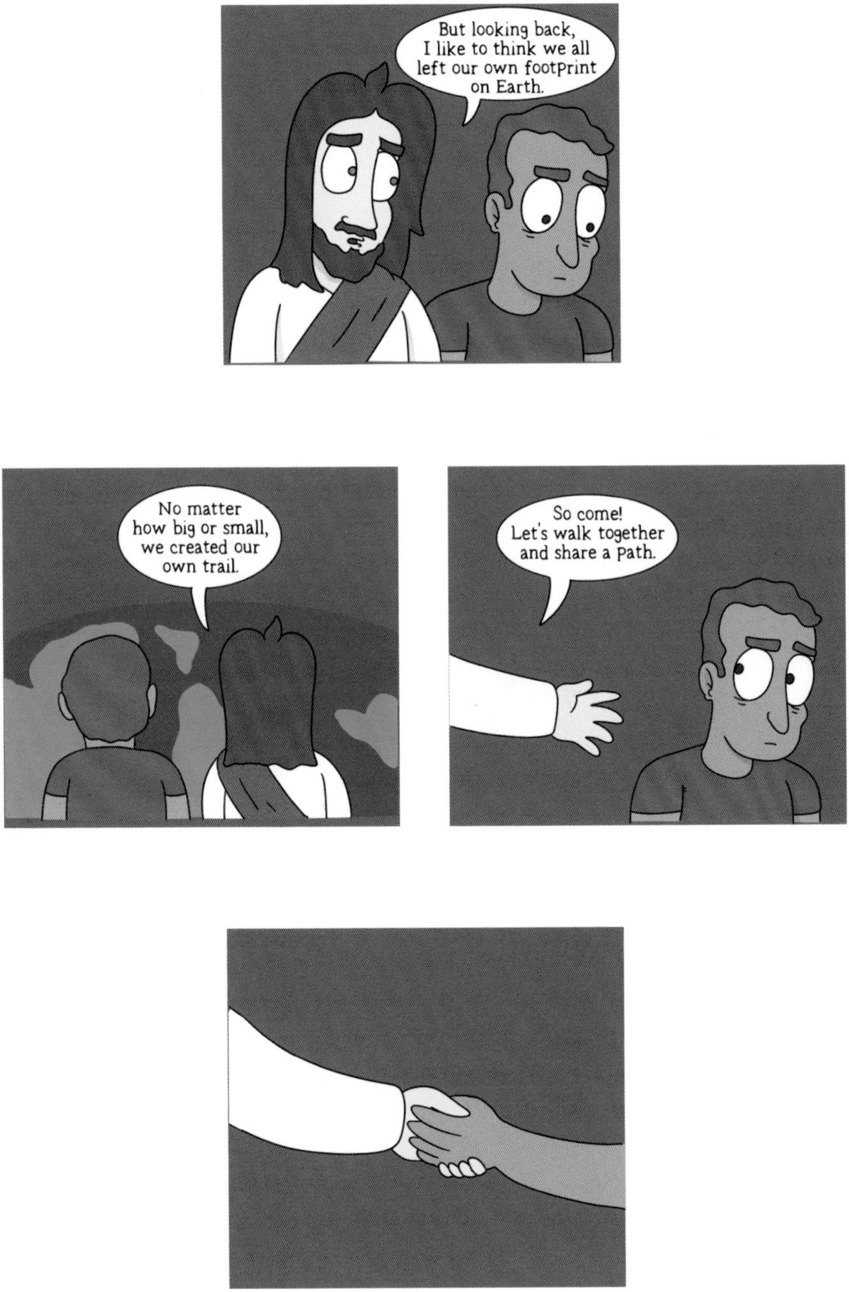
But looking back, I like to think we all left our own footprint on Earth.
No matter how big or small, we created our own trail.
So come! Let's walk together and share a path.

Poof

creak...

BONUS

Patel, is that you? You still owe me $50!
See? You did leave a mark!

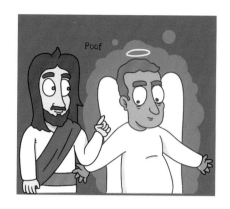

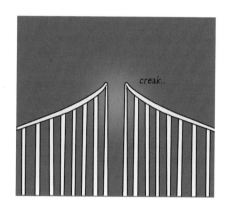

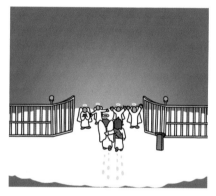

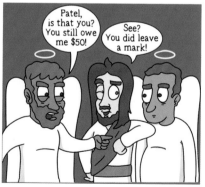

Image

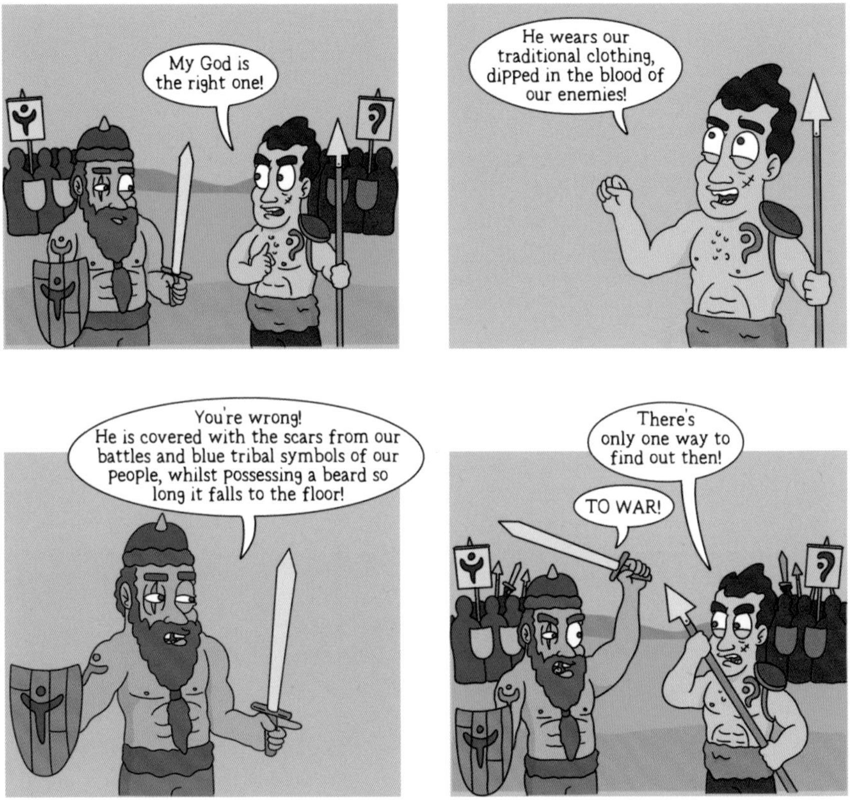
My God is the right one!
He wears our traditional clothing, dipped in the blood of our enemies!
You're wrong! He is covered with the scars from our battles and blue tribal symbols of our people, whilst possessing a beard so long it falls to the floor!
There's only one way to find out then!
TO WAR!

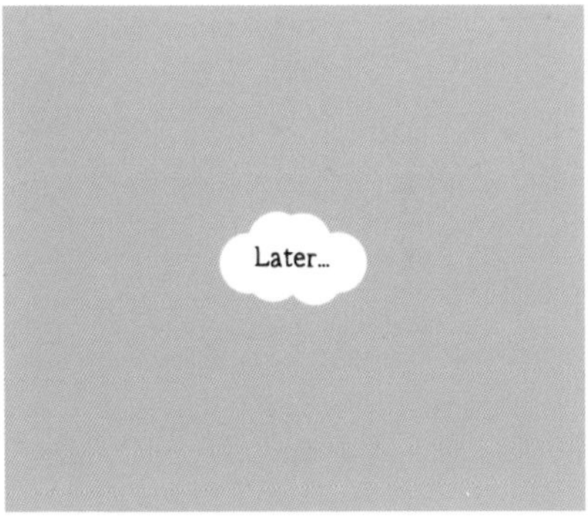
Later...

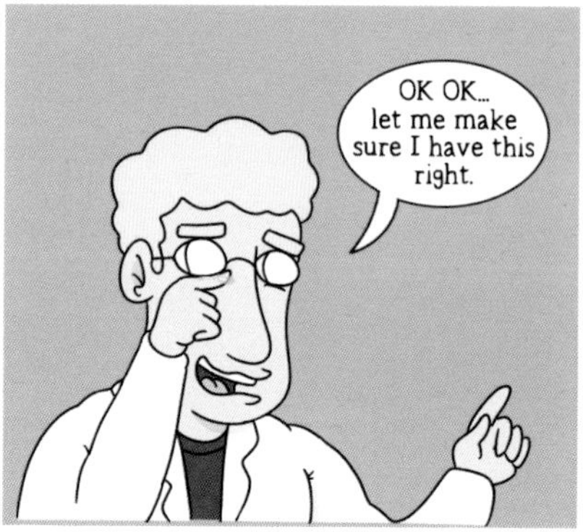
OK OK...
let me make
sure I have this
right.

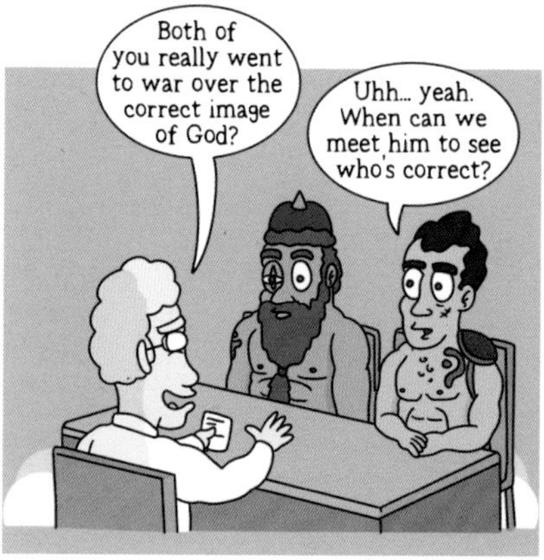
Both of
you really went
to war over the
correct image
of God?
Uhh... yeah.
When can we
meet him to see
who's correct?

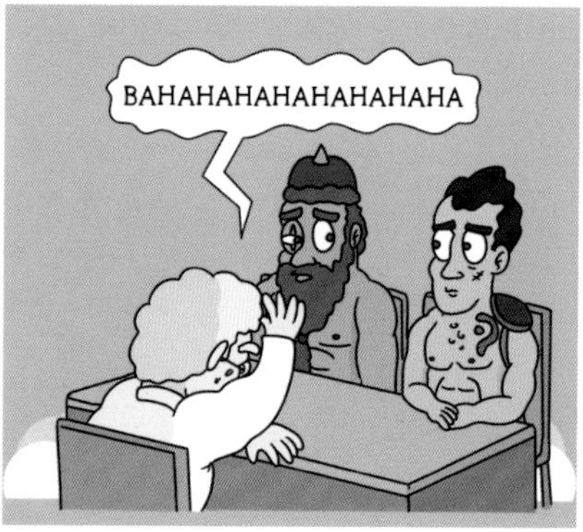
BAHAHAHAHAHAHAHAHA

BONUS

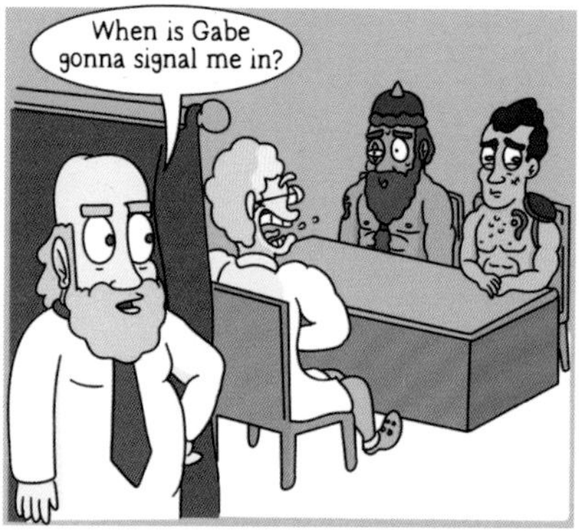
When is Gabe
gonna signal me in?

Fast

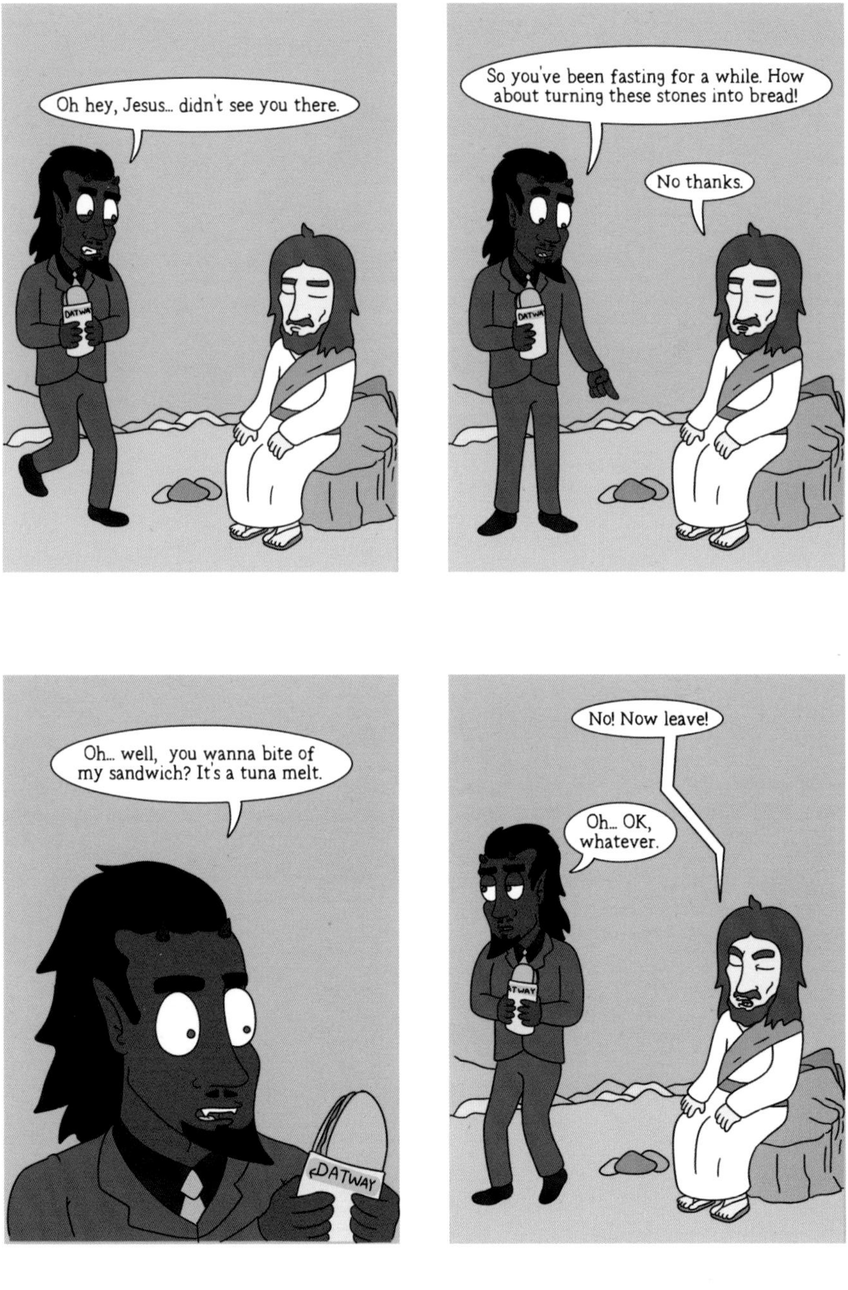
Oh hey, Jesus... didn't see you there.
DATWAY
So you've been fasting for a while. How about turning these stones into bread!
No thanks.
DATWAY
Oh... well, you wanna bite of my sandwich? It's a tuna melt.
DATWAY
No! Now leave!
Oh... OK, whatever.

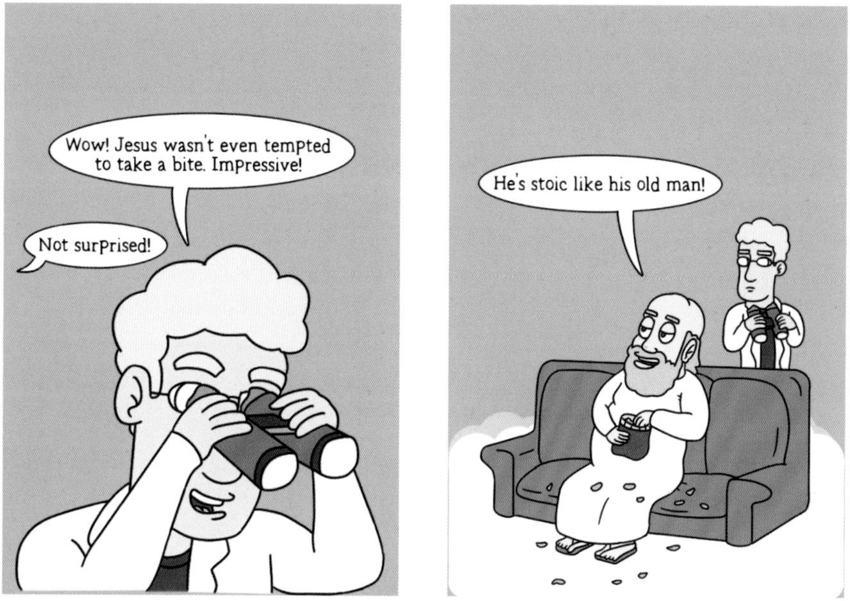
Wow! Jesus wasn't even tempted to take a bite. Impressive!
Not surprised!
He's stoic like his old man!

BONUS

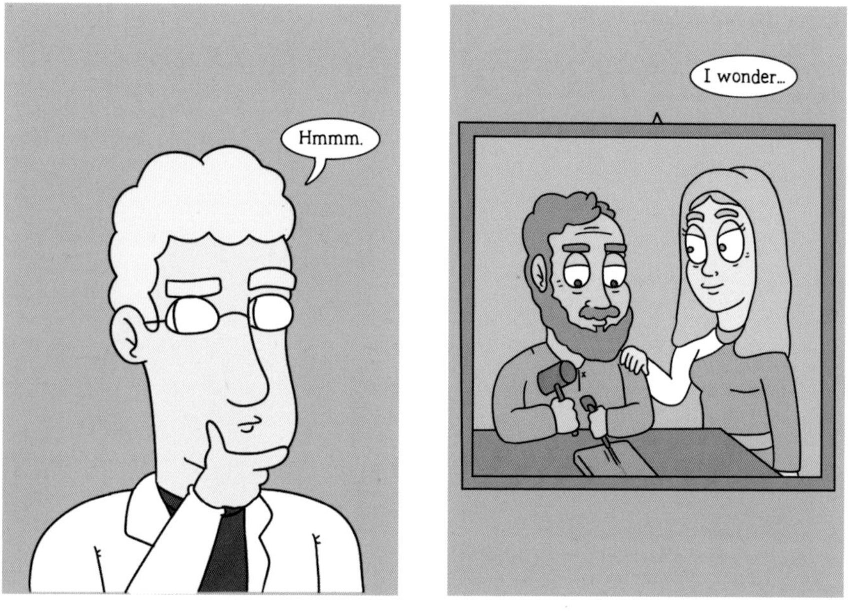
Hmmm.
I wonder...

Saint?

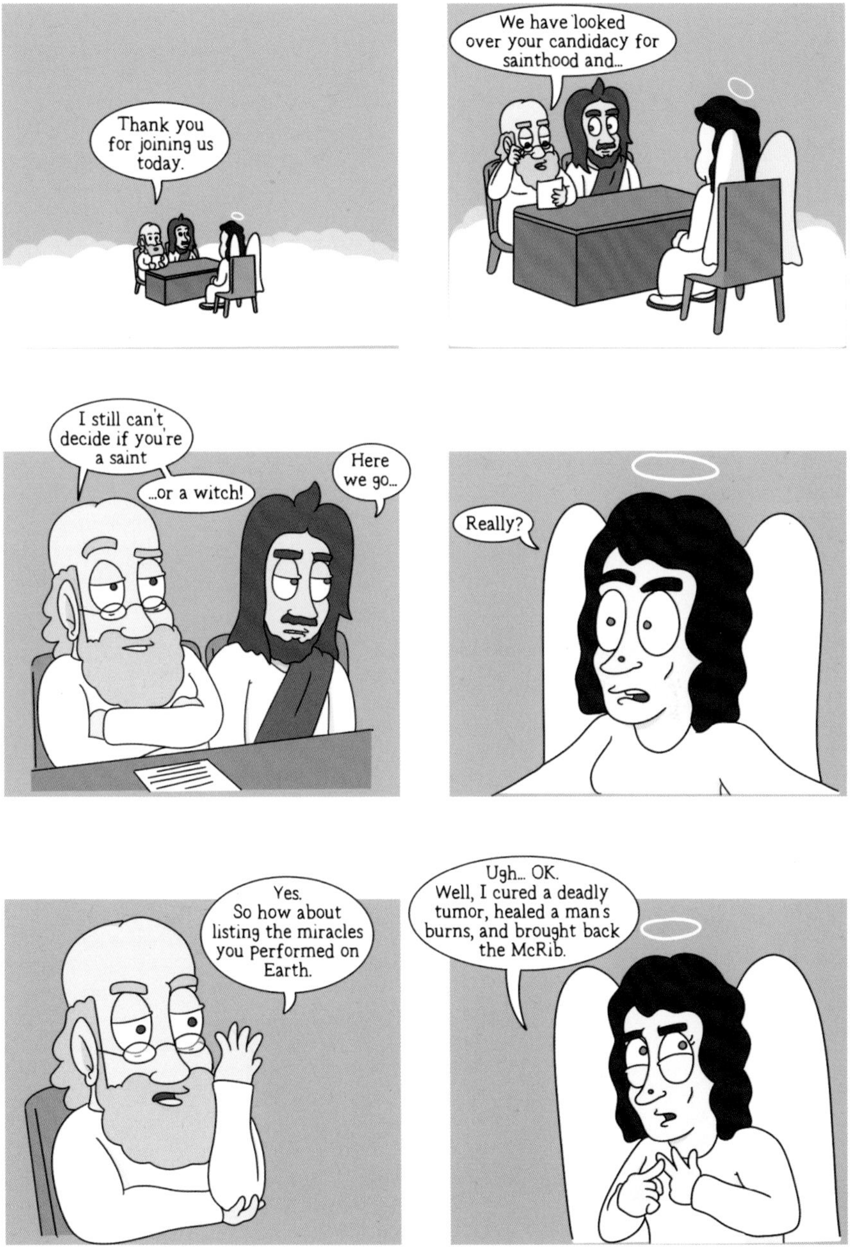
Thank you for joining us today.
We have looked over your candidacy for sainthood and...
I still can't decide if you're a saint
...or a witch!
Here we go...
Really?
Yes. So how about listing the miracles you performed on Earth.
Ugh... OK. Well, I cured a deadly tumor, healed a man's burns, and brought back the McRib.

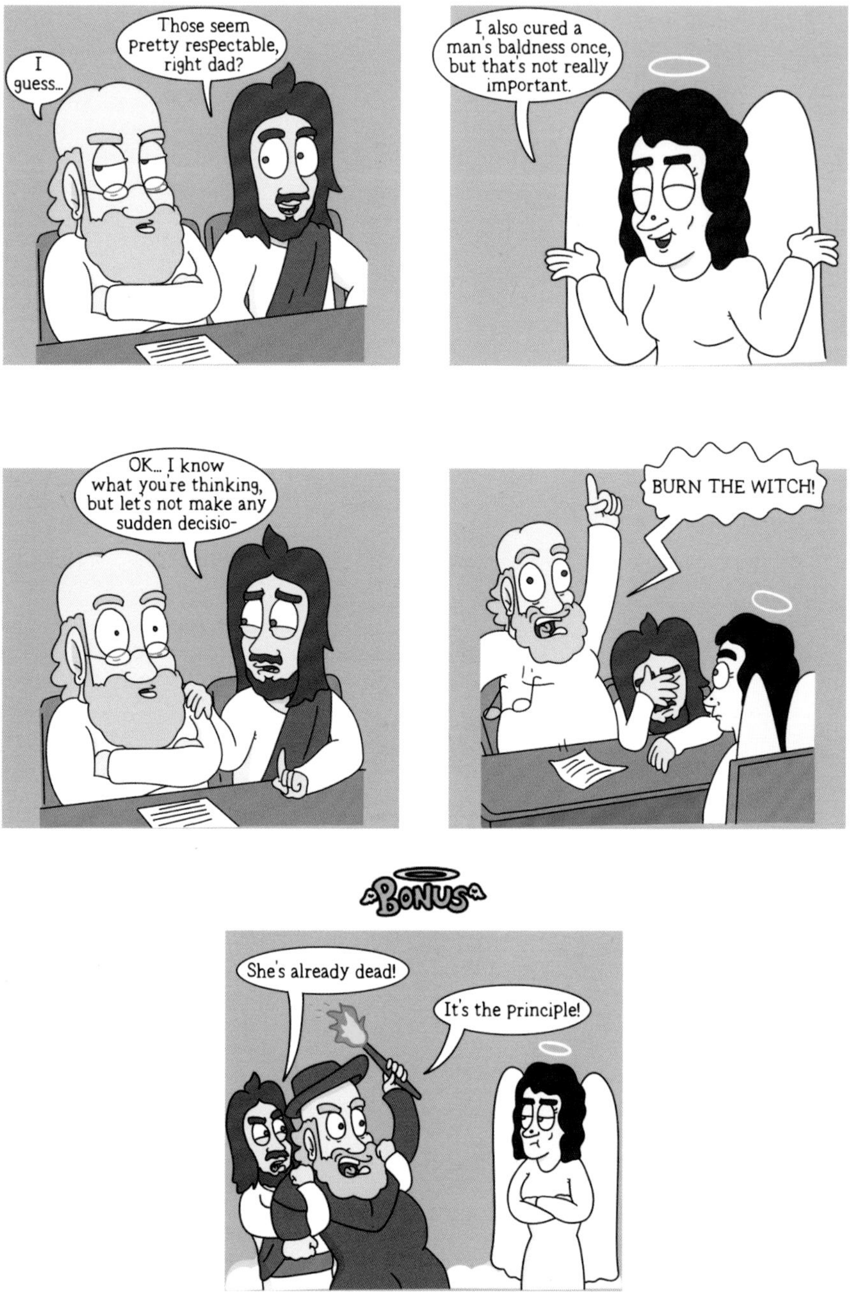
I guess...
Those seem pretty respectable, right dad?
I also cured a man's baldness once, but that's not really important.
OK... I know what you're thinking, but let's not make any sudden decisio-
BURN THE WITCH!
BONUS
She's already dead!
It's the principle!

St. Patrick

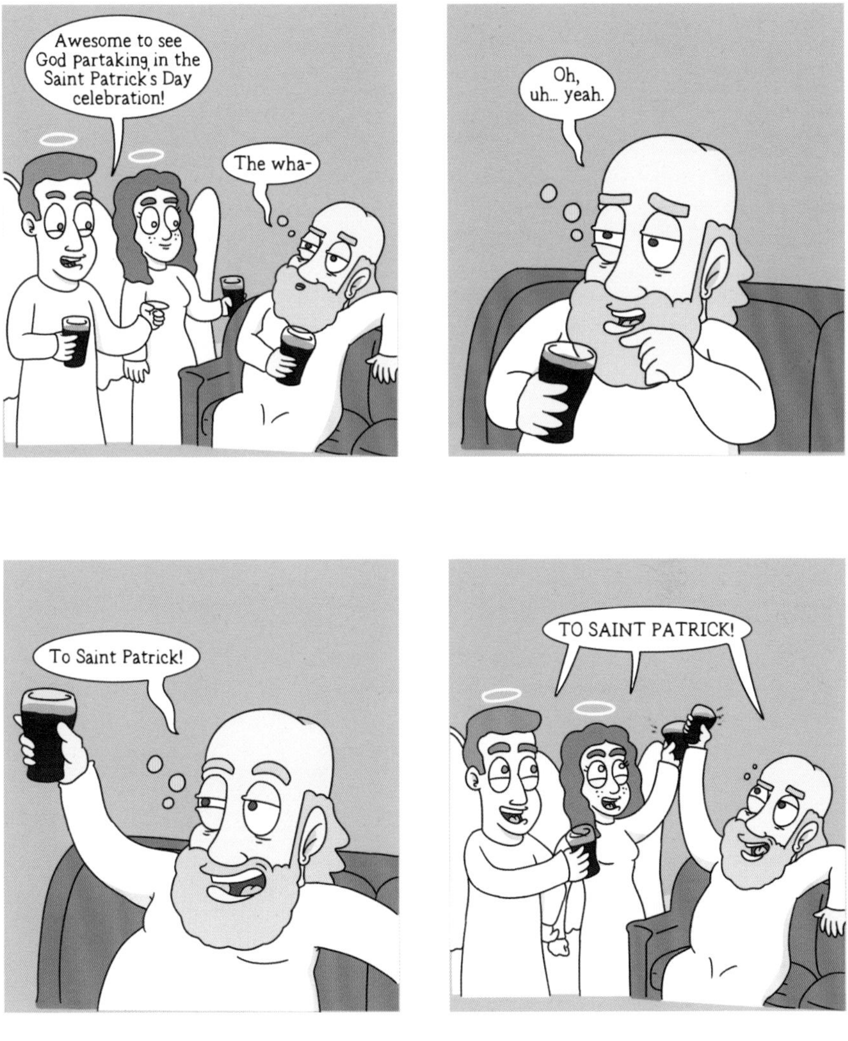
Awesome to see God partaking in the Saint Patrick's Day celebration!
The wha-
Oh, uh... yeah.
To Saint Patrick!
TO SAINT PATRICK!

Just an excuse to drink, am I right, my dude?

BONUS

Look at that lush getting drunk.
Are you even Irish!?

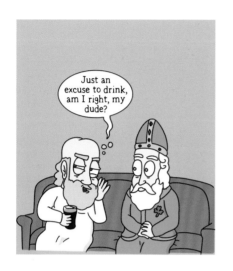

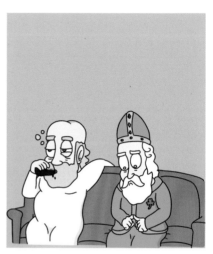

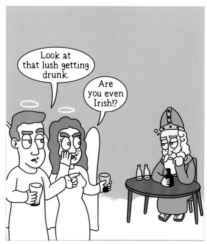

Business Trip

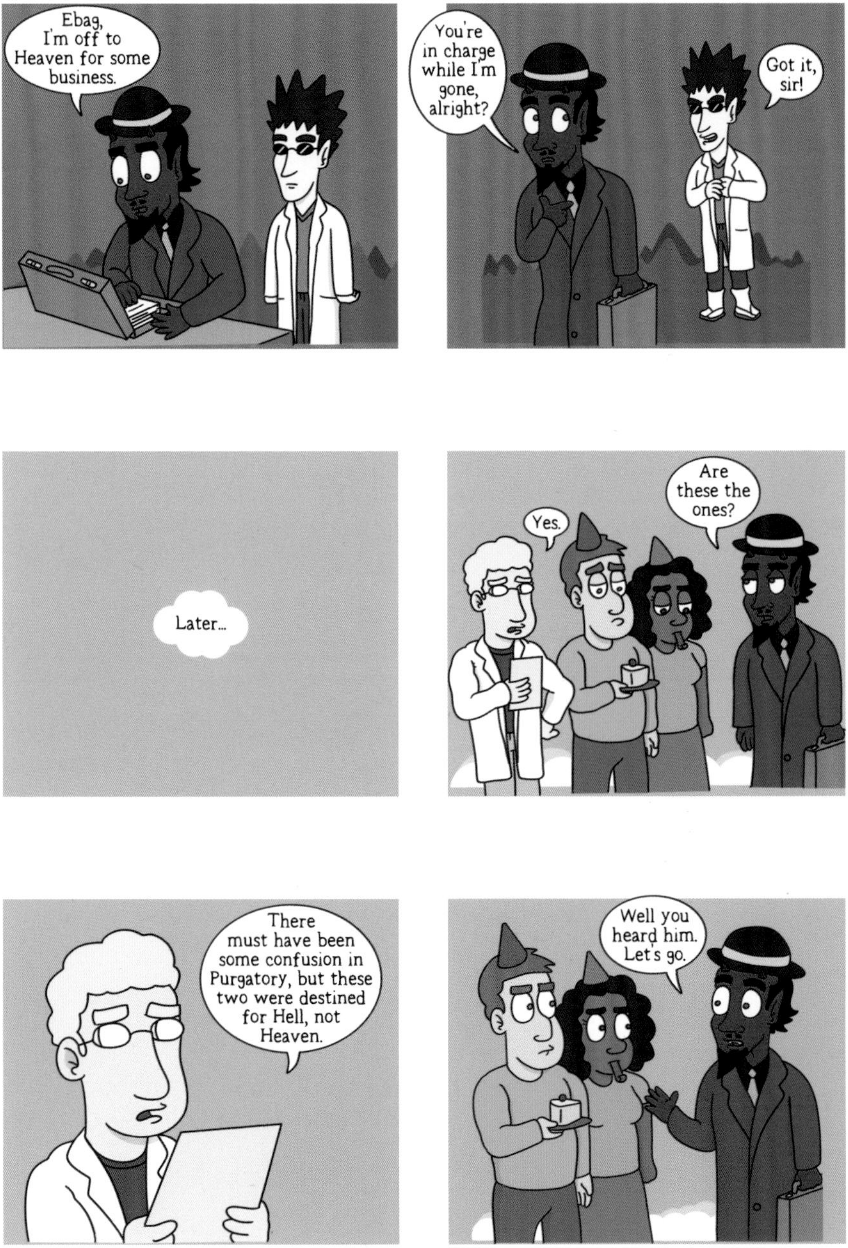
Ebag, I'm off to Heaven for some business.
You're in charge while I'm gone, alright?
Got it, sir!
Later...
Are these the ones?
Yes.
There must have been some confusion in Purgatory, but these two were destined for Hell, not Heaven.
Well you heard him. Let's go.

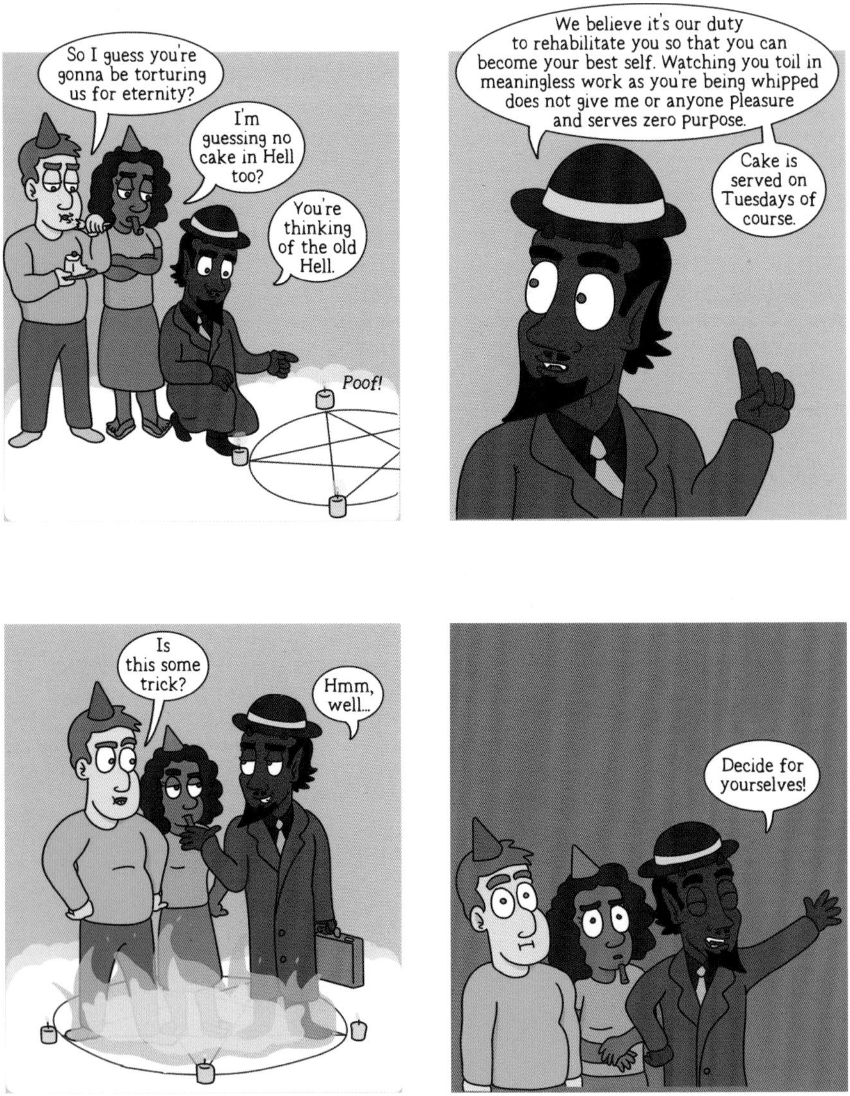
So I guess you're gonna be torturing us for eternity?
I'm guessing no cake in Hell too?
You're thinking of the old Hell.
Poof!
We believe it's our duty to rehabilitate you so that you can become your best self. Watching you toil in meaningless work as you're being whipped does not give me or anyone pleasure and serves zero purpose.
Cake is served on Tuesdays of course.
Is this some trick?
Hmm, well...
Decide for yourselves!

HAHAHA BOW DOWN TO YOUR EMPEROR AND SUFFER! YOU'RE IN HELL NOW BABY!
Uhh... he's just a temp.

BONUS

I just don't understand what I did so wrong?
...Same...

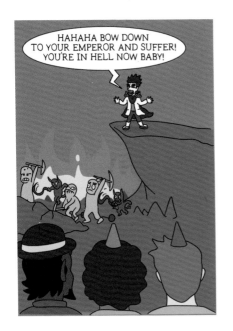

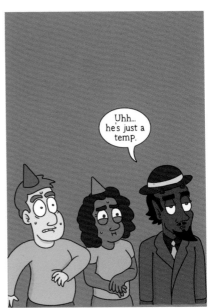

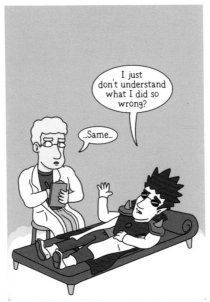

Business Trip 2

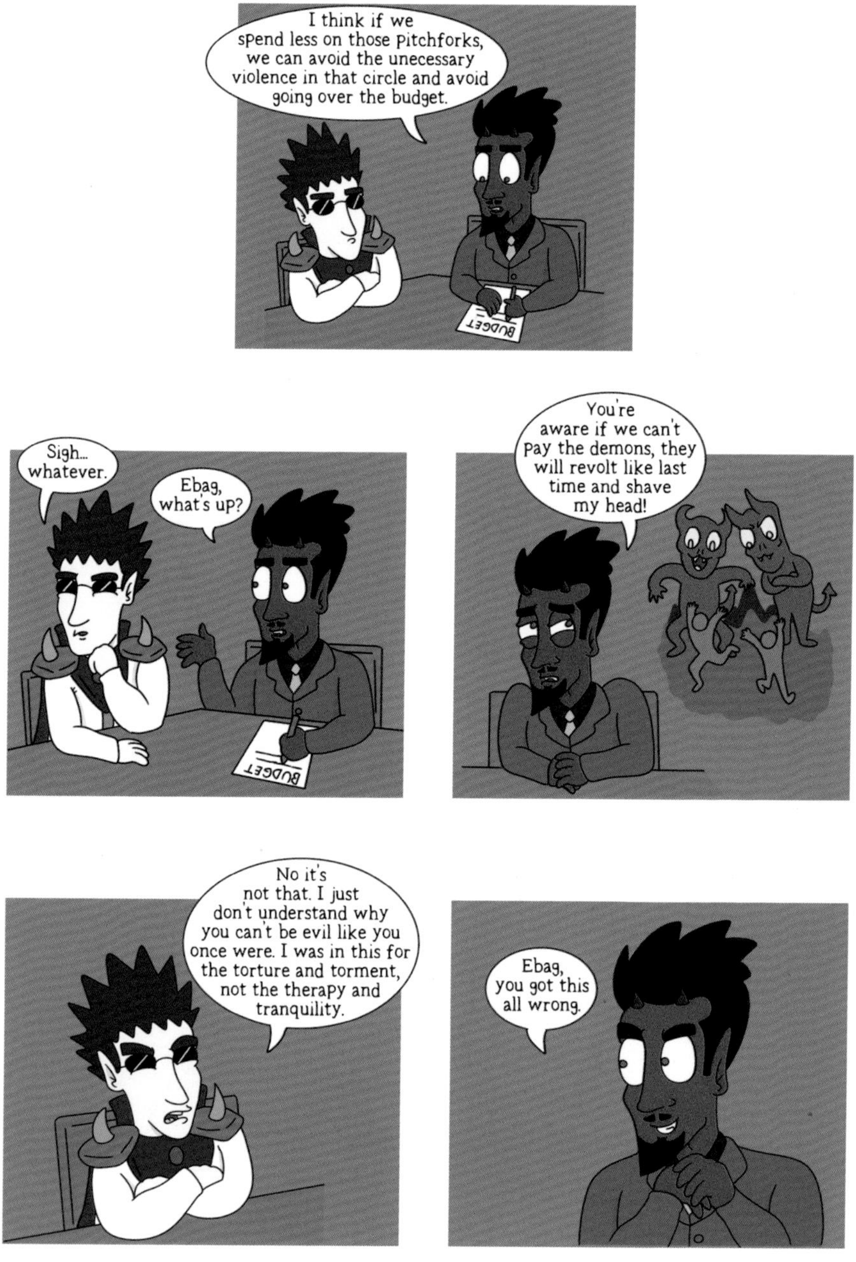
I think if we spend less on those pitchforks, we can avoid the unecessary violence in that circle and avoid going over the budget.
Sigh... whatever.
Ebag, what's up?
You're aware if we can't pay the demons, they will revolt like last time and shave my head!
No it's not that. I just don't understand why you can't be evil like you once were. I was in this for the torture and torment, not the therapy and tranquility.
Ebag, you got this all wrong.

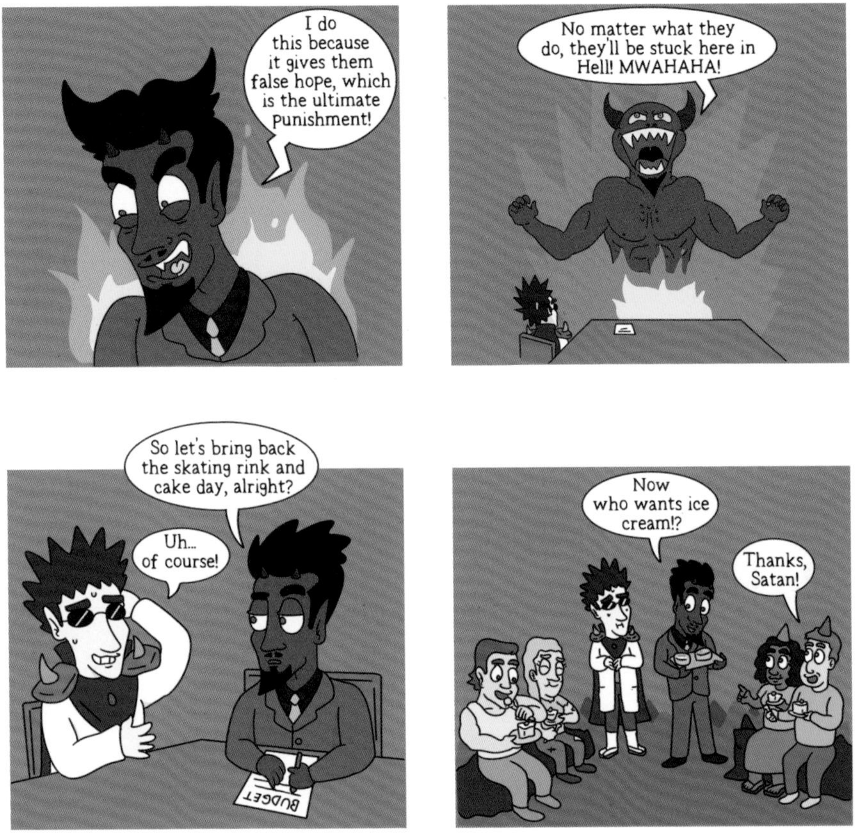
I do this because it gives them false hope, which is the ultimate punishment!
No matter what they do, they'll be stuck here in Hell! MWAHAHA!
So let's bring back the skating rink and cake day, alright?
Uh... of course!
BUDGET
Now who wants ice cream!?
Thanks, Satan!

BONUS

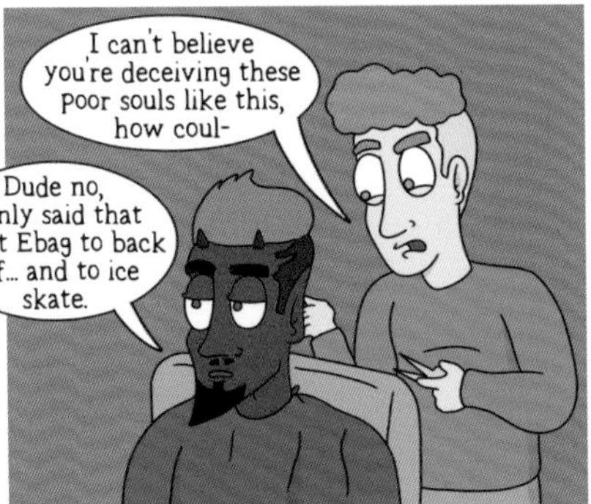
I can't believe you're deceiving these poor souls like this, how coul-
Dude no, I only said that to get Ebag to back off... and to ice skate.

The Whole Truth

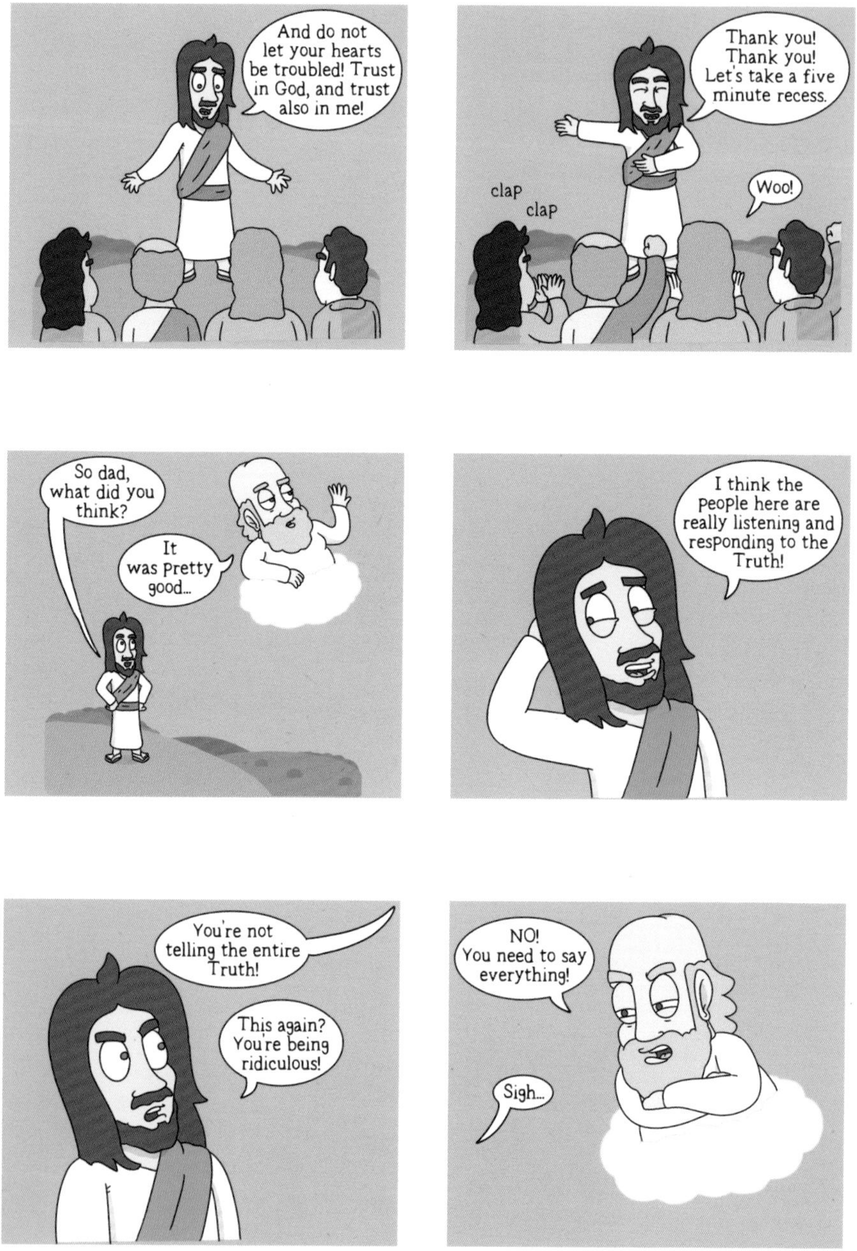

And do not let your hearts be troubled! Trust in God, and trust also in me!
Thank you! Thank you! Let's take a five minute recess.
clap
clap
Woo!
So dad, what did you think?
It was pretty good...
I think the people here are really listening and responding to the Truth!
You're not telling the entire Truth!
This again? You're being ridiculous!
NO! You need to say everything!
Sigh...

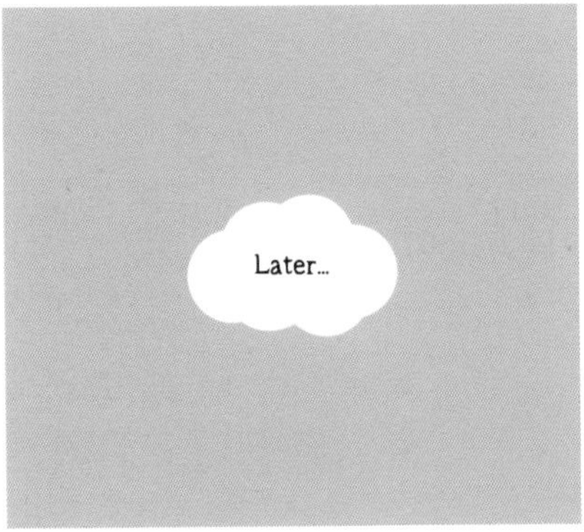
Later...

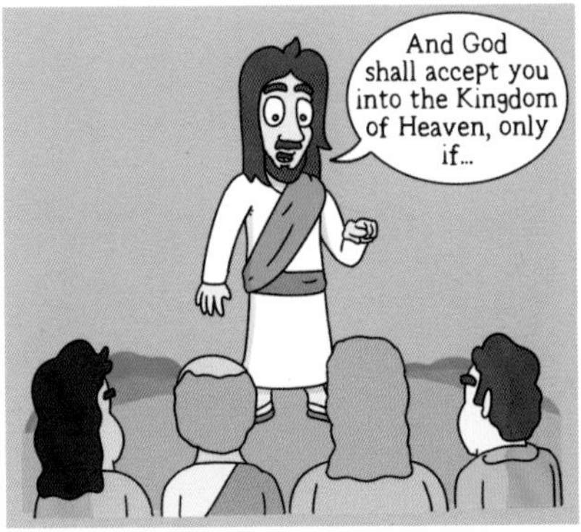
And God shall accept you into the Kingdom of Heaven, only if...

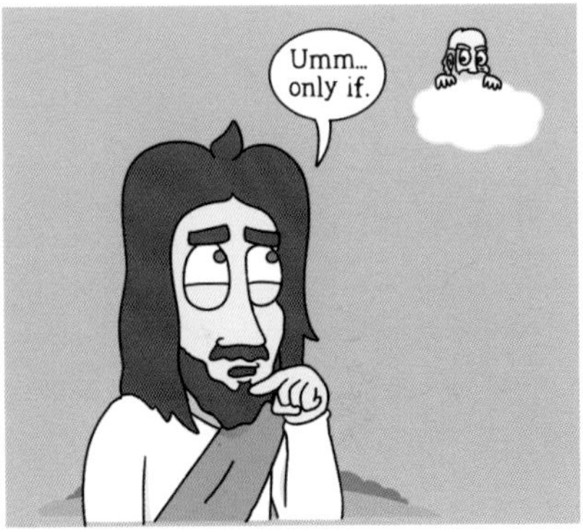
Umm... only if.

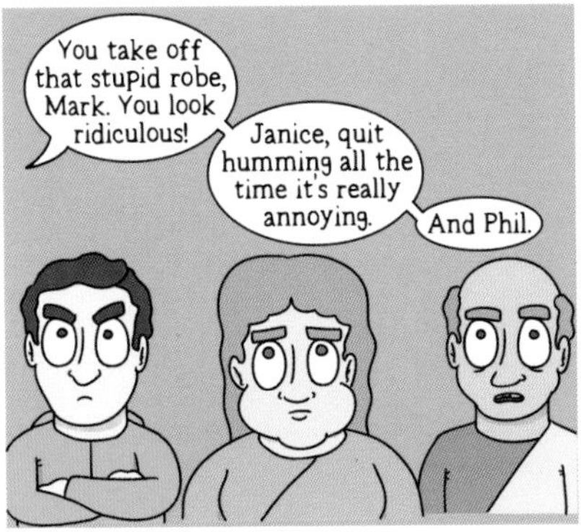
You take off that stupid robe, Mark. You look ridiculous!
Janice, quit humming all the time it's really annoying.
And Phil.

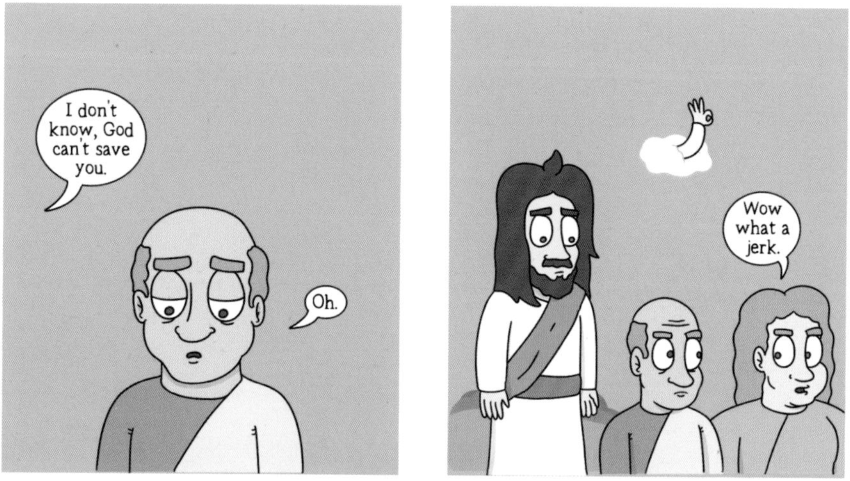
I don't know, God can't save you.
Oh.
Wow what a jerk.

BONUS

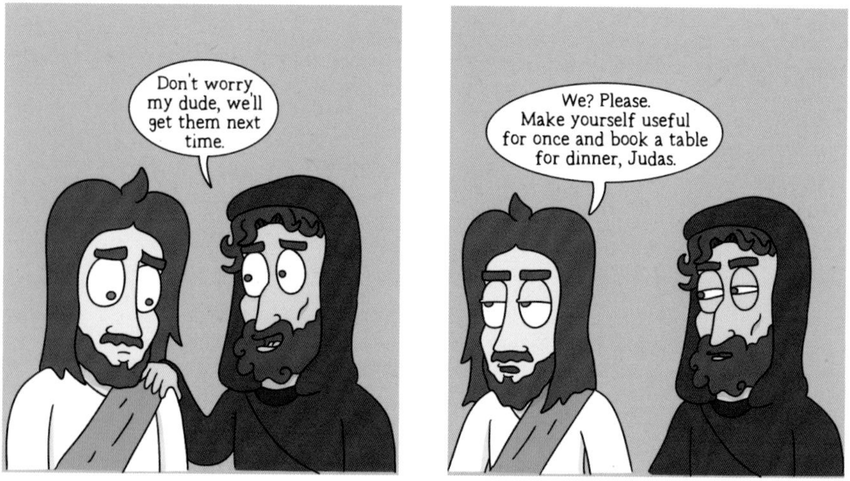
Don't worry my dude, we'll get them next time.
We? Please. Make yourself useful for once and book a table for dinner, Judas.

Monk

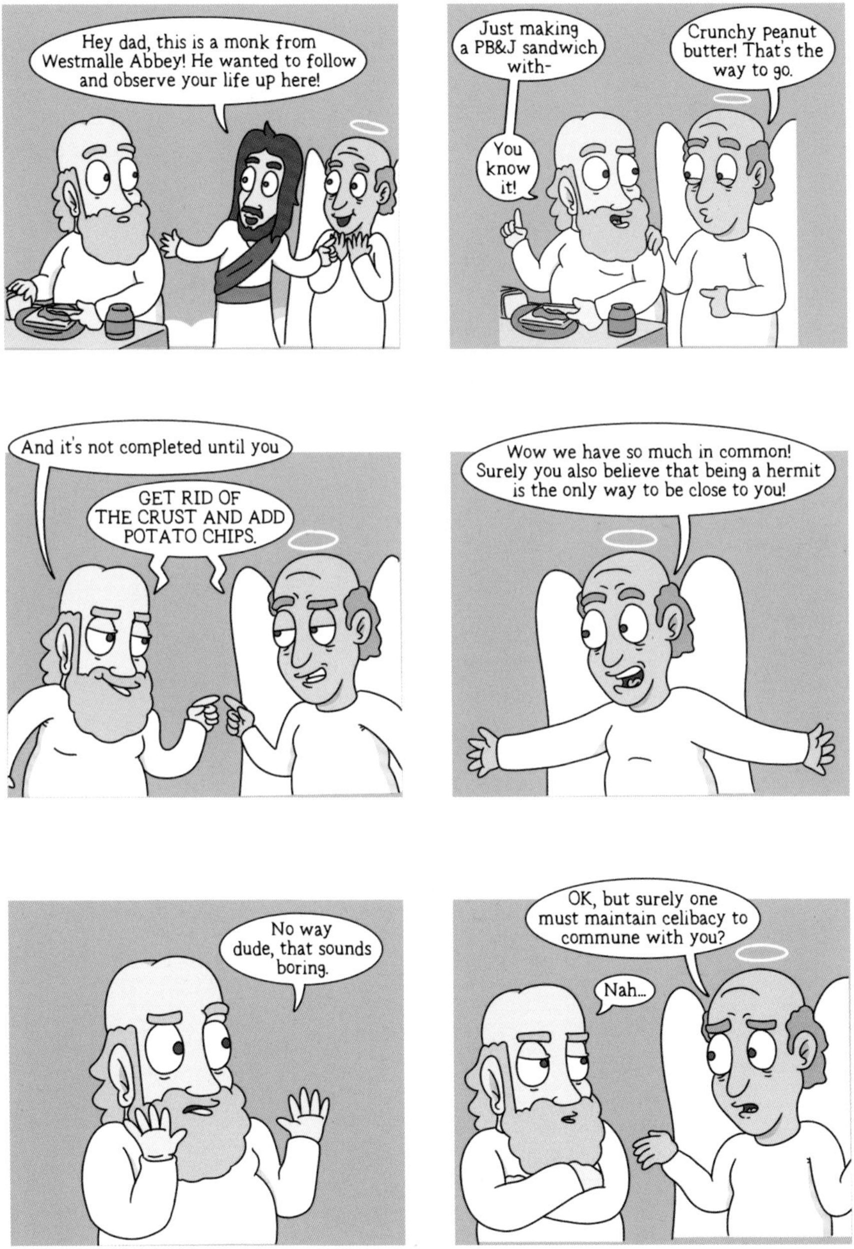
Hey dad, this is a monk from Westmalle Abbey! He wanted to follow and observe your life up here!
Just making a PB&J sandwich with-
Crunchy peanut butter! That's the way to go.
You know it!
And it's not completed until you
GET RID OF THE CRUST AND ADD POTATO CHIPS.
Wow we have so much in common! Surely you also believe that being a hermit is the only way to be close to you!
No way dude, that sounds boring.
OK, but surely one must maintain celibacy to commune with you?
Nah...

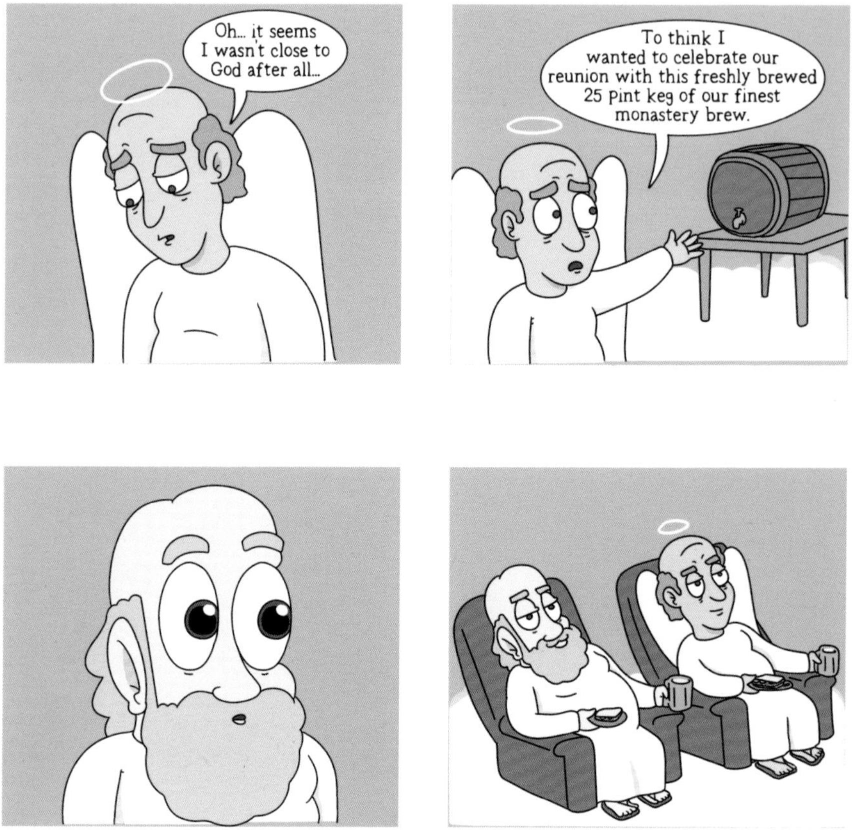
Oh... it seems
I wasn't close to
God after all...
To think I
wanted to celebrate our
reunion with this freshly brewed
25 pint keg of our finest
monastery brew.

BONUS

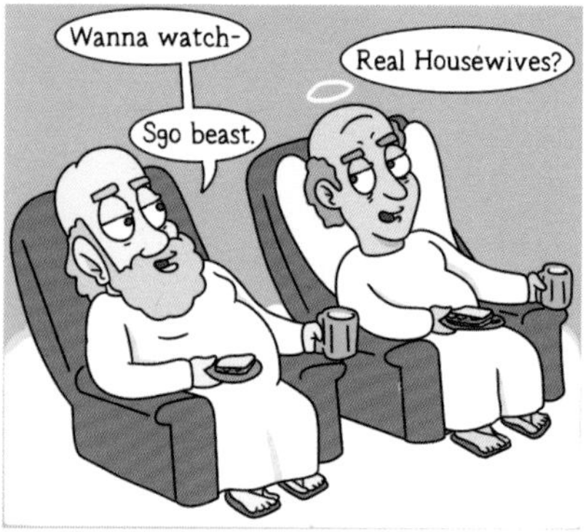
Wanna watch-
Real Housewives?
Sgo beast.

Last Words

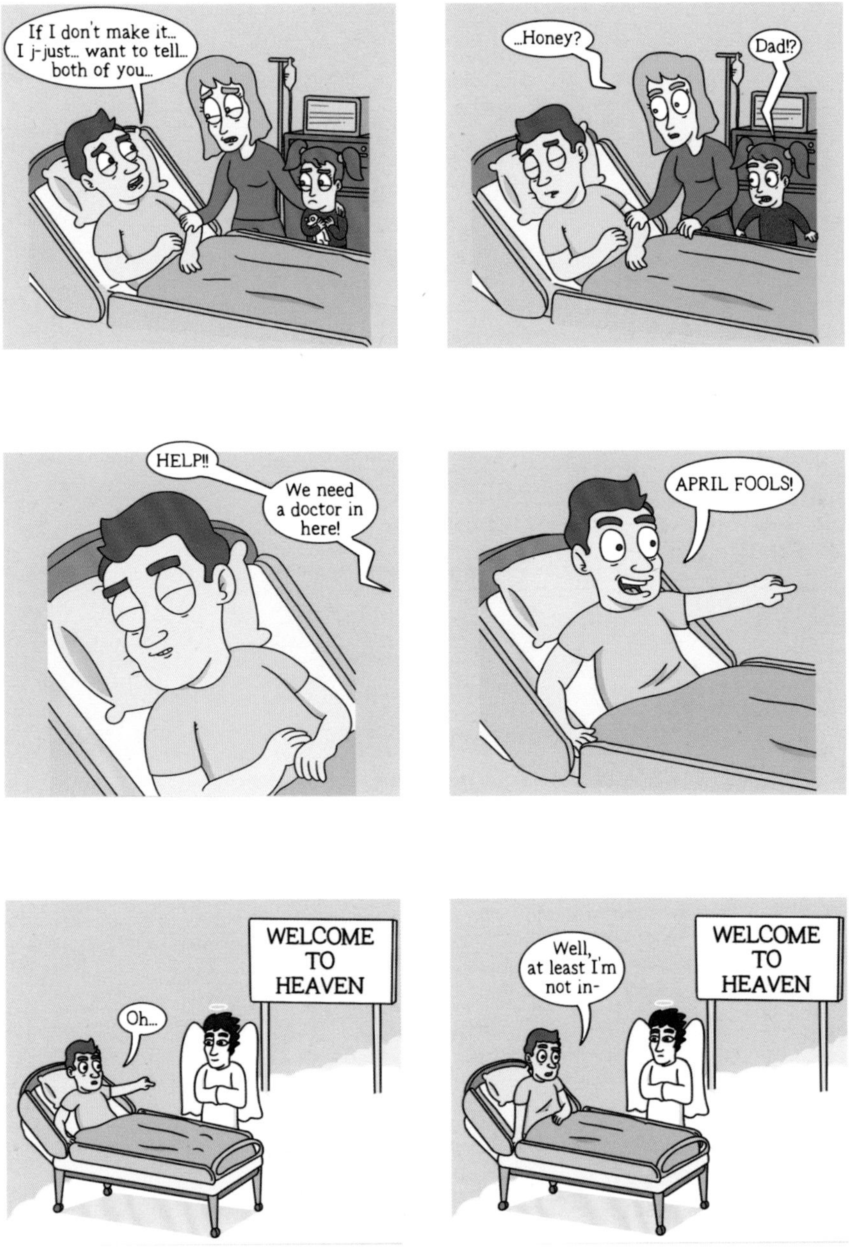
If I don't make it... I j-just... want to tell... both of you...
...Honey?
Dad!?
HELP!!
We need a doctor in here!
APRIL FOOLS!
WELCOME TO HEAVEN
Oh...
WELCOME TO HEAVEN
Well, at least I'm not in-

APRIL FOOLS!
WELCOME TO HELL
WELCOME TO HEAVEN

BONUS

Meanwhile

My children, I have risen!

Oh har har har, April Fools!
Greg is that you?

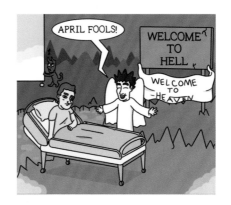

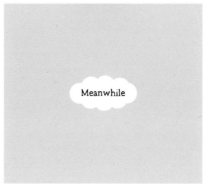

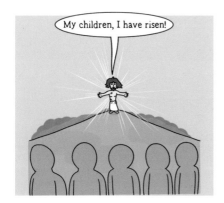

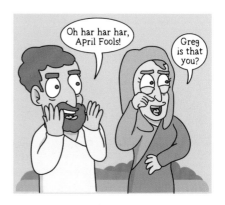

Spring Cleaning

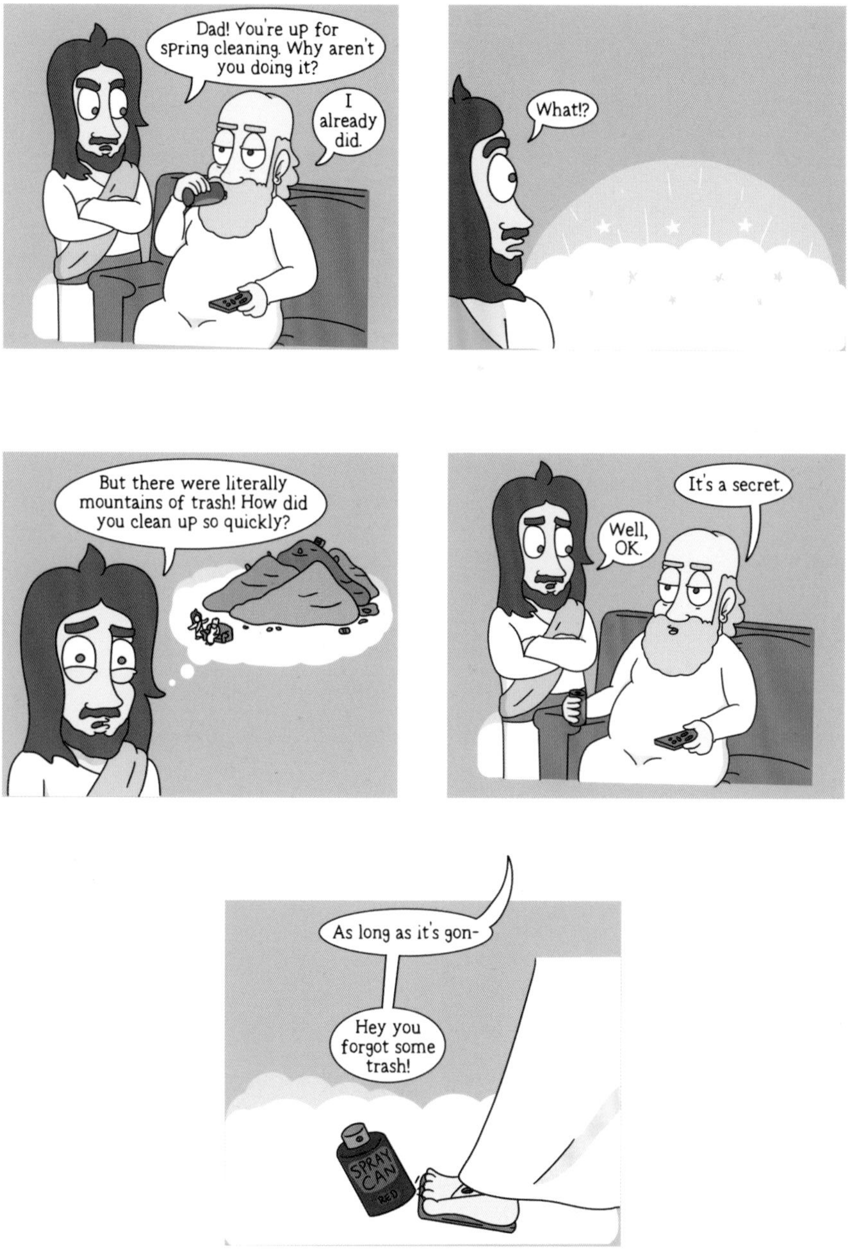
Dad! You're up for spring cleaning. Why aren't you doing it?
I already did.
What!?
But there were literally mountains of trash! How did you clean up so quickly?
It's a secret.
Well, OK.
As long as it's gon-
Hey you forgot some trash!
SPRAY CAN

Hmm?

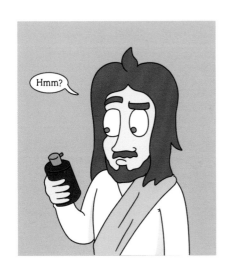

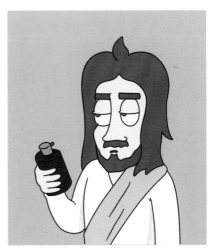

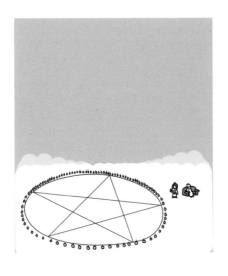

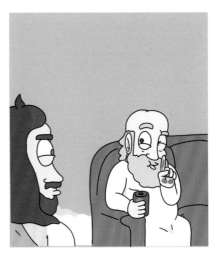

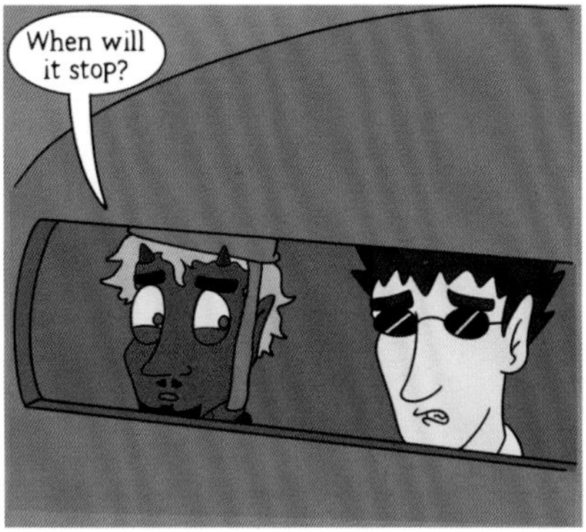
When will it stop?

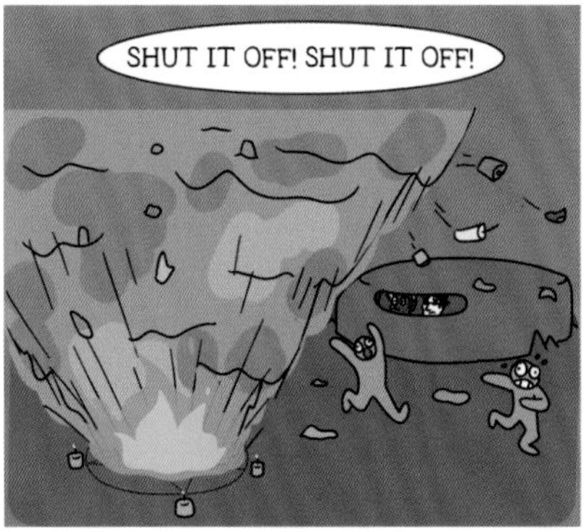
SHUT IT OFF! SHUT IT OFF!

BONUS

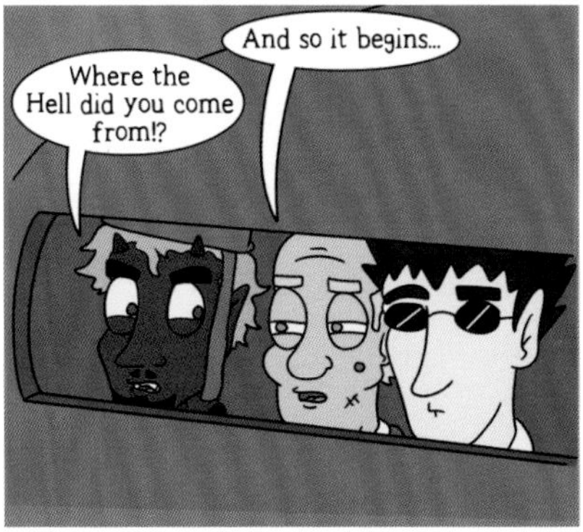
Where the Hell did you come from!?
And so it begins...

Spring Cleaning 2

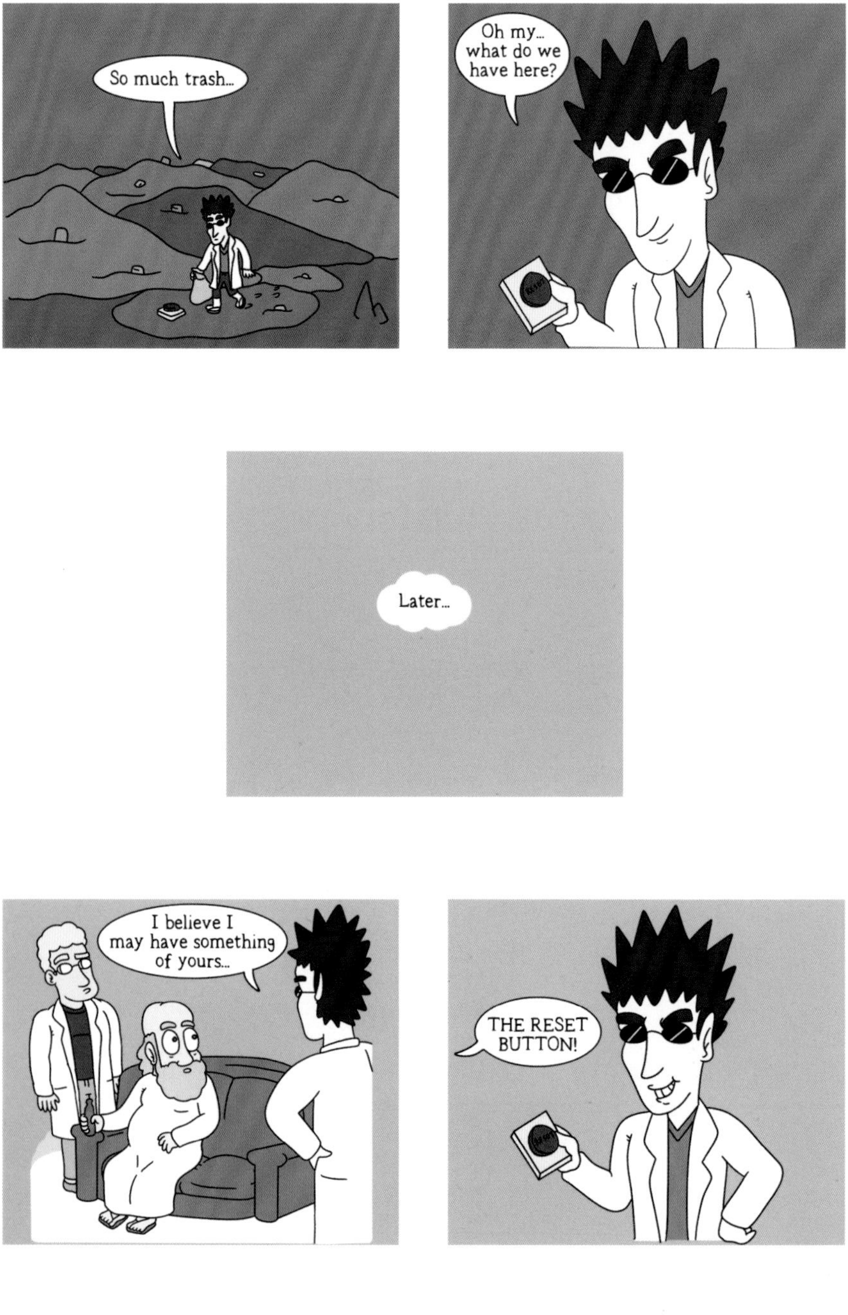
So much trash...
Oh my... what do we have here?
Later...
I believe I may have something of yours...
THE RESET BUTTON!

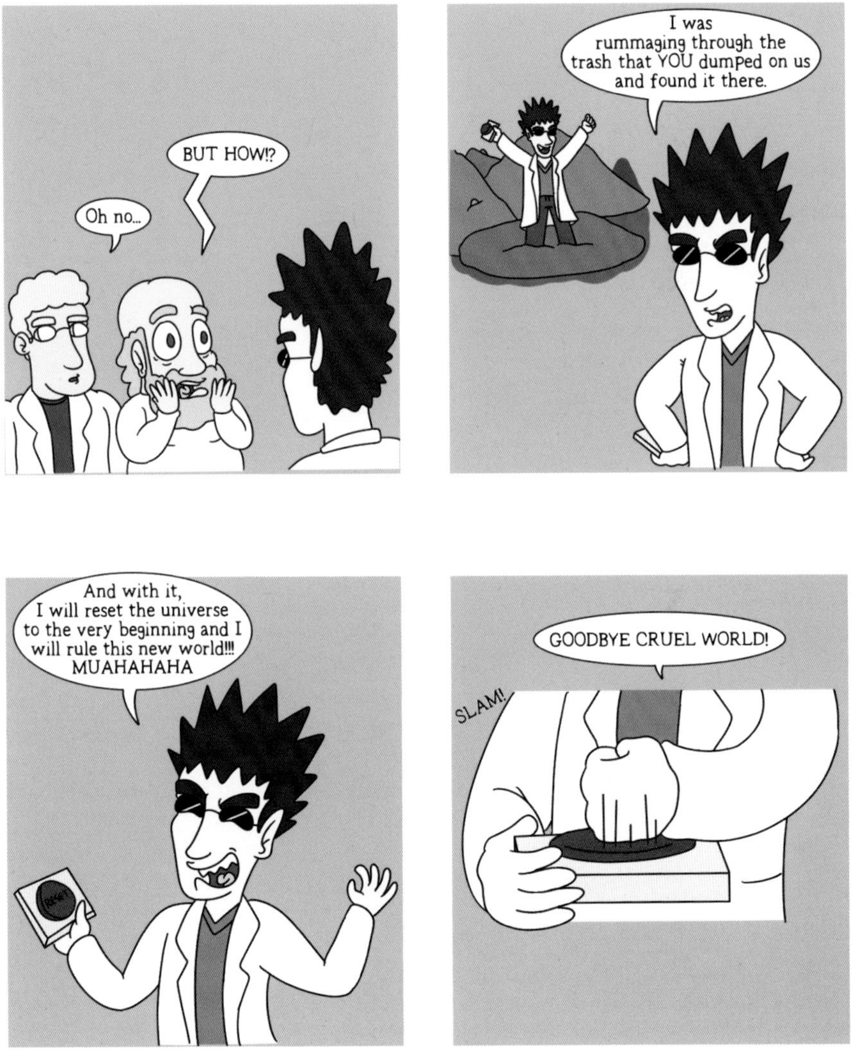
Oh no...
BUT HOW!?
I was rummaging through the trash that YOU dumped on us and found it there.
And with it, I will reset the universe to the very beginning and I will rule this new world!!! MUAHAHAHA
GOODBYE CRUEL WORLD!
SLAM!

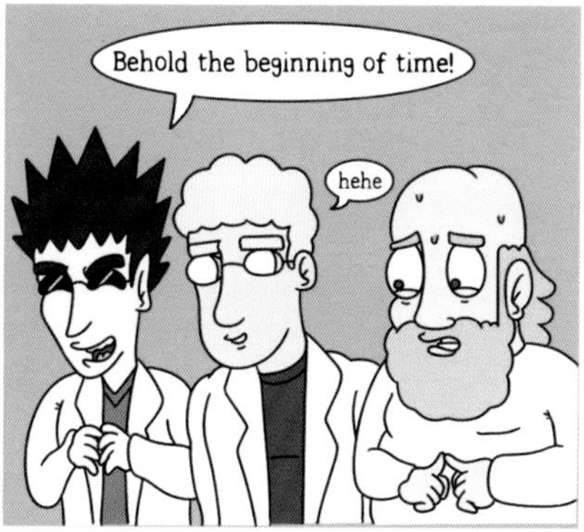
Behold the beginning of time!
hehe

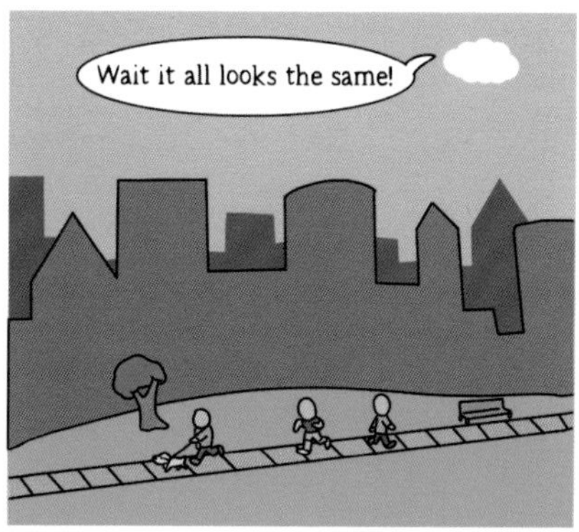
Wait it all looks the same!

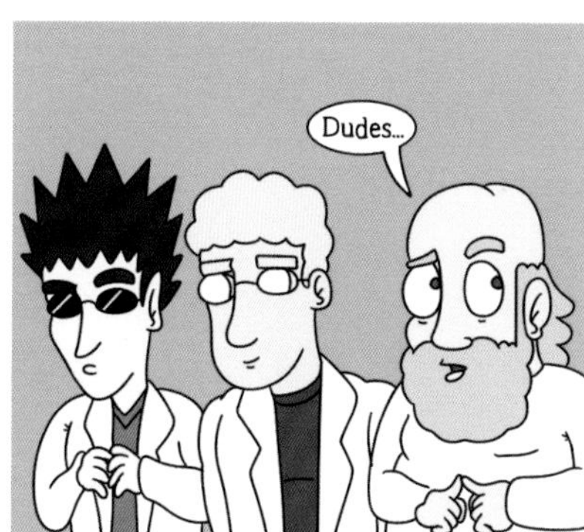
Dudes...

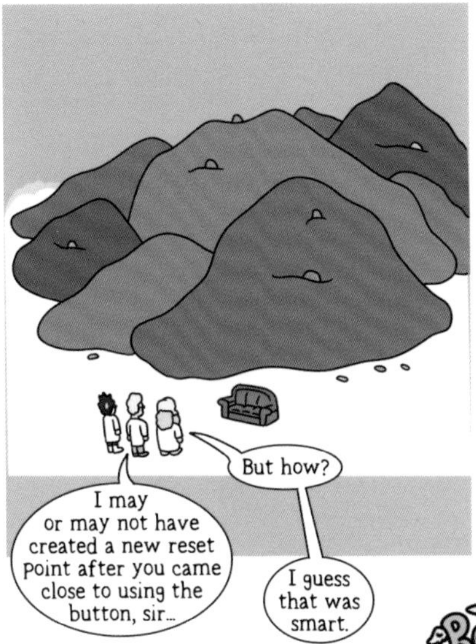
But how?
I may or may not have created a new reset point after you came close to using the button, sir...
I guess that was smart.

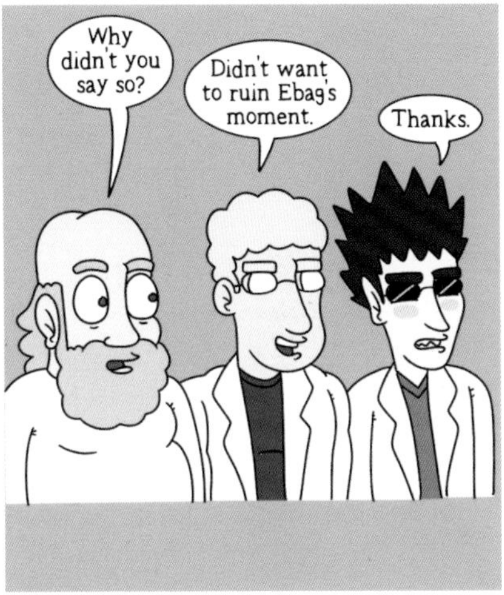
Why didn't you say so?
Didn't want to ruin Ebag's moment.
Thanks.

BONUS

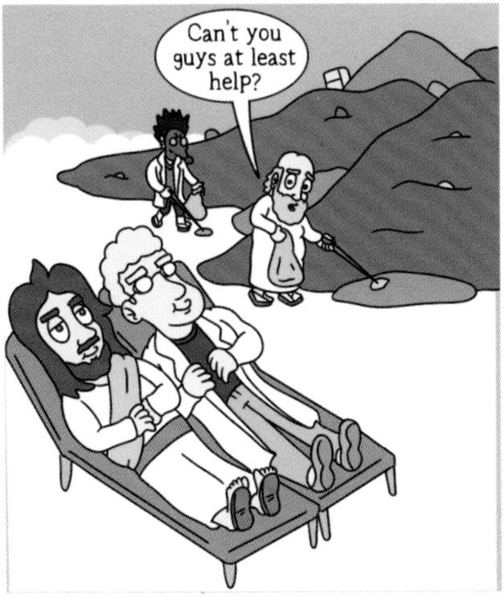
Can't you guys at least help?

III

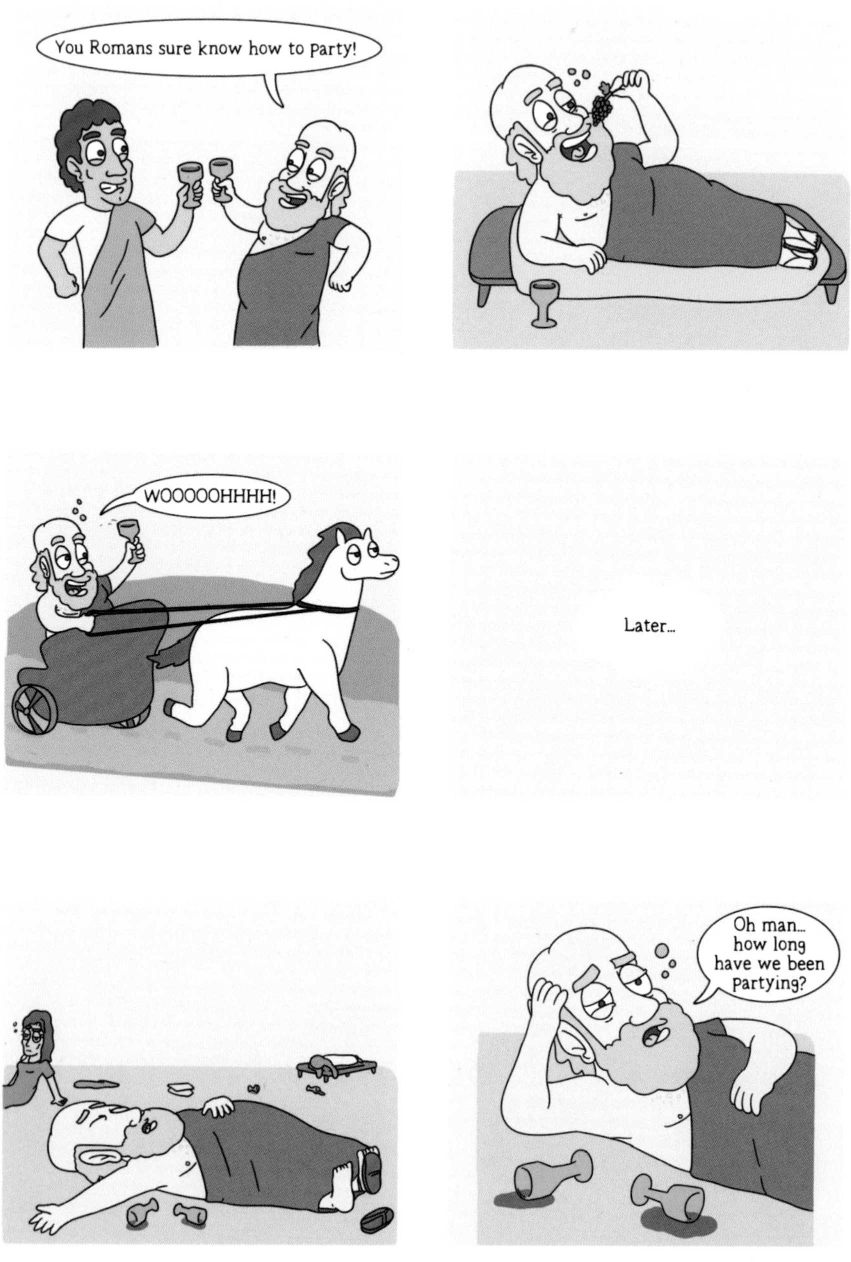
You Romans sure know how to party!
WOOOOOHHHH!
Later...
Oh man... how long have we been partying?

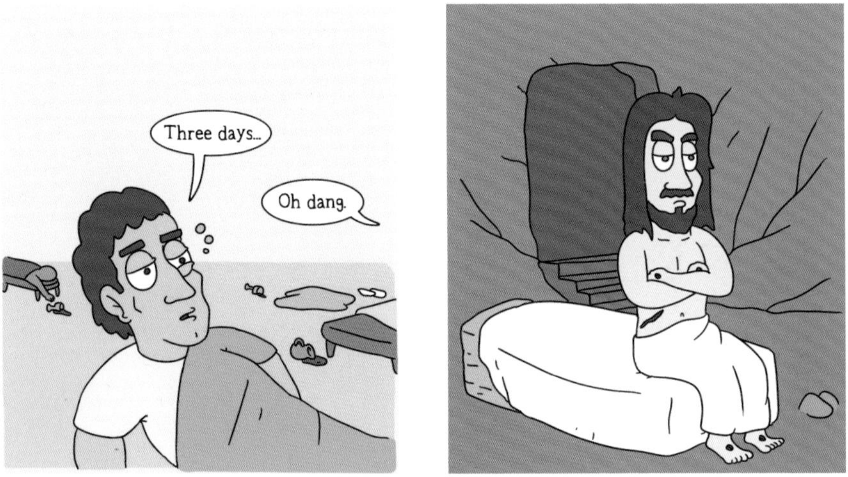
Three days...
Oh dang.

BONUS

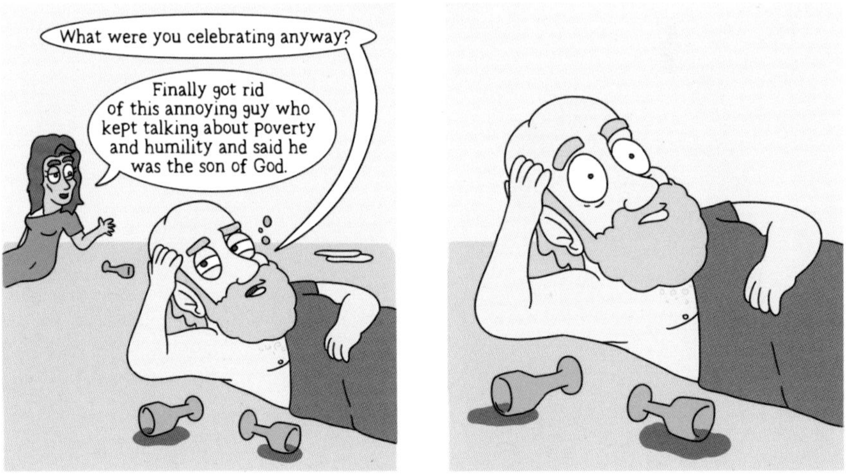
What were you celebrating anyway?
Finally got rid of this annoying guy who kept talking about poverty and humility and said he was the son of God.

Contract

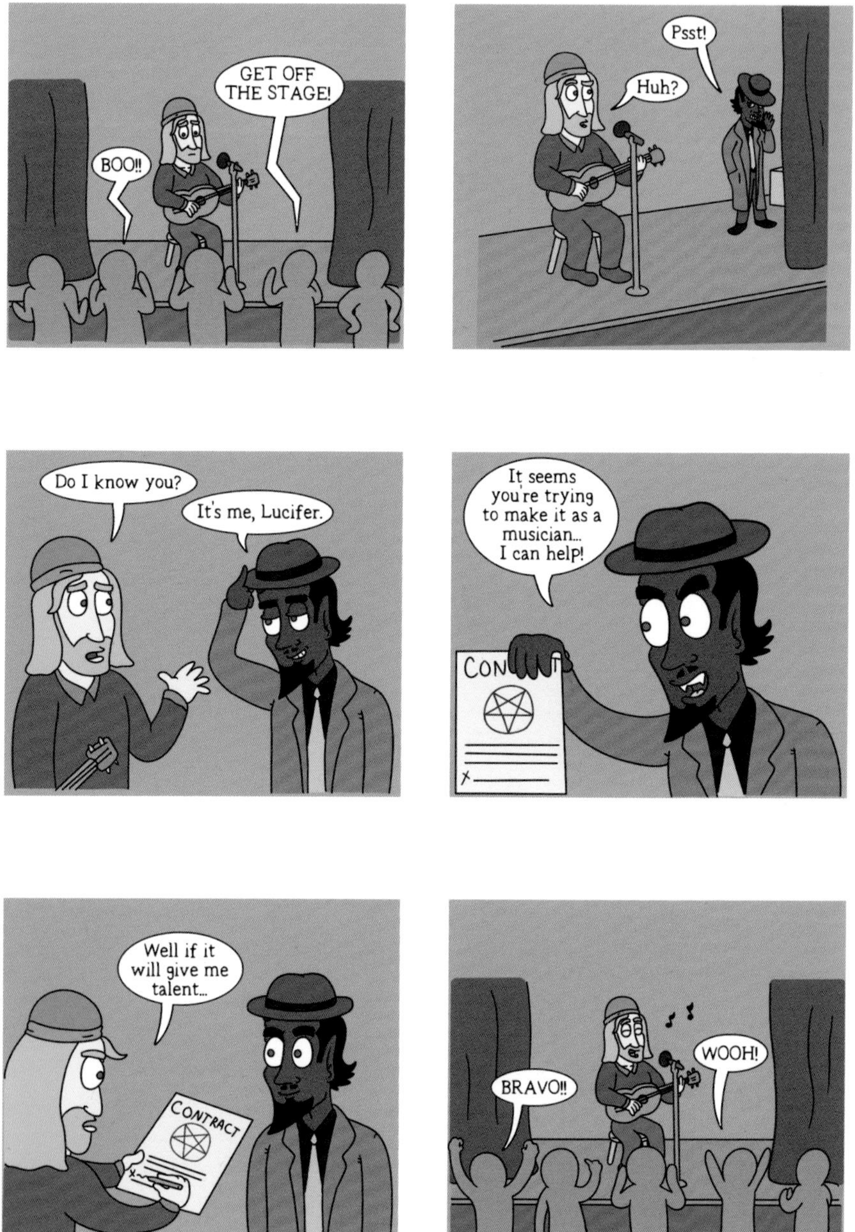
GET OFF THE STAGE!
BOO!!
Psst!
Huh?
Do I know you?
It's me, Lucifer.
It seems you're trying to make it as a musician... I can help!
CON
Well if it will give me talent...
CONTRACT
WOOH!
BRAVO!!

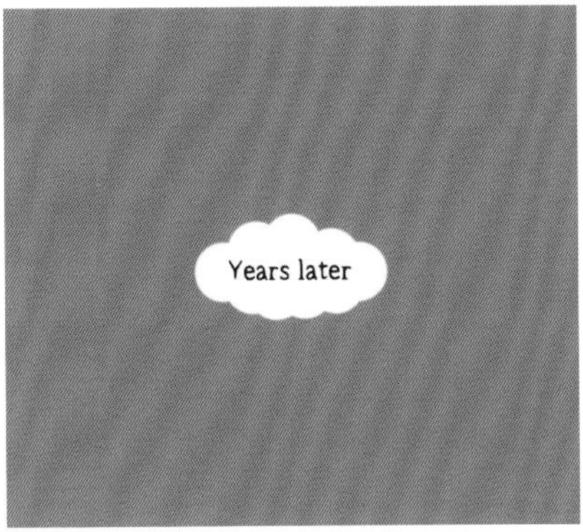
Years later

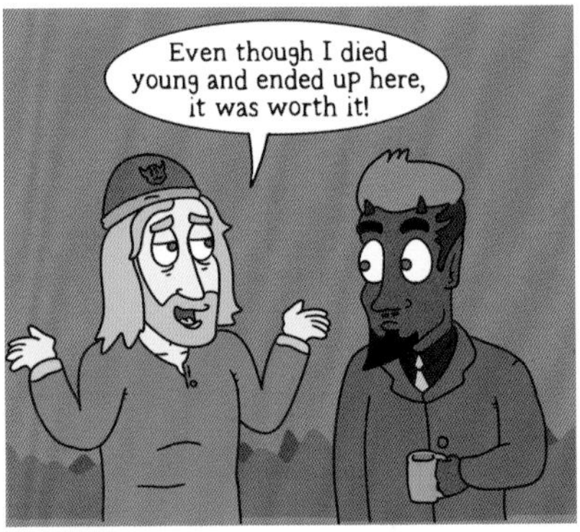
Even though I died young and ended up here, it was worth it!

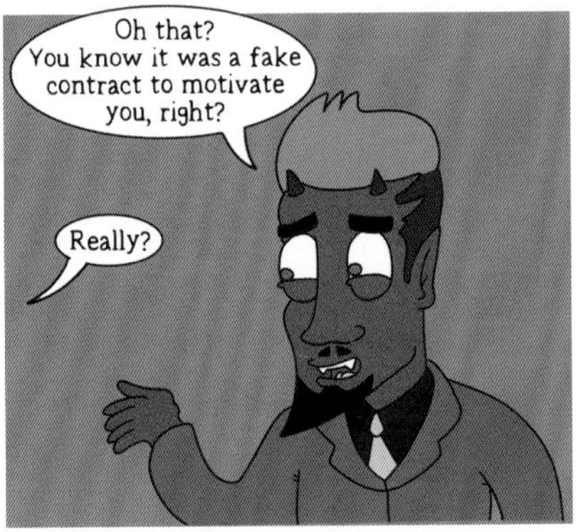
Oh that?
You know it was a fake contract to motivate you, right?
Really?

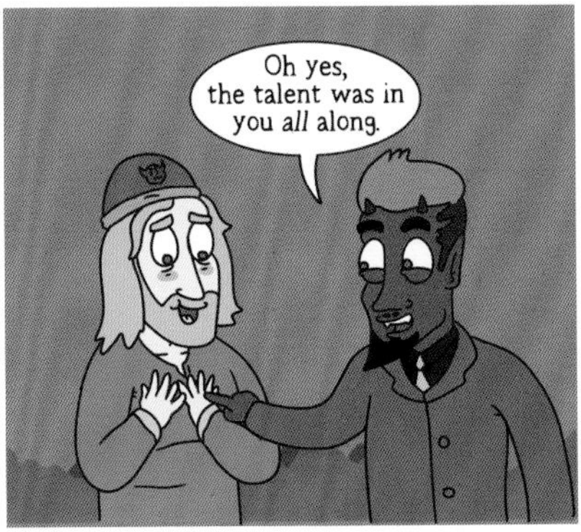
Oh yes, the talent was in you *all* along.

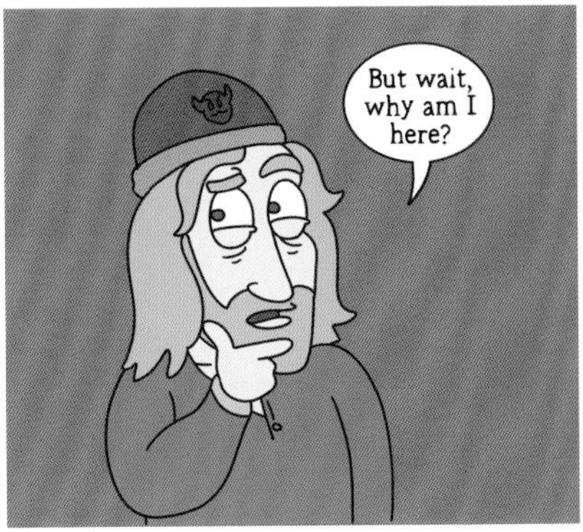
But wait, why am I here?

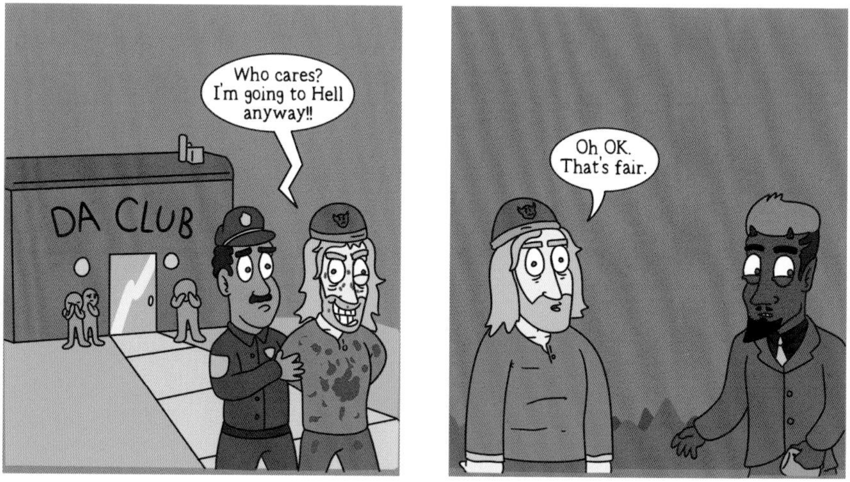
Who cares? I'm going to Hell anyway!!
DA CLUB
Oh OK. That's fair.

BONUS

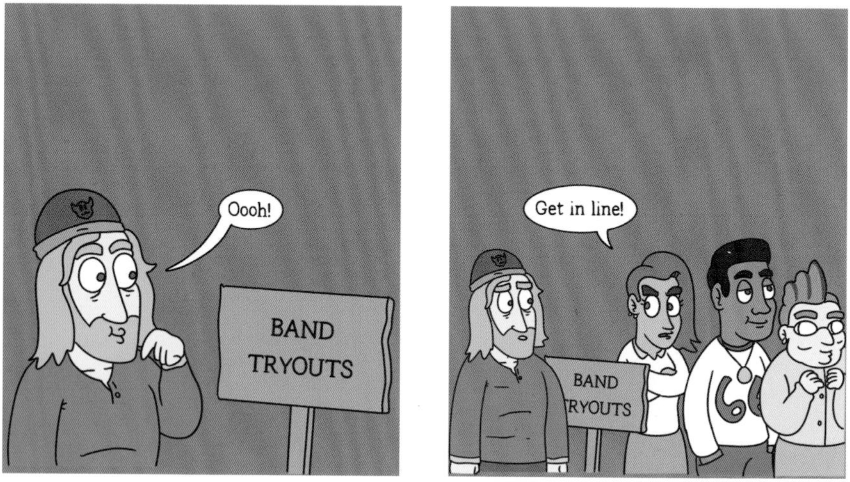
Oooh!
BAND TRYOUTS
Get in line!
BAND TRYOUTS

Contract 2

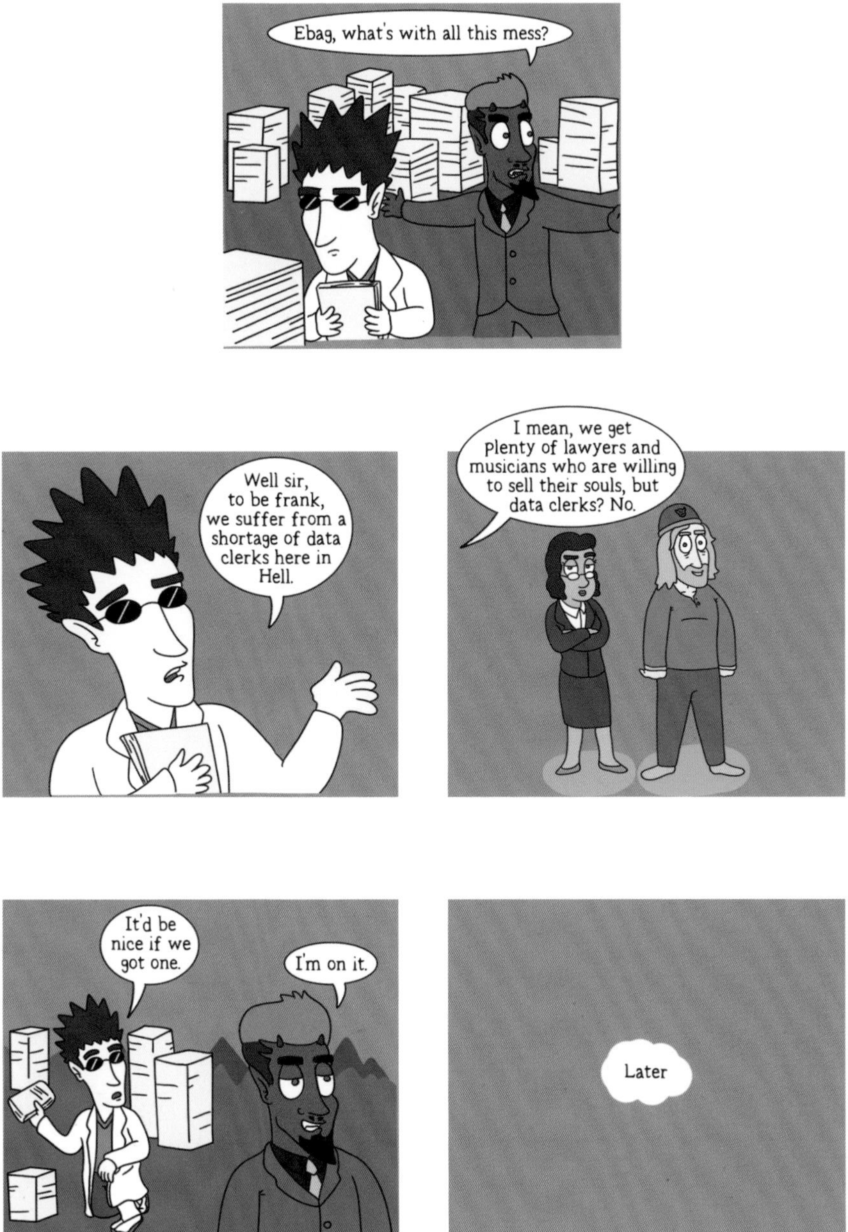
Ebag, what's with all this mess?
Well sir, to be frank, we suffer from a shortage of data clerks here in Hell.
I mean, we get plenty of lawyers and musicians who are willing to sell their souls, but data clerks? No.
It'd be nice if we got one.
I'm on it.
Later

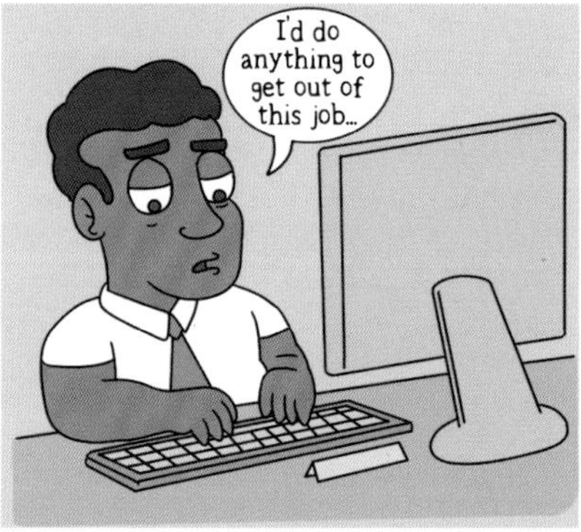
I'd do anything to get out of this job...

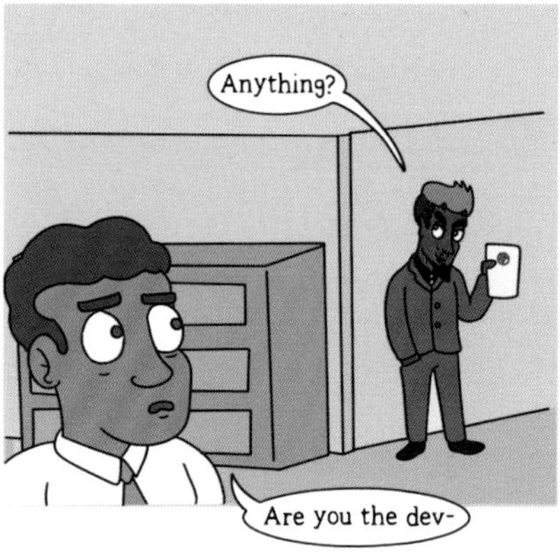
Anything?
Are you the dev-

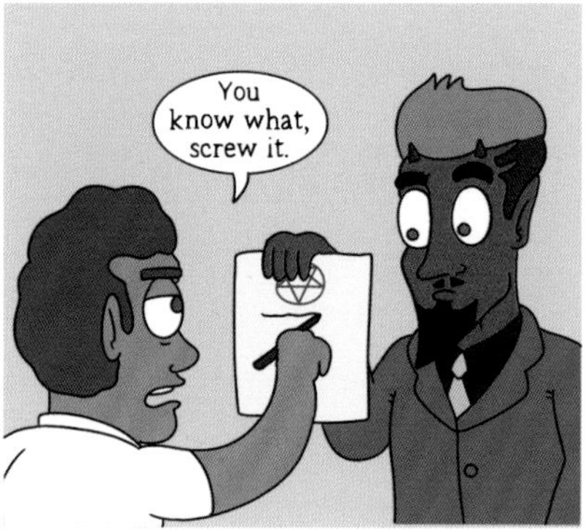
You know what, screw it.

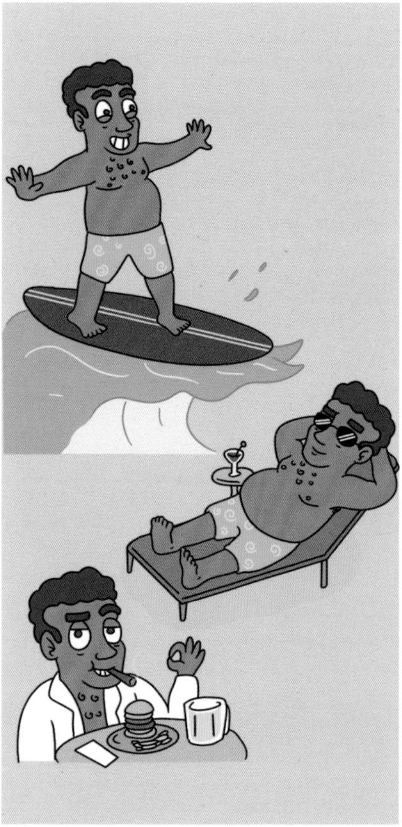

Get back to work!

BONUS

This wasn't in the contract! I'm going to sue you.
Good luck with that buddy.

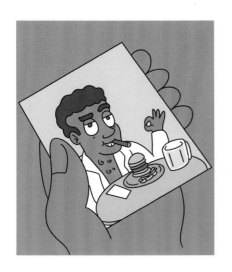

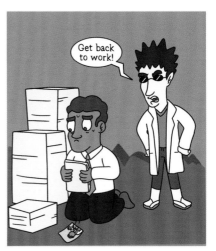

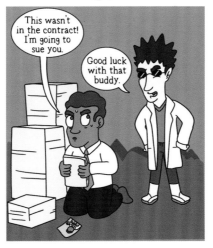

Note

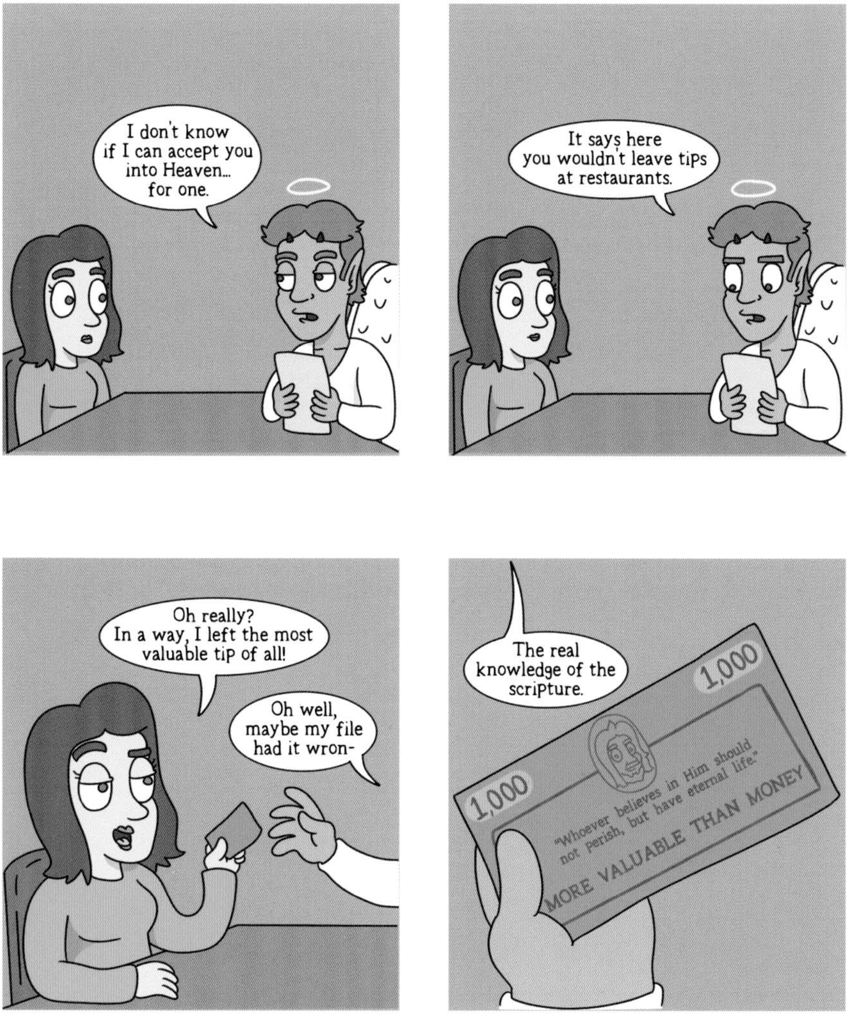
I don't know if I can accept you into Heaven... for one.
It says here you wouldn't leave tips at restaurants.
Oh really? In a way, I left the most valuable tip of all!
Oh well, maybe my file had it wron-
The real knowledge of the scripture.
1,000
1,000
"Whoever believes in Him should not perish, but have eternal life."
MORE VALUABLE THAN MONEY

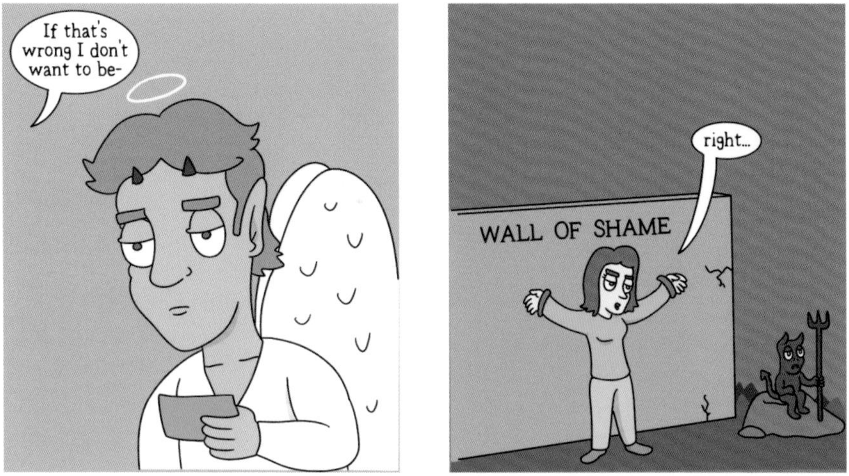
If that's wrong I don't want to be-
right...
WALL OF SHAME

BONUS

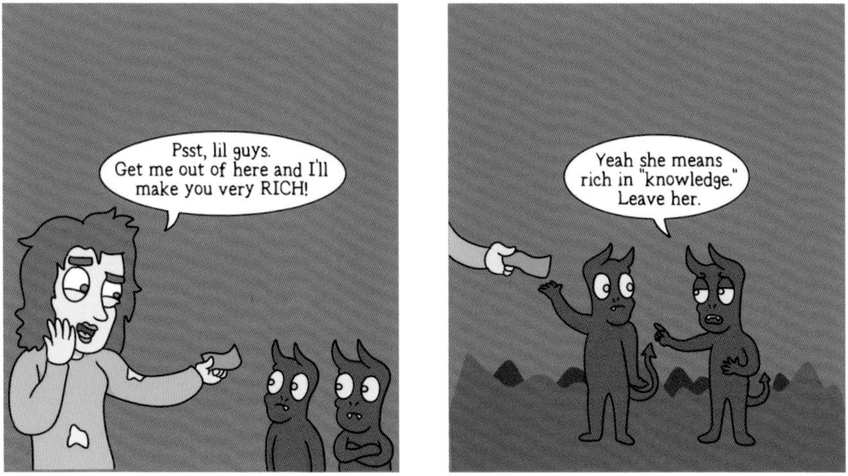
Psst, lil guys. Get me out of here and I'll make you very RICH!
Yeah she means rich in "knowledge." Leave her.

A Match Made in Heaven

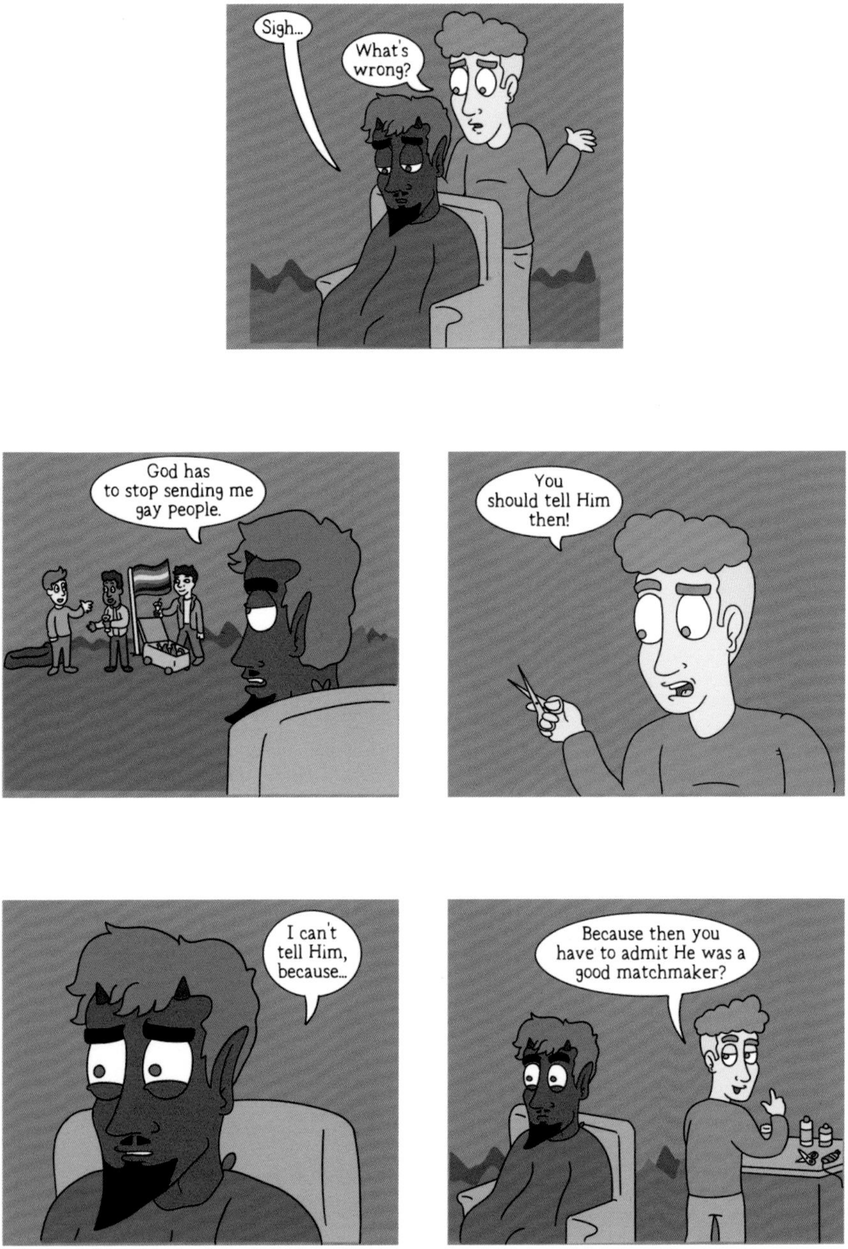
Sigh...
What's wrong?
God has to stop sending me gay people.
You should tell Him then!
I can't tell Him, because...
Because then you have to admit He was a good matchmaker?

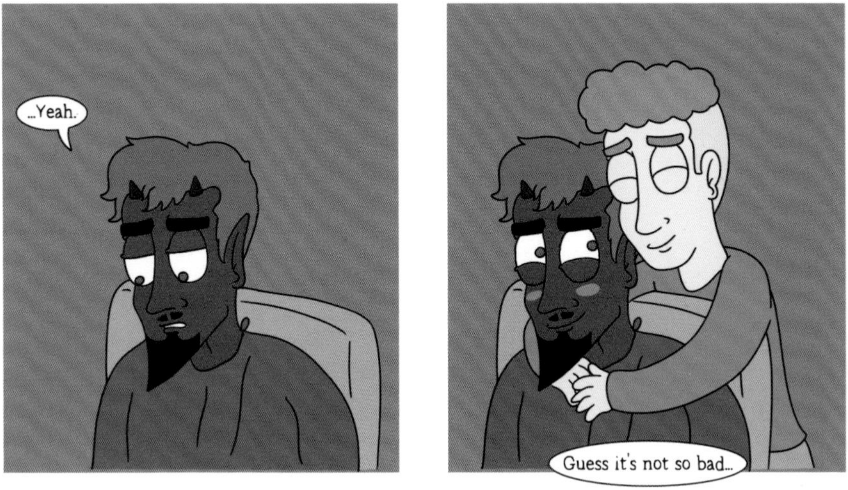
...Yeah.
Guess it's not so bad...

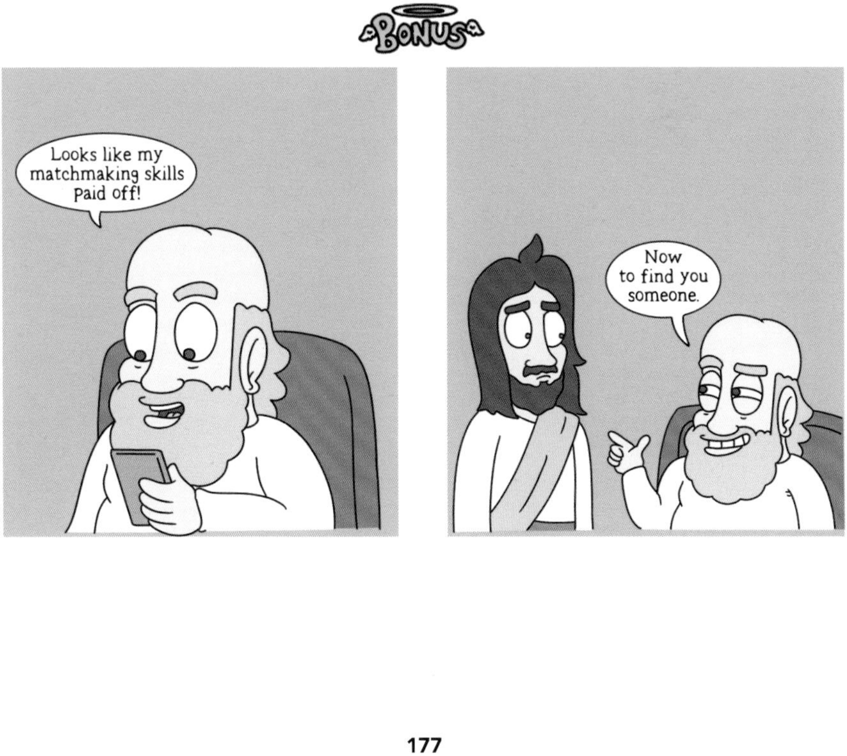
BONUS
Looks like my matchmaking skills paid off!
Now to find you someone.

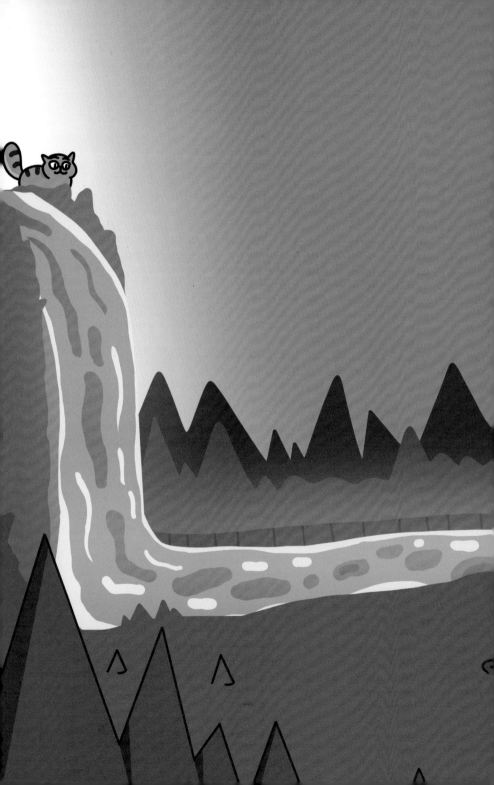

ADVENTURES of GOD Vol. 2

GALLERY

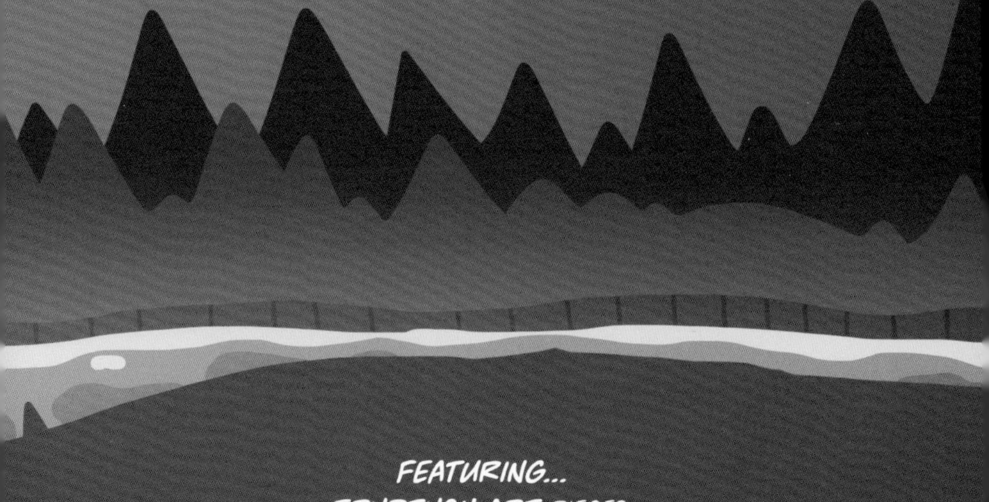

FEATURING...
TRYPTYCH ART PIECES,
PROCESS FOR THE **COLLECTED EDITION COVER**
AND **EXCLSUIVE ART POSTER**

OVERLEAF: TRYPTYCH ART PIECES

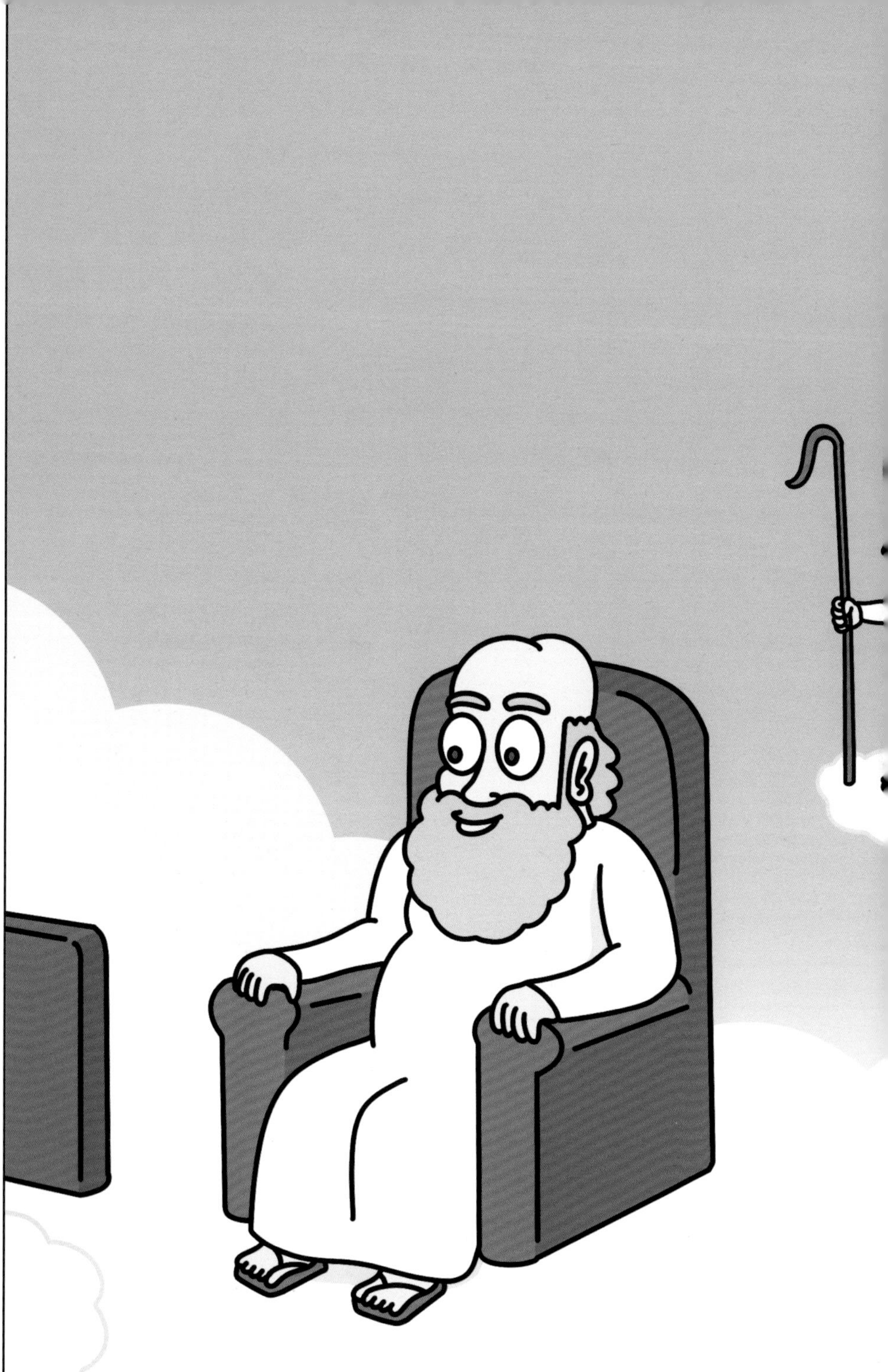

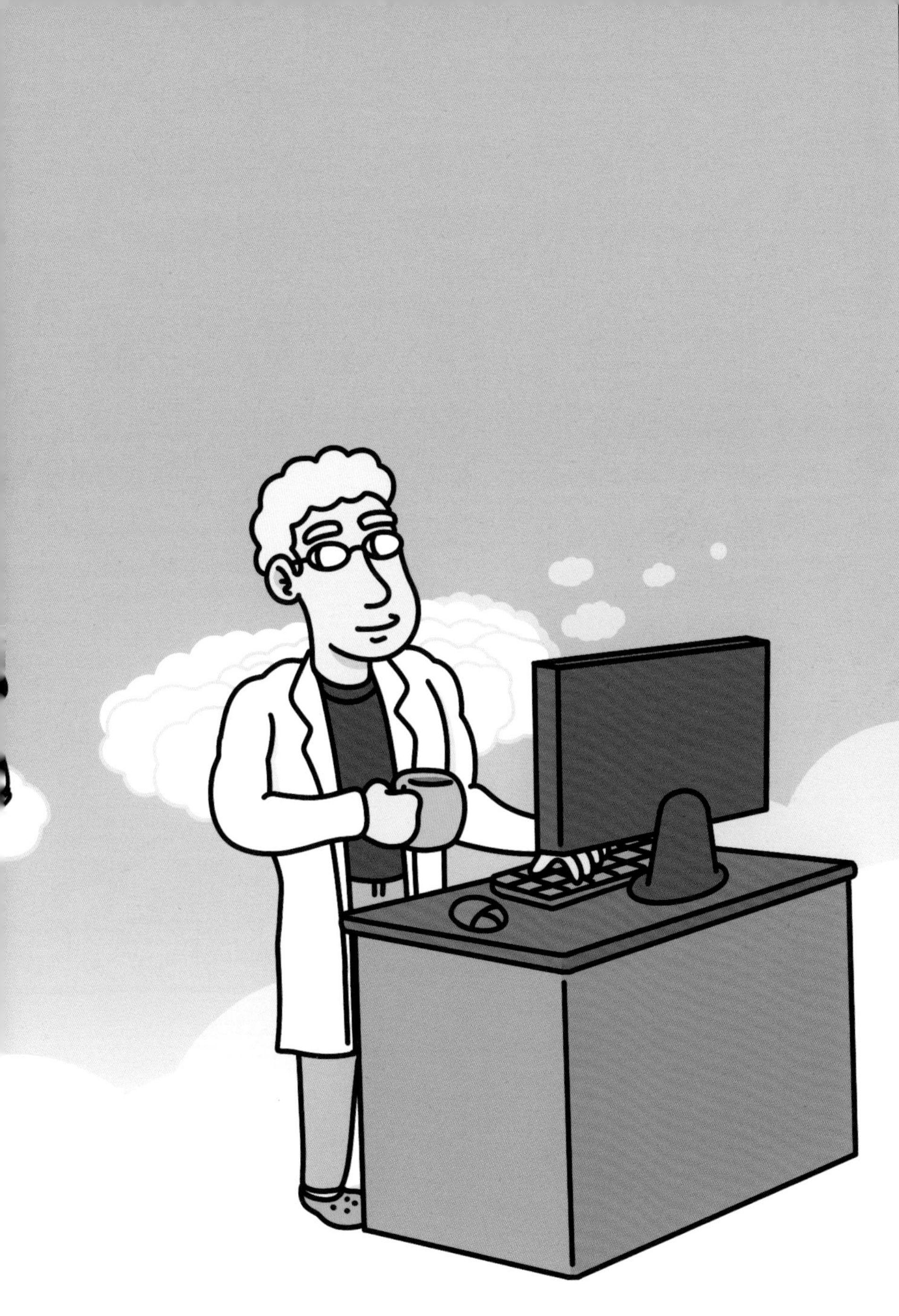

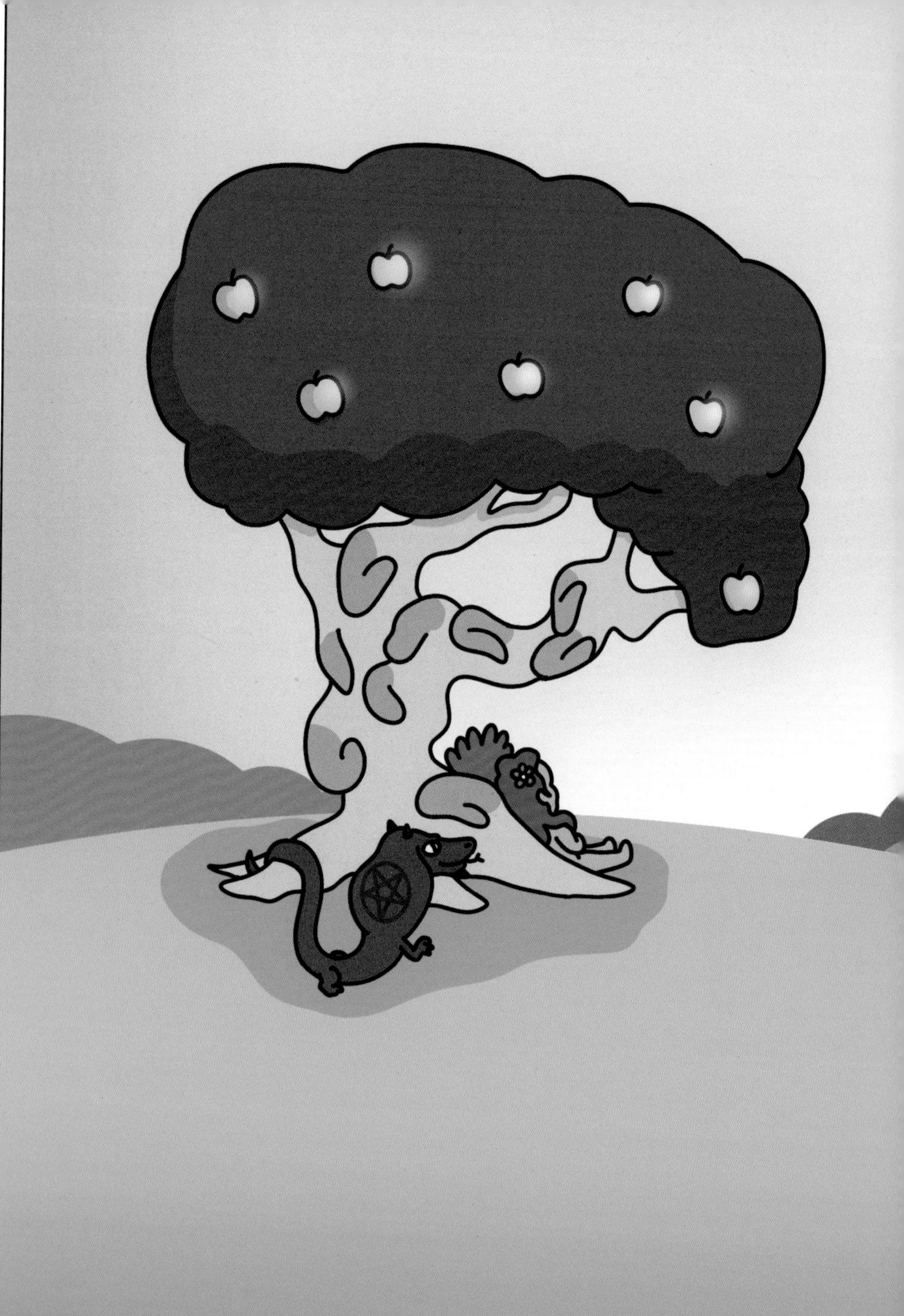

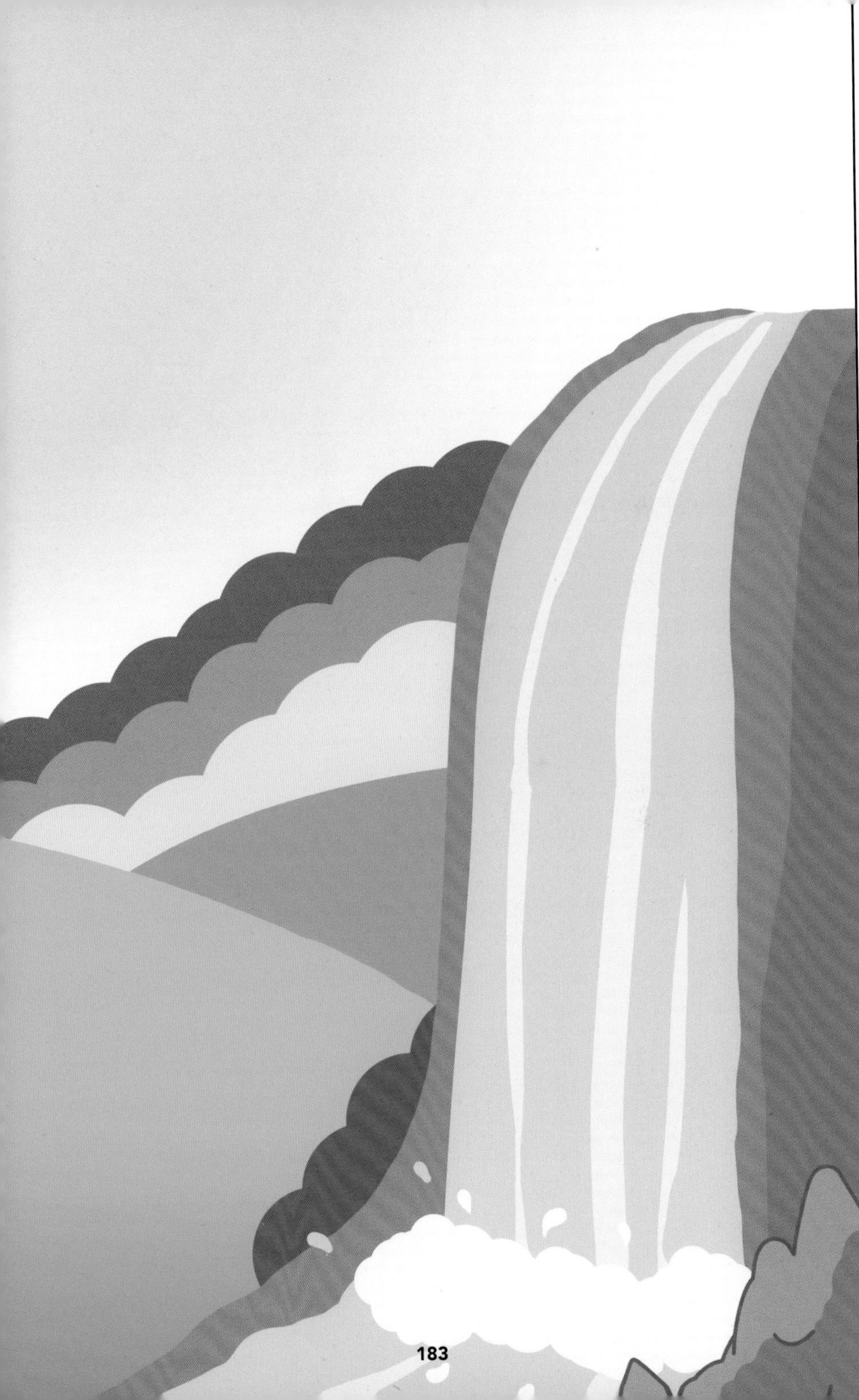

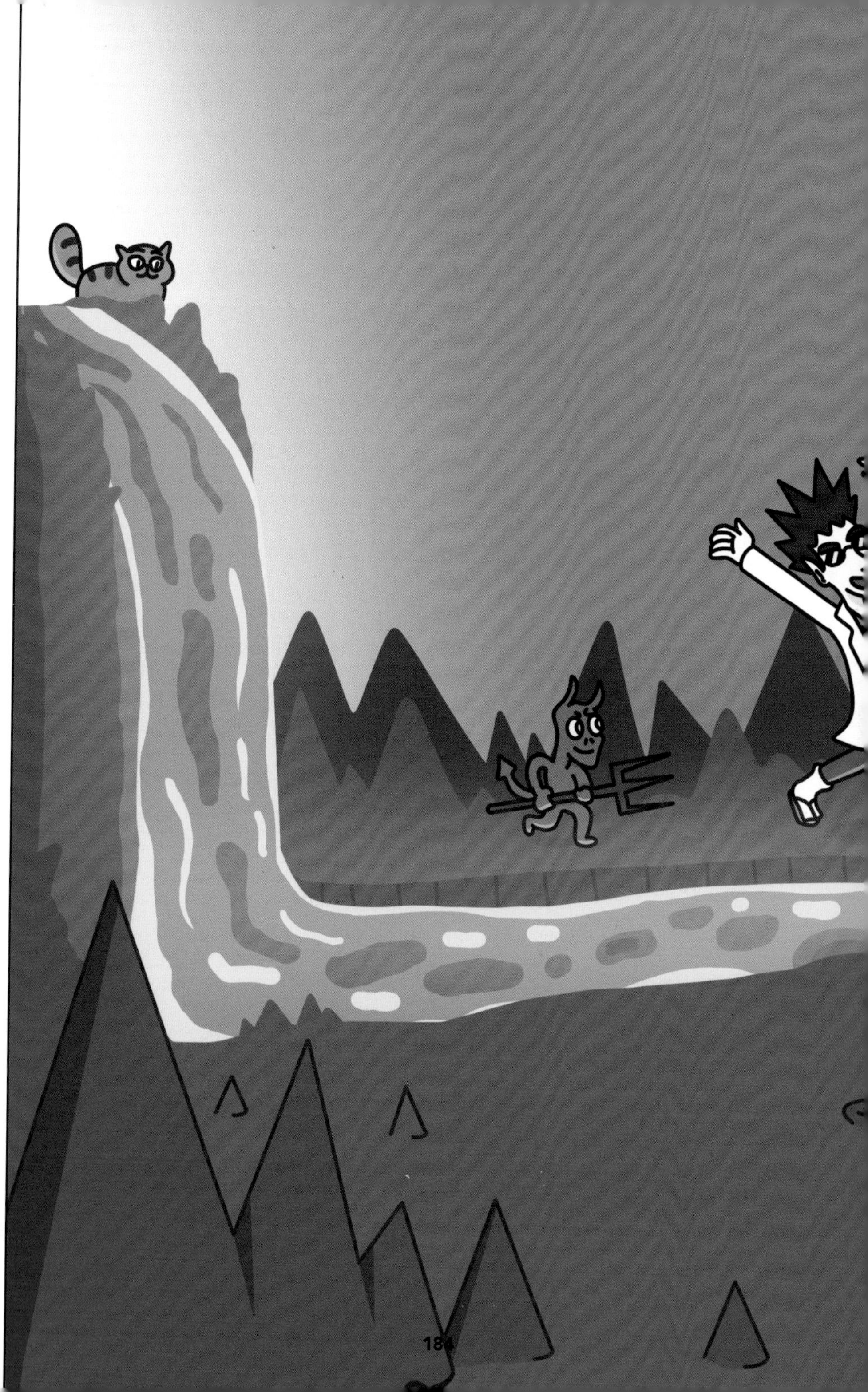

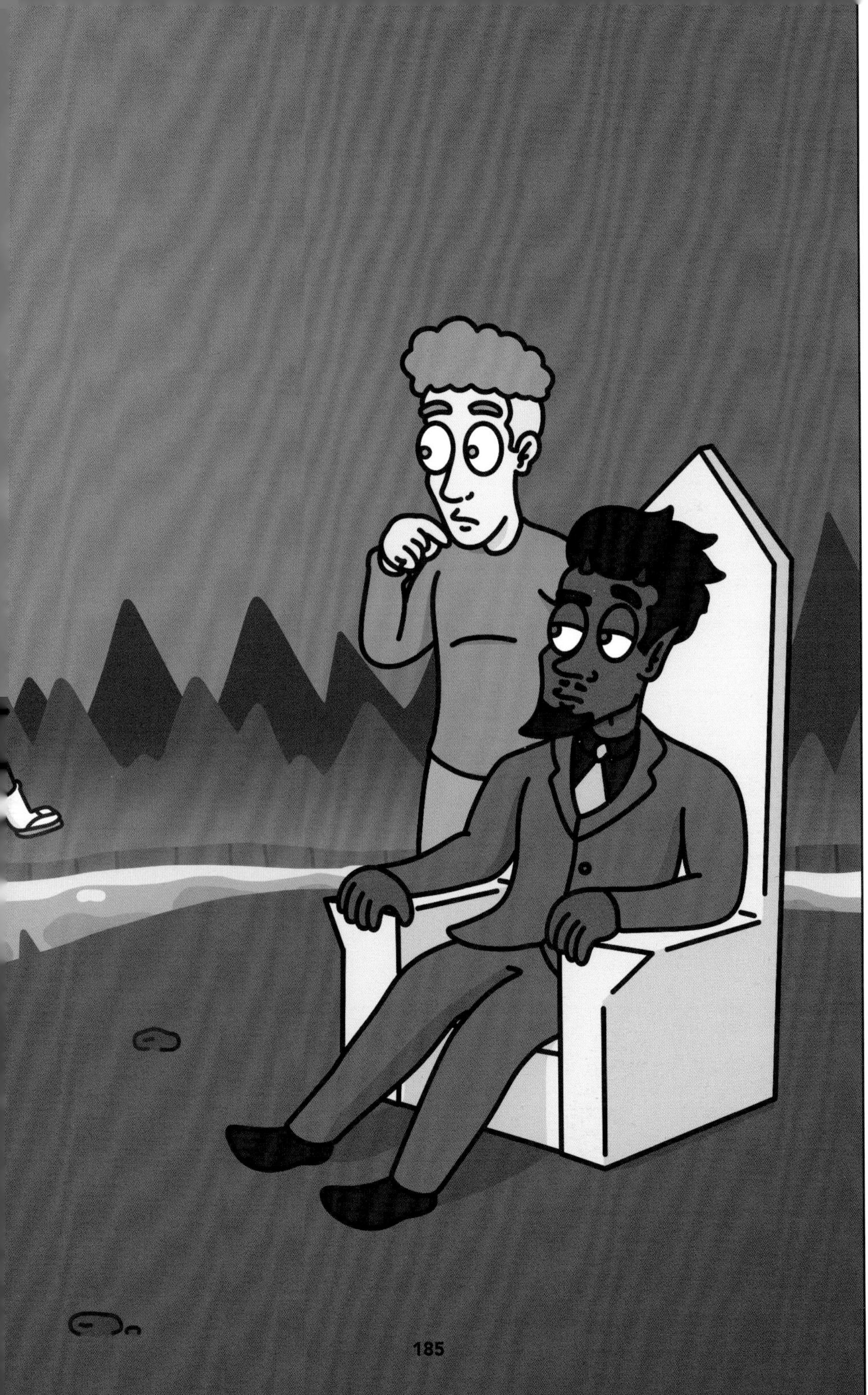

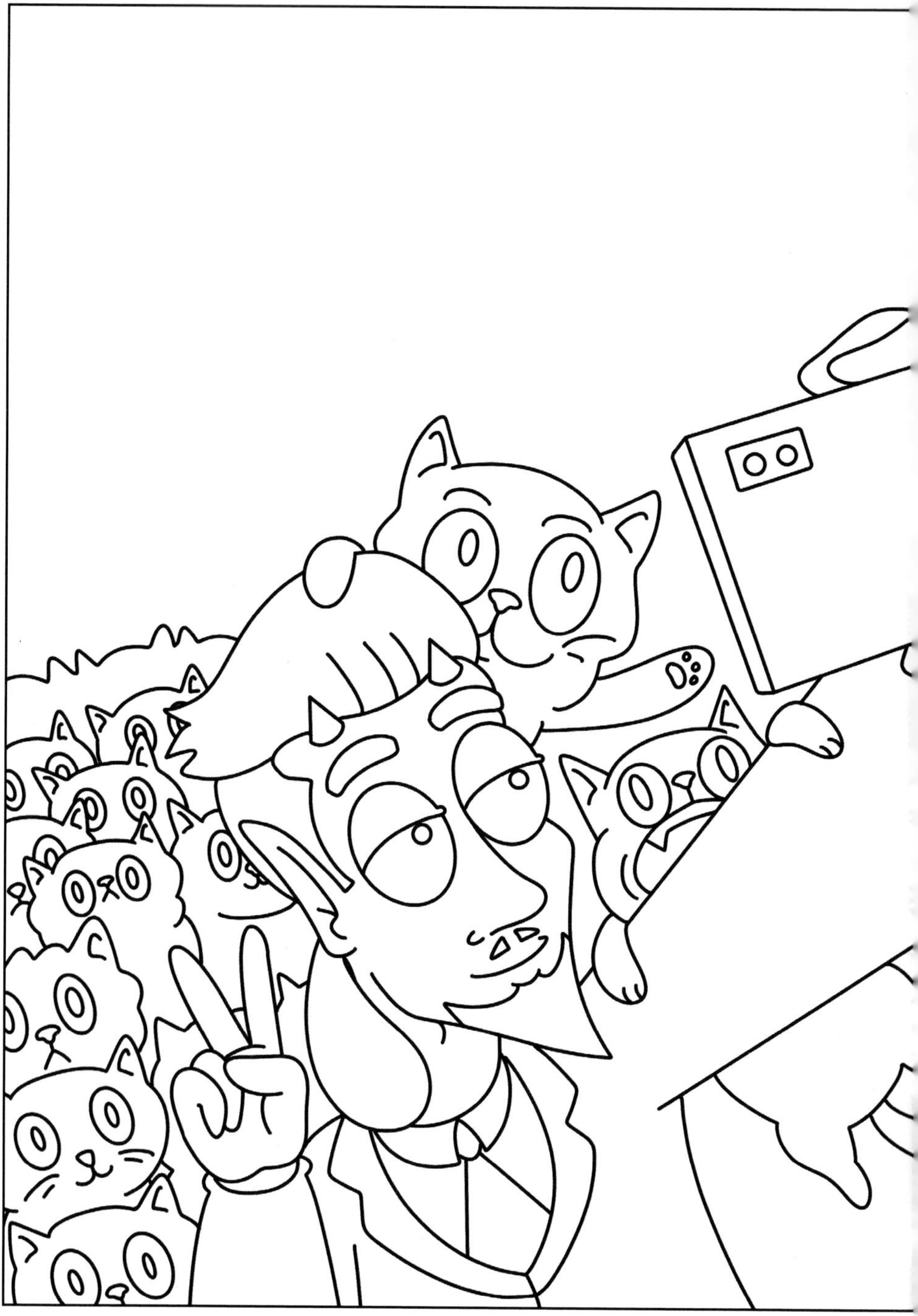

ABOVE: ADVENTURES OF GOD VOLUME 2 - COVER LINE ART

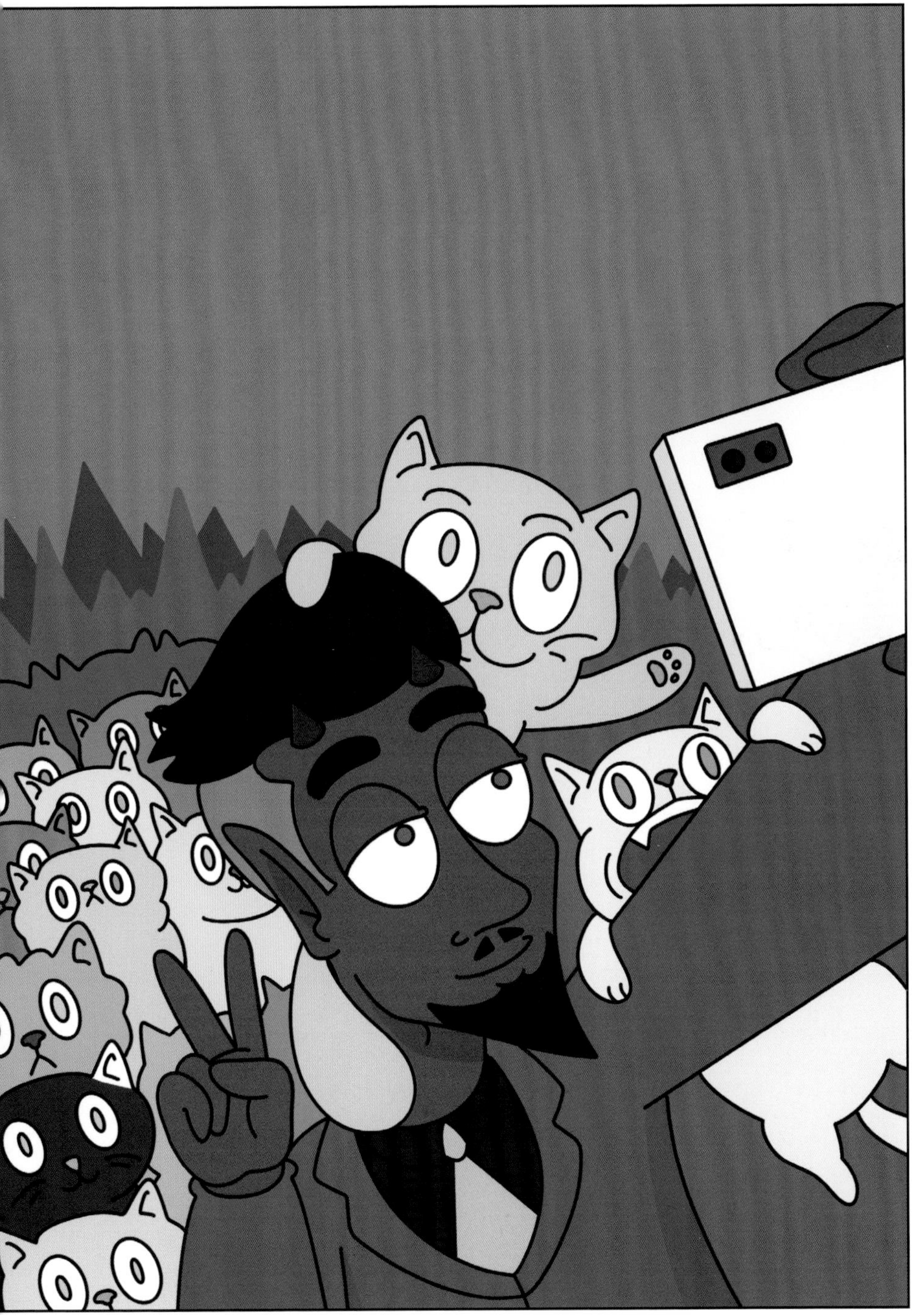

ABOVE: ADVENTURES OF GOD VOLUME 2 - COVER COLORS

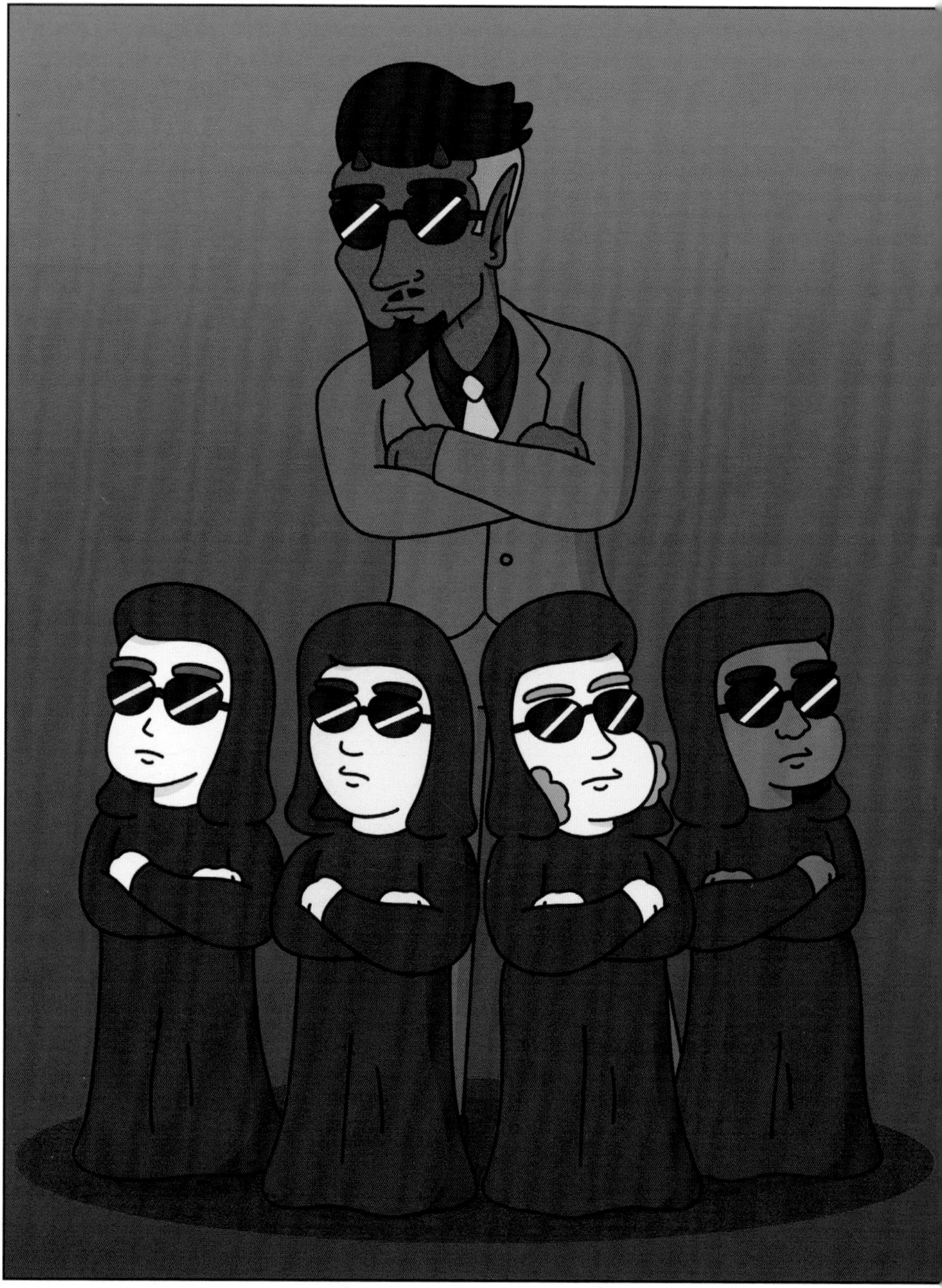

ABOVE: ADVENTURES OF GOD VOLUME 2 - EXCLUSIVE POSTER